GOD, ISRAEL, AND THE GENTILES

SOCIETY
OF BIBLICAL
LITERATURE

DISSERTATION SERIES
Saul Olyan, Old Testament Editor
Mark Allan Powell, New Testament Editor

Number 176
GOD, ISRAEL, AND THE GENTILES
Rhetoric and Situation in Romans 9–11

by
Johann D. Kim

Johann D. Kim

GOD, ISRAEL, AND THE GENTILES
Rhetoric and Situation in Romans 9–11

Society of Biblical Literature
Atlanta, Georgia

GOD, ISRAEL, AND THE GENTILES
Rhetoric and Situation in Romans 9–11

by
Johann D. Kim
Ph.D., Union Theological Seminary and
Presbyterian School of Christian Education, 1999
Paul J. Achtemeier, Dissertation Advisor

Library of Congress Cataloging-in-Publication Data

Kim, Johann D., 1962–
     God, Israel, and the gentiles : rhetoric and situation in Romans 9–11 /
by Johann D. Kim.
          p. cm.— (Dissertation series ; no. 176)
     Includes bibliographical references.
     ISBN 0-88414-014-8 (alk. paper)
     1. Bible. N.T., Romans IX–XI—Socio-rhetorical criticism. 2. Jews in the
New Testament. I. Title. II. Dissertation series (Society of Biblical
Literature); no. 176.

BS2665.6.J44 K56 2000
227'.1066—dc21   99-089676

08 07 06 05 04 03 02 01 00 99   5 4 3 2 1

Printed in the United States of America
on acid-free paper

For Terri

TABLE OF CONTENTS

ACKNOWLEDGMENTS

As I think about the people to whom I wish to express my gratitude, I realize that there are too many to name all. At the risk of omissions, I must be brief in this acknowledgment. First of all, the professors in my committee, Dr. John T. Carroll, Dr. Jack D. Kingsbury, and Dr. Paul J. Achtemeier, have all been patient and gracious in all proceedings since the commencement of my doctoral study through its formal conclusion in the oral defense. Dr. Carroll always responded promptly and saved me from many errors despite his busy schedule as Dean of Faculty. Dr. Achtemeier has been in the fullest sense of the word, *Doktorvater,* one who has not only academically but also spiritually guided me throughout the writing process. He graciously took time to read through Romans in Greek with me for almost a year when I was thinking about dissertation topics. Being one of his last students, I will carry the honor of having been his student for the rest of my life. I would be amiss if I did not acknowledge Dr. William P. Brown, who has always encouraged and shown great interest in my work. He taught me not only Hebrew and OT but also modeled the kind of scholar I would like to be someday.

I have been tremendously privileged to study with great Biblical scholars over the years: the late Dr. Robert Guelich (then, at Fuller Seminary) was the one who inspired and encouraged me to be a scholar; later at Yale, Dr. Leander Keck taught me Romans among other things and Dr. Abraham Malherbe opened my eyes to the Hellenistic milieu of NT, especially the importance of Greco-Roman rhetoric. It was a great privilege to seat in the seminars of Dr. Wayne Meeks on Christology, Dr. B. S. Childs on the history of Biblical interpretation, and Dr. J. Louis Martyn (who was visiting) on Galatians. To all of my teachers, my heart-felt thanks.

My friends and colleagues at Union also deserve my deep appreciation. My classmate (now Prof.) Nancy Lee has been a source of great encouragement; Peter Chang also has always been there to encourage and strengthen me; and Nate Kamano frequently reminded me that I should keep writing in his interesting emails (now, finish yours, Nate!). J. P. Kang read most of the following pages and suggested many stylistic improvements. Without his help, I doubt that I could have finished this dissertation on time. I will cherish those long computer sessions and listening to music together.

Many members at my home church, Young Nak Presbyterian Church of L.A., supported me and my family financially and through prayer. Especially when I went back to Union to write, their gifts surprised and overwhelmed me. Rev. Joseph Kim and the congregation of Great Light Korean Church where I am currently serving, lifted me up with constant prayers as I finished up the project. Deacon Heejoo Kim, college students at Young Nak, and members of CCM at Great Light are also ones who always rallied to support me.

My children, Pauline, Sean, and Daniel suffered with their daddy for completion of the dissertation. When asked what daddy is doing, Daniel always answers "gongbu" (study in Korean). They are the reason that I did not give up on the study. My wife, Terri, should take more than half of the credit for this dissertation. For almost ten years now, she has supported me and our family with great patience and strength. It is only natural, therefore, that this dissertation is dedicated to her.

Finally, looking back all these years, I can't help but to praise and give thanks to our God. It is solely by his grace that I was able to start and finish the doctoral study. When God called me into ministry, I had no idea that I was going to pass through this path but now it is clear that he is the one who has led me. Therefore, I would like to say with Paul,

"Μόνῳ σοφῷ θεῷ διὰ Ἰησοῦ Χριστοῦ, ᾧ ἡ δόξα εἰς τοὺς αἰῶνας, ἀμήν" (Rom 16:27).

LIST OF ABBREVIATIONS

I. BIBLICAL BOOKS (WITH THE APOCRYPHA)

Gen	Nah	1-2-3-4 Kgdms	John
Exod	Hab	Add Esth	Acts
Lev	Zeph	Bar	Rom
Num	Hag	Bel	1-2 Cor
Deut	Zech	1-2 Esdr	Gal
Josh	Mal	4 Ezra	Eph
Judg	Ps (*pl.*: Pss)	Jdt	Phil
1-2 Sam	Job	Ep Jer	Col
1-2 Kgs	Prov	1-2-3-4 Macc	1-2 Thess
Isa	Ruth	Pr Azar	1-2 Tim
Jer	Cant	Pr Man	Titus
Ezek	Eccl (*or* Qoh)	Sir	Phlm
Hos	Lam	Sus	Heb
Joel	Esth	Tob	Jas
Amos	Dan	Wis	1-2 Pet
Obad	Ezra	Matt	1-2-3 John
Jonah	Neh	Mark	Jude
Mic	1-2 Chr	Luke	Rev

II. ANCIENT LITERATURE

Ar. *Poet.*	Aristotle, *Poetica*
Ar. *Rhet.*	Aristotle, *Rhetorica*
Ar. *Top.*	Aristotle, *Topica*
Aug. *De Doct. Chr.*	Augustine, *De Doctrina Chrisitiana*
Cic. *Brut.*	Cicero, *Brutus*
Cic. *De Or.*	Cicero, *De Oratore*
Cic. *Inv.*	Cicero, *De Inventione*
Cic. *Opt. Gen.*	Cicero, *De Optimo Genera*
Cic. *Or.*	Cicero, *Orator*
Cic. *Part. Or.*	Cicero, *De Partitione Oratoriae*

Cic. *Top.*	Cicero, *Oratorum Topica*
Cic. *Ad Fam.*	Cicero, *Letters to his Friends*
Cic. *Ad Att.*	Cicero, *Letters to Atticus*
Demetr. *Eloc.*	Demetrius, *Elocutione*
Ad. Her.	[Cicero], *Rhetorica ad Herennium*
Long. *Subl.*	Longinus, *De Sublime*
Pl. *Phdr.*	Plato, *Phaedrus*
Quint.	Quintilian, *Institutio Oratoria*
Rhet. Ad Alex.	*Rhetorica ad Alexandrum*
Hermog. *Stat.*	Hermogenes, περὶ τῶν στάσεων
Sext. Emp. *Math.*	Sextus Empiricus, *Adversus Mathematicos*

III. MODERN LITERATURE

AB	Anchor Bible
AGJU	Arbeiten zur Geschichte des antiken Judentums und des Urchristentums
AnBib	Analecta biblica
ANRW	*Aufstieg und Niedergang der römischen Welt*
BAGD	W. Bauer, W. F. Arndt, F. W. Gingrich, and F. W. Danker, *Greek-English Lexicon of the NT*
BDF	F. Blass, A. Debrunner, and R. W. Funk, *A Greek Grammar of the New Testament*
BETL	Bibliotheca ephemeridum theologicarum lovaniensium
BEvT	Beiträge zur evangelischen Theologie
BHT	Beiträge zur historischen Theologie
Bib	*Biblica*
BTB	*Biblical Theology Bulletin*
BWANT	Beiträge zur Wissenschaft vom Alten und Neuen Testament
BZ	*Biblische Zeitschrift*
CBQ	*Catholic Biblical Quarterly*
ConBNT	Coniectanea biblica, New Testament
ConNT	Coniectanea neotestamentica
CRINT	Compendia rerum iudaicarum ad novum testamentum
CTM	*Concordia Theological Monthly*
CurTM	*Currents in Theology and Mission*

EKKNT	Evangelisch-katholischer Kommentar zum Neuen Testament
ETL	*Ephemerides theologicae lovanienses*
EvK	Evangelische Kommentare
ExpTim	*Expository Times*
FRLANT	Forschungen zur Religion und Literatur des Alten und Neuen Testaments
GBS	Guides to Biblical Scholarship
GRBS	*Greek, Roman, and Byzantine Studies*
GTA	Göttinger theologische Arbeiten
HBC	J. L. Mays, et al. (eds.), *Harper's Bible Commentary*
HBD	P. J. Achtemeier, et al. (eds.), *Harper's Bible Dictionary*
HBT	*Horizons in Biblical Theology*
HKNT	Handkommentar zum Neuen Testament
HNT	Handbuch zum Neuen Testament
HNTC	Harper's NT Commentaries
HTKNT	Herders theologischer Kommentar zum Neuen Testament
HTR	*Harvard Theological Review*
HUT	Hermeneutische Untersuchungen zur Theologie
IBC	Interpretation: A Bible Commentary for Teaching and Preaching
ICC	International Critical Commentary
IDB	G. A. Buttrick (ed.), *Interpreter's Dictionary of the Bible*
IDBSup	Supplementary volume to *IDB*
Int	*Interpretation*
JBL	*Journal of Biblical Literature*
JBR	*Journal of Bible and Religion*
JETS	*Journal of the Evangelical Theological Society*
JQR	*Jewish Quarterly Review*
JR	*Journal of Religion*
JSNT	*Journal for the Study of the New Testament*
JSNTSup	Journal for the Study of the New Testament Supplement Series
JSOT	*Journal for the Study of the Old Testament*
JTC	*Journal for Theology and the Church*
JTS	*Journal of Theological Studies*
KD	*Kerygma und Dogma*
LCL	Loeb Classical Library

LD	Lectio divina
LSJ	Liddell-Scott-Jones, *Greek-English Lexicon*
LT	*Literature and Theology*
MeyerK	H. A. W. Meyer, Kritisch-exegetischer Kommentar über das Neue Testament
MNTC	Moffatt NT Commentary
NICNT	New International Commentary on the New Testament
NIV	New International Version
NovT	*Novum Testamentum*
NovTSup	Novum Testamentum, Supplements
NRSV	New Revised Standard Version
NTAbh	Neutestamentliche Abhandlungen
NTF	Neutestamentliche Forschungen
NTL	New Testament Library
NTS	*New Testament Studies*
NTTS	New Testament Tools and Studies
QD	Quaestiones disputatae
RB	*Revue biblique*
RevExp	*Review and Expositor*
RSV	Revised Standard Version
SacPag	Sacra Pagina
SBLDS	SBL Dissertation Series
SBLSP	SBL Seminar Papers
SBLSS	SBL Semeia Studies
SBT	Studies in Biblical Theology
SJT	*Scottish Journal of Theology*
SNT	Studien zum Neuen Testament
SNTSMS	Society for New Testament Studies Monograph Series
ST	*Studia theologica*
SUNT	Studien zur Umwelt des Neuen Testaments
TBei	*Theologische Beiträge*
TDNT	G. Kittel and G. Friedrich (eds.), *Theological Dictionary of the New Testament*
TGl	*Theologie und Glaube*
THKNT	Theologischer Handkommentar zum Neuen Testament
TynBul	*Tyndale Bulletin*
TZ	*Theologische Zeitschrift*
WBC	Word Biblical Commentary

WTJ	*Westminster Theological Journal*
WUNT	Wissenschaftliche Untersuchungen zum Neuen Testament
ZNW	*Zeitschrift für die neutestamentliche Wissenschaft*
ZTK	*Zeitschrift für Theologie und Kirche*

INTRODUCTION

In Rom 9:6a, Paul declares, "It is not as though the word of God had failed." In what context did he utter such a sentence? Had someone, in fact, maintained that the word of God had failed? If so, on what basis did that person sustain such a bold, if not blasphemous, challenge? What is the situation in which Paul faces such a question or challenge? To whom does Paul make an argument about such a subject? In other words, who is his audience? What does he hope to achieve by his argumentation in Rom 9-11? Finally, what does he want his audience to do? Before we can ask this last question, however, we need to know what he argues for in these chapters or, even more fundamentally, whether he is consistent or not. Is Paul "wrestling with a 'burning personal problem,'[1] attempting to 'square the circle,'"[2] or "trying different solutions"[3] in these chapters?

These are the questions that this study explores. A rhetorical critical method is employed in this investigation because it best helps to decipher the question of Paul's rhetoric and situation in Rom 9-11. The task and methodology is introduced in more detail in chapter one, where the research on Rom 9-11 is described and the need for a new method in approaching these chapters is explored. The methodology of George A. Kennedy, employed in this study, is briefly but critically re-

---

[1] Bent Noack, "Current and Backwater in the Epistle to the Romans," *ST* 19 (1965): 165-66.

[2] N. Walter, "Zur Interpretation von Römer 9-11," *ZTK* 81 (1984): 173, 6.

[3] R. Ruether, *Faith and Fratricide: The Theological Roots of Anti-Semitism* (New York: Crossroad, 1974), 105; H. Räisänen, "Paul, God, and Israel: Romans 9-11 in Recent Research," in *The Social World of Formative Christianity and Judaism: Essays in Tribute to Howard Clark Kee*, ed. J. Neusner, *et al.* (Philadelphia: Fortress, 1988), 196.

1

viewed to see whether it needs refinement. Also, the theory of *stasis* is examined closely for its feasibility for our purposes.

Chapter two explores the relationship between the historical situation and the rhetorical situation. We will see whether historical criticism and rhetorical criticism stand in an antithetical relationship or can complement each other in their basic orientation in methodology. Then, the theory of the rhetorical situation, as advocated by Lloyd F. Bitzer, is critically examined. After surveying developments in the theory of the rhetorical situation, a summary of how New Testament scholars have used the theory in their works is offered. The similarities and differences between the historical situation and the rhetorical situation are examined and evaluated in terms of their applicability in this study.

Chapter three deals with the rhetorical situation of Romans as a whole. Emphasis is concentrated on the beginning and the ending of the letter, namely, the *exordium* and the *peroratio*, in order to gain an understanding of the rhetorical situation of Romans. The verses that constitute each part are determined first before proceeding to the investigation of the rhetorical situation of Romans. Focus is on the rhetorical exigence, the speaker, and the audience which are manifested on the text level of Romans, especially as detected in the *exordium* and the *peroratio*.

With the results of chapter three, the rhetorical unit and the rhetorical situation of Rom 9-11 are explored in chapter four. Whether Rom 9-11 is an integral part of Romans as a whole or stands independently, detached from its larger argument, is closely examined. How the speaker is presented throughout Romans is traced and compared with the presentation in the narrower context of Rom 9-11. The portrait of the audience in these three chapters is critically examined and assessed, and in this way, the question "Who is Paul's rhetorical audience?" is answered. The rhetorical exigence of Rom 9-11 is examined on the basis of the evidence that is present in the text itself. Of foremost importance for the investigation is whether the exigence of Rom 9-11 corresponds to the overall exigence of Romans, examined in chapter three.

Chapter five presents a rhetorical analysis of Rom 9-11. The arrangement of the passage is examined and the rhetorical species is determined. The invention and style of Rom 9-11 are examined with a focus on the argumentative flow of Paul's presentation. The *stasis* theory (utilized to understand the invention of the unit) is used to understand the rhetorical strategy that Paul employs. Pertinent exegetical issues are also discussed in this chapter but historical critical issues such as the source of Paul's quotation of scripture or his use of traditional materials (e.g., whether 11:33-36 contains early Christian hymnic materials) are not engaged here. The investigation focuses on the text level of Rom 9-11, where Paul's rhetorical arguments are presented. That will help us to hear what Paul wants to say in these chapters. The conclusion summarizes the findings and discusses their implications for our understanding of rhetoric and situation in Rom 9-11.

CHAPTER ONE

THE TASK AND METHODOLOGY

I. THE TASK

Romans 9-11 has become an exegetical and theological battle ground in recent years. Interest in these three chapters in the middle of Paul's letter to the Christians in Rome has been intense but there seems to have been little consensus among scholars concerning what Paul means in Rom 9-11. More than two decades ago, Werner Kümmel invited scholars to solve the problem of these chapters, which he called a *crux interpretum* in Pauline studies.[1] The problem that Rom 9-11 has posed for scholars has not been purely exegetical in nature but has been complicated by theological and even political issues intertwined with exegetical problems.[2] For example, preoccupation with the so-called

---

[1] Werner Georg Kümmel, "Die Probleme von Römer 9-11 in der gegenwärtigen Forschungslage," in *Die Israelfrage Nach Römer 9-11*, ed. L. de Lorenzi (Rome: Abtei van St. Paul vor den Mauern, 1977), 13.

[2] See Guenter Wasserberg, "Romans 9-11 and Jewish Christian Dialogue: Prospects and Provisos," in *1998 SBL Seminar Papers: Part One* (Atlanta: Scholars, 1998), 1-11, from a German point of view. From American point of view, see Sidney G. Hall III, *Christian Anti-Semitism and Paul's Theology* (Minneapolis: Fortress, 1993), especially pp. 113-130. For reviews of scholarship, see Christian Müller, *Gottes Gerechtigkeit und Gottes Volk: Eine Untersuchung zu Römer 9-11*, FRLANT 86 (Göttingen: Vandenhoeck & Ruprecht, 1964), 5-27; Peter Stuhlmacher, "Zur Interpretation von Römer 11,25-32," *Probleme biblischer Theologie: Gerhard von Rad zum 70. Geburtstag,* ed. H. W. Wolff (Munich: Kaiser, 1971), 555-70; Kümmel, "Römer 9-11," 13-33; W. D. Davies, "Paul and the People

Israelfrage has led European and American scholars to concentrate on rather peripheral issues even though the growing consensus among scholars is that the central issue that Paul deals with in Rom 9-11 is the "trustworthiness of God"[3] or "impartiality and faithfulness of God."[4]

Since Romans itself has been considered Paul's systematic theology in letter form, it is not surprising to see that Rom 9-11 has been a gold mine for the debates on Paul's theology, regardless of these chapters' context. For example, many disputes have occurred in connection with "predestination and human responsibility,"[5] "the righteousness of God,"[6] "the relation between Jews and Gentiles,"[7] "the church and Israel,"[8] and "salvation."[9] Reviewing some of these discussions, James Aageson claims that "scholarship on Romans 9-11 has reached an im-

---

of Israel," *NTS* 24 (1977-1978): 24-5; John E. Toews, "The Law in Paul's Letter to the Romans: A Study of Romans 9:30-10:13" (Ph.D. dissertation, Northwestern University, 1977), 107-10; Paul E. Dinter, "The Remnant of Israel and the Stone of Stumbling According to Paul (Romans 9-11)" (Ph.D. dissertation, Union Theological Seminary in New York, 1979), 8-9; P. Gorday, *Principles of Patristic Exegesis: Romans 9-11 in Origen, John Chrysostom, and Augustine*, Studies in the Bible and Early Christianity 4 (New York and Toronto: E. Mellen, 1983), 1-10, especially his notes in pp. 243-56; H. Räisänen, "Römer 9-11: Analyse eines geistigen Ringens," *ANRW* 2:25.4 (1987): 2891-939; and idem, "Romans 9-11," 178-206.

[3] Räisänen, "Romans 9-11," 178.

[4] E. Elizabeth Johnson, "Romans 9-11: The Faithfulness and Impartiality of God," in *Pauline Theology III: Romans*, ed. David M. Hay and E. Elizabeth Johnson (Minneapolis: Fortress, 1995), 211-39. Johnson illustrates well how this preoccupation plays in the exegesis of various scholars in pp. 211-15.

[5] See G. B. Caird, "Predestination—Romans ix.-xi.," *ExpTim* 68 (1956-57): 324-27; R. Bring, "Paul and the Old Testament: A Study of the Ideas of Election, Faith and Law in Paul with Special Reference to Rom ix:30-x:21," *ST* 25 (1971): 21-60; and E. Dinkler, "The Historical and the Eschatological Israel in Romans, Chapters 9-11: A Contribution to the Problem of Predestination and Individual Responsibility," *JR* 36 (1956): 109-27.

[6] Müller, *Gottes Gerechtigkeit*.

[7] Dieter Zeller, *Juden und Heiden in der Mission des Paulus*, 2d ed., FB 8 (Stuttgart: Katholisches Bibelwerk, 1976), 202-69; Johannes Munck, *Christ and Israel: An Interpretation of Romans 9-11*, trans. Ingeborg Nixon (Philadelphia: Fortress, 1967); and Davies, "Paul and the People of Israel," 4-39.

[8] Michael Theobald, "Kirche und Israel nach Röm 9-11," *Kairos* 29 (1987): 1-22; M. Rese, "Israel und Kirche in Römer 9," *NTS* 34 (1988): 208-17; and Paul M. van Buren, "The Church and Israel: Romans 9-11," *Princeton Seminary Bulletin* Supp. 1 (1990): 5-18.

[9] Christoph Plag, *Israels Wege zum Heil: Eine Untersuchung zu Römer 9 bis 11*, Arbeiten zur Theologie 40 (Stuttgart: Calwer, 1969); more recently, Daniel Jong-Sang Chae, *Paul As Apostle to the Gentiles: His Apostolic Self-Awareness and Its Influence on the Soteriological Argument in Romans*, Paternoster Biblical and Theological Monographs (Carlisle: Paternoster, 1997), especially, pp. 215-88.

passe"[10] and calls for an alternative way to resolve the impasse.[11] It is true that excessive focus on "Paul's theoretical theological ideas"[12] has created such deadlock that a new method is seriously called for. I believe that the most neglected aspect of Rom 9-11 has been its rhetorical composition, namely, the way Paul presents his argumentation in the context of Greco-Roman rhetorical conventions.[13] When this is not properly understood, Paul is accused of inconsistency: "Romans 9-11 is simply inconsistent in its argumentation";[14] "There is nothing unclear about the goal of the argument in chaps. 9-11.... But the route he traces

---

[10] James W. Aageson, "Scripture and Structure in the Development of the Argument in Romans 9-11," *CBQ* 48 (1986): 266.

[11] His solution is to pay closer attention to Paul's "scriptural argumentation" (ibid.): "... if our understanding of these three chapters is to be advanced, the theological concepts and ideas expressed in Romans 9-11 must be viewed in light of the method which Paul has used to construct his response to a troublesome issue in the early church." In his recent dissertation, John G. Lodge approaches Rom 9-11 with a reader-response criticism and presents an interesting study (*Romans 9-11: A Reader-Response Analysis,* University of Florida International Studies in Formative Christianity and Judaism 6 [Atlanta: Scholars, 1996]). Lodge uses "radical" reader-oriented theories to resolve the tensions in Rom 9-11 (e.g., whether 9:6a or 9:6b is the theme of the passage; contradiction between Rom 9 and 11 or Rom 9 and 10) and he finds that "the tensions and incompatibilities are not so much to be resolved as to be experienced" (x). Apart from a suspicion whether Paul's letter can be analyzed as such with success, I am not convinced, however, that this study provides any new understanding of the passage to help "the readers," whether "implied," "real," or "actual," that may be.

[12] Räisänen, "Romans 9-11," 179.

[13] Hans Hübner, *Biblische Theologie des Neuen Testaments, Band 2: Die Theologie des Paulus und ihre neutestamentaliche Wirkungsgeschichte* (Göttingen: Vandenhoeck & Ruprecht, 1993), 252, n. 689: "Für die rhetorische Analyse von Röm 9-11 nenne ich so gut wie keine Lit." The work of Folker Siegert, *Argumentation bei Paulus: gezeigt an Röm 9-11,* WUNT 34 (Tübingen: Mohr, 1985) analyzes Rom 9-11 strictly from perspective of the New Rhetoric advocated by C. Perelman and L. Olbrechts-Tyteca (*The New Rhetoric: A Treatise on Argumentation,* trans. J. Wilkinson and P. Weaver [Notre Dame: Notre Dame University Press, 1969]). Hermeneutically interesting, but this study has a completely different goal from mine in its investigation. Siegert first catalogues 105 examples of rhetorical examples from LXX in terms of argumentation, using the New Rhetoric's terminology (pp. 23-84). These examples in turn are used as background for Pauline argumentation in Rom 9-11. Since Perelman and Olbrechts-Tyteca's rhetorical theories have little to do with the ancient rhetoric (even though they claim that their theories are based on it), Siegert's analysis does not advance in our understanding of Rom 9-11 in terms of Greco-Roman rhetoric.

[14] J. C. Beker, "Romans 9-11 in the Context of the Early Church," *Princeton Seminary Bulletin* Supp.1 (1990): 45.

out to reach it is virtually unnavigable";[15] "Of the many problems which trouble interpreters of Romans 9-11, none rises more massively from its pages or casts a more impenetrable shadow than the relationship between Paul's argument in 9:6-13 and his argument in 11:25-31."[16] Is Paul really inconsistent in his argumentation in Rom 9-11?

We will have to judge him after we examine the rhetorical aspect of his argumentation. Paul Achtemeier puts this point well when he says:

> Paul was a coherent thinker—and often far more skilled in rhetoric than his critics want to believe. Careful attention to language, rhetorical structure, and context will often show supposed contradictions to rest more with careless exegesis than with Paul.[17]

It is my contention that our understanding of Rom 9-11 can only be advanced if we pay more attention to Paul's argumentative structure from the perspective of his sophisticated use of Greco-Roman rhetorical theories. Since the Greco-Roman rhetorical theories are thoroughly catalogued and explained by various rhetorical handbooks in the Hellenistic periods,[18] it is not too difficult to find much correspondence between Paul's arguments and these theories. Yet, discovering such correspondence does not mean much because the purpose of "using the classical handbooks in an analysis of Paul's letters is not to prove his dependence upon them but to be guided by them in a *description* of Paul's arguments."[19] The goal should be to utilize these theories described in the handbooks to decipher and analyze Paul's argumentation

---

[15] Terence L. Donaldson, "'Riches for the Gentiles' (Rom 11:12): Israel's Rejection and Paul's Gentile Mission," *JBL* 112 (1993): 89.

[16] Frank Thielman, "Unexpected Mercy: Echoes of a Biblical Motif in Romans 9-11," *SJT* 47 (1994): 169. See also François Refoulé, "Cohérence ou incohérence de Paul en Romains 9-11?," *RB* 98 (1991): 51-79.

[17] "Finding the Way to Paul's Theology: A Response to J. Christiaan Beker and J. Paul Sampley," in *Pauline Theology, Volume I: Thessalonians, Philippians, Galatians, Philemon,* ed. Jouette M. Bassler (Minneapolis: Fortress, 1991), 27.

[18] See, e.g., Aristotle's *Rhetorica,* Quintilian's *Institutio Oratoria,* or Cicero's *De Oratore* and *De Inventione.* The best and succinct introduction to classical rhetoric with useful examples is still Edward P. J. Corbett, *Classical Rhetoric for the Modern Student,* 3d ed. (Oxford: Oxford University Press, 1990).

[19] G. W. Hansen, "Rhetorical Criticism," in *Dictionary of Paul and His Letters,* ed. G. Hawthorn, *et al.* (Downers Grove, Ill.: InterVarsity, 1993), 822 (my emphasis). Therefore, "[r]hetorical criticism of Paul's letters uses the parallels which are applicable from the rhetorical handbooks as descriptive tools" (ibid.).

in order to gain a better understanding of what he is trying to say in Rom 9-11.

Also, the place of Rom 9-11 should be clarified in the letter as a whole, as to whether its content has any continuity with what Paul argues in the rest of the letter. Without proper understanding of its place in the letter, exegesis will be misguided and misled. For this purpose, the letter framework (beginning and ending) will be examined to put Rom 9-11 into the context of the whole letter.

II. THE METHODOLOGY

In order to understand Paul's argumentation in light of Greco-Roman rhetoric, a method of rhetorical criticism developed in recent years by various scholars will be employed.[20]   There should be no doubt that it was Hans-Dieter Betz's commentary on Galatians[21] that revived interest in rhetorical criticism.[22] Betz was not the first modern scholar who utilized Greco-Roman rhetoric in New Testament exegesis, but his work is distinguished by his emphasis on the invention and arrangement of arguments in contrast to previous works which concentrated on style.[23]   Indeed, it is true that Betz's approach

---

[20] Useful surveys of development of the New Testament rhetorical criticism abound. See especially Dennis L. Stamps, "Rhetorical Criticism of the New Testament: Ancient and Modern Evaluations of Argumentation," in *Approaches to New Testament Studies,* eds. Stanley E. Porter and David Tombs, JSNTSup 120 (Sheffield: Sheffield Academic, 1995), 129-69 and Duane F. Watson, "Rhetorical Criticism of the Pauline Epistle Since 1975," *Critical Reviews in Biblical Studies* 3 (1995): 219-48.

[21] Hans-Dieter Betz, *Galatians: A Commentary on Paul's Letter to the Churches in Galatia,* Hermeneia (Philadelphia: Fortress, 1979); see also idem, "The Literary Composition and Function of Paul's Letter to the Galatians," *NTS* 21 (1975): 353-79.

[22] J.-N. Aletti, "La présence d'um modèle rhétorique en Romains: Son rôle et son importance," *Bib* 71 (1990): 1; Carl Joachim Classen, "St. Paul's Epistles and Ancient Greek and Roman Rhetoric," in *Rhetoric and the New Testament: Essays from the 1992 Heidelberg Conference,* ed. Stanley E. Porter and Thomas H. Olbricht, JSNTSup 90 (Sheffield: Sheffield Academic, 1993), 265-6.

[23] Margaret M. Mitchell, *Paul and the Rhetoric of Reconciliation: An Exegetical Investigation of the Language and Composition of 1 Corinthians,* HUT 28 (Tübingen: Mohr, 1991), 5-6. See the surveys in Michael Bünker, *Briefformular und rhetorische disposition im 1. Korintherbrief,* Göttingen Theologische Arbeiten 28 (Göttingen: Vandenhoeck und Ruprecht, 1983), 13-5; Siegert, *Argumentation bei Paulus,* 5-15; Hans-Dieter Betz, "The Problem of Rhetoric and Theology Ac-

realizes that Paul's letters undeniably contain argumentation, which can be elucidated by comparison with the conventions for the invention and arrangement of arguments in rhetorical compositions in Greco-Roman antiquity.[24]

Turning from mere stylistic analysis of rhetoric toward argumentation is hailed by Burton Mack as "the single most important feature" that modern rhetorical criticism has contributed to New Testament interpretation.[25]

While Betz's contribution should be recognized, he did not clearly systematize or schematize the methodology itself.[26] It was George A. Kennedy, one of the foremost experts in the field of ancient rhetoric, who laid down the procedure of rhetorical criticism.[27] He argues that since James Muilenburg's 1969 SBL presidential address,[28] although a few rhetorical critical works on the New Testament had appeared, there had been no "vigorous methodology," and thus he provides one.[29] His methodology is quite simple to follow but it has defied the outlining efforts of several scholars who have attempted to summa-

---

cording to the Apostle Paul," in *L'Apôtre Paul. Personalitè, style et concêption du ministère*, ed. A. Vanhoye, BETL 73 (Leuven: Leuven University Press, 1986), 16-21; Burton L. Mack, *Rhetoric and the New Testament* (Minneapolis: Fortress, 1990), 9-17; R. Meynet, "Histoire de 'l'analyse rhétorique' en exégèse biblique," *Rhetorica* 8 (1990): 291-312; S. M. Pogoloff, *Logos and Sophia: The Rhetorical Situation of 1 Corinthians*, SBLDS 134 (Atlanta: Scholars, 1992), chapter 1; Duane F. Watson and Alan J. Hauser, eds., *Rhetorical Criticism of the Bible: A Comprehensive Bibliography with Notes on History and Method*, Biblical Interpretation Series 4 (Leiden: E. J. Brill, 1994), 101-9; R. Dean Anderson, Jr., *Ancient Rhetorical Theory and Paul*, Contribution to Biblical Exegesis and Theology 18 (Kampen: Kok Pharos, 1996), 13-28, whose rhetorical analysis is, however, heavily concentrated on the stylistic issues; Brian K. Peterson, *Eloquence and the Proclamation of the Gospel in Corinth*, SBLDS 163 (Atlanta: Scholars, 1998), 7-16.

[24] Mitchell, *Paul and the Rhetoric*, 6.

[25] Mack, *Rhetoric and the New Testament*, 21.

[26] The reason is, I think, that he still operated in the scheme of historical criticism, that he did not think he was not developing a new methodology. Betz's own description of his *Galatians* commentary illustrates this well: "the work of an historian whose goal is to understand a historical phenomenon with the help of a set of methods called the historical-critical method" (*Galatians*, xv; cited by Mitchell, *Paul and the Rhetoric*, 6, n. 17).

[27] George A. Kennedy, *New Testament Interpretation Through Rhetorical Criticism* (Chapel Hill: University of North Carolina Press, 1984).

[28] "Form Criticism and Beyond," *JBL* 88 (1969): 1-18.

[29] Kennedy, *Rhetorical Criticism*, 3-4.

rize it in their works.[30] This is chiefly because his language is rather ambiguous towards the end of his description; but we can briefly summarize his methodology in the following way:[31]

1) Determination of the *rhetorical unit*. The first step is to determine the rhetorical unit just as form critics identify discrete pericopes. Kennedy compares determining the rhetorical unit to the practice of form critics, but cautions that the goal of rhetorical criticism is not to dig into the original sources of certain texts but "to understand the effect of the text" (p. 33). The clues for a certain rhetorical unit include the use of *inclusio,* which often marks the beginning and the end of the rhetorical unit. One of Kennedy's caveats is that the rhetorical critic should be aware of the overall rhetoric of the larger unit if the unit investigated is contained in the larger work. Also, "the rhetoric of large units has to be built up from an understanding of the rhetoric of smaller units" (p. 33). In the case of this study, it is important to be aware of the rhetoric of the larger unit (the whole of Romans) in the analysis of Rom 9-11. In the discussion in the next chapter, it will be clear that some interpreters ignore this warning and simply work on smaller units without due consideration of the larger rhetorical situation.

2) Determination of the *rhetorical situation*. This is an area that needs to be refined in terms of its definition and application to rhetorical criticism. The next chapter is devoted to examining the problems related to the rhetorical situation, especially in relationship to the historical situation.

3) Determination of the *rhetorical problem*. Kennedy suggests two methods for determining the overriding rhetorical problem: the use of *stasis* theory and the theory of the three *species of rhetoric*. Kennedy warns that "Stasis theory is exceedingly complex, and discussion of it probably should not be undertaken by a student before extensive reading in the rhetorical sources" (p. 36). With these words, Kennedy opts not to explain further *stasis* theory, which the present writer be-

---

[30] See the six step division of C. C. Black, "Rhetorical Criticism and Biblical Interpretation," *ExpTim* 100 (1989): 254-5 and four step scheme of A. H. Snyman, "Style and the Rhetorical Situation of Romans 8:31-39," *NTS* 34 (1988): 218. The five step division is most common. See Wilhelm Wuellner, "Where Is Rhetorical Criticism Taking Us?," *CBQ* 49 (1987): 455-58; Duane F. Watson, *Invention, Arrangement, and Style: Rhetorical Criticism of Jude and 2 Peter*, SBLDS 104 (Atlanta: Scholars, 1988), 8-28; Anderson, *Rhetorical Theory and Paul*, 23-4; Peterson, *Eloquence and the Proclamation*, 24-5. I prefer to see it in six steps, similar to Black's explanation.

[31] Kennedy, *Rhetorical Criticism*, 33-8.

lieves holds the key to understanding our rhetorical unit of Rom 9-11. Therefore, the theory itself will be reviewed in the next section before moving on to the next chapter. Determining the rhetorical species, whether judicial, deliberative, or epideictic, involves examination of the time frame of the goal of rhetoric, whether it "seeks to bring about a judgment about events in the past" (judicial), "aims at effecting a decision about future action" (deliberative), or "celebrates or condemns someone or something... increasing or undermining assent to some value," thus concerning the present (epideictic) (p. 36).

4) Determination of the *arrangement of material*. The arrangement (τάξις) of the material is largely dependent upon the species of rhetoric. The subdivisions of material (*exordium, narratio, propositio, probatio, refutatio, peroratio,* etc.) should be examined in terms of their persuasive effectiveness in meeting the rhetorical situation.

5) Determination of *invention* and *style*. In order to examine the rhetorical effectiveness just described, the rhetorical critic should consider how the proofs are crafted by the author. Inartificial proofs or external evidence include ancient authorities (e.g., scripture), sworn testimony, and laws. Artificial proofs are created by the rhetor, which are *logos,* the mode of inductive or deductive argument, *pathos,* appealing to the audience's emotions, and *ethos,* establishing the rhetor's good character. When the *devices of style* are examined, figures of thought, figures of speech, and diction (λέξις), among other things, should be considered carefully. Kennedy emphasizes that the oral nature of rhetoric should be kept in mind in examining the style of New Testament rhetoric.[32]

6) Evaluation of *rhetorical effectiveness*. The last step of Kennedy's methodology is to evaluate the rhetoric investigated to see if it meets the rhetorical exigence.

This procedure will be followed generally, but two areas, as noted, the theory of rhetorical situation and *stasis*, will be critically examined before applying this methodology.[33] The theory of *stasis* needs to be examined carefully since it has not been clearly explained, let alone applied satisfactorily to New Testament scholarship.[34] The reason

---

[32] On the oral aspect of the New Testament writings, see Paul J. Achtemeier, "*Omne Verbum Sonat*: The New Testament and the Oral Environment of Late Western Antiquity," *JBL* 109 (1990): 3-27.

[33] The theory of rhetorical situation will be discussed in chapter 2 in conjunction with the question of history in rhetorical criticism.

[34] It is puzzling why Kennedy ignores the importance of *stasis* theory even though he makes some useful comments throughout the book (e.g., pp. 46-7, 88,

why the theory of the rhetorical situation needs to be examined in detail, despite the fact that it is not a part of the ancient rhetorical theories (and therefore the reason why some practitioners reject its use [see chapter 2]), is because of my conviction that it holds an important key to bridging the gap between rhetorical criticism and historical criticism. Further, when the theory is applied properly, it will guide and control our exegesis in a very effective way.

EXCURSUS

WHAT DOES ARISTOTLE HAVE TO DO WITH PAUL?

This study assumes that Paul not only was educated in Greco-Roman rhetoric but also consciously and skillfully used it to persuade his audience. There are some scholars, however, who still question whether Paul used in his letters, or even knew, Greco-Roman rhetorical theories at all. Most recently, for example, Jeffrey A. Weima[35] argues that Paul had not received any formal rhetorical training and even if he knew or had been trained in ancient rhetoric, he "deliberately chose not to engage in such oratory practices."[36] First, concerning Paul's educational background, he argues that "[t]here is no concrete evidence that Paul knew or was ever trained in ancient rhetoric."[37] Of course, there is no mention in the New Testament that he received rhetorical training, either in his letters or in Acts. It is a mistake, however, to assume that Paul did not receive any rhetorical training because we have so much external evidence that illuminates his probable educational background. Most of all, it is well-known that rhetoric had become the primary dis-

---

147). See Peterson, *Eloquence and the Proclamation*, 36-38, for a survey of its applications to New Testament interpretation. Peterson utilizes the theory well in his rhetorical analysis of 2 Cor 10-13 in pp. 144-59.

[35] "What Does Aristotle Have to Do with Paul? An Evaluation of Rhetorical Criticism." *Calvin Theological Journal* 32 (1997): 458-68.

[36] Ibid., 464-5. Even from the beginning of his essay, it is plainly seen that his statements are contradictory simply because he cannot maintain both of these positions. If he is successful in his first argument that Paul had not had any rhetorical training, then his second argument that Paul chose not to use his rhetorical skills cannot be made and vice versa.

[37] Ibid., 464.

cipline of Roman higher education in the first century.[38] Being a Roman citizen from Tarsus, which was the center of philosophy and rhetoric, it is very likely that Paul received Roman higher education which began at the age of eighteen. Even if Paul was being educated in Jerusalem as a Pharisee,[39] which has been strongly supported recently,[40] there is still a high probability that he was educated in rhetoric. Jerusalem was fully hellenized by the time of Paul's youth, and had become cosmopolitan, similar to any other Hellenistic city.[41] Hengel's research has sufficiently shown that the education that the typical Jewish boy received in the first century was conducted in a *gymnasium,* which had become a center of education in Palestine along with the synagogues.[42] Even the rabbis studied Greco-Roman rhetorical theories and were familiar with Greek language and culture.[43] Furthermore, there is evidence that instructing and learning Greco-Roman rhetoric was so popular in Jerusalem that even Herod the Great learned rhetoric from Nico-

---

[38] Henri I. Marrou, *A History of Education in Antiquity,* tr. George Lamb (New York: Sheed & Ward, 1956), 267, 87: "Hellenistic culture was above all a rhetorical culture, and its typical literary form was the public lecture... and it ran through Hellenistic culture as a whole. For a thousand years—possibly two—from Demetrius Phaleron to Ennodius (later still Byzantium), this was the standard type of teaching in all higher education." See also S. Bonner, *Education in Ancient Rome: From the Elder Cato to the Younger Pliny* (Berkeley: University of California Press, 1977); M. L. Clarke, *Higher Education in the Ancient World* (Albuquerque: University of New Mexico Press, 1971); and Mack, *Rhetoric and the New Testament,* 29-31.

[39] "I am a Jew, born in Tarsus in Cilicia, but brought up in this city at the feet of Gamaliel, educated strictly according to our ancestral law" (Acts 22:3). See W. C. van Unnik, "Tarsus or Jerusalem: The City of Paul's Youth," in *Sparsa Collecta I* (Leiden: Brill, 1973), 259-320.

[40] Martin Hengel and R. Deines, *The Pre-Christian Paul* (Valley Forge, Penn: Trinity Press International, 1991), 27-30.

[41] Martin Hengel, *Judaism and Hellenism: Studies in their Encounter in Palestine during the Early Hellenistic Period,* tr. John Bowden (Minneapolis: Fortress, 1974), I, 6-57. See also Hengel and Deines, *Pre-Christian Paul,* 54-60.

[42] Hengel, *Judaism and Hellenism,* 70-78.

[43] J. L. Kinneavy, *Greek Rhetorical Origins of Christian Faith: An Inquiry* (New York: Oxford University Press, 1987), 90-91. See also Saul Lieberman, *Hellenism in Jewish Palestine* (New York: Jewish Theological Seminary of America, 1954), 104: "They probably did not read Plato and certainly not the pre-Socratic philosophers. Their main interest was centered on Gentile legal studies and their methods of rhetoric" (cited by Emil Schürer, *The History of the Jewish People in the Age of Jesus Christ [175 B.C.—A.D. 135],* a new English version rev. and ed. Geza Vermes, Fergus Millar, and Matthew Black; original trans. by John Macpherson [Edinburgh: T. & T. Clark, 1979], II, 78, n. 265).

laus of Damascus.[44]   All this evidence leads to the idea that Paul received some rhetorical training as a part of his education. Ben Witherington observes: "Paul had the motive, the means and the opportunity to obtain these skills, even in Jerusalem, and he is likely to have done so before he even took up formal training outside the home."[45]

Weima also argues that Paul himself denies he was trained in rhetoric, and that even if he had been trained, he consciously chose not to use it. Weima refers to 2 Cor 11:6 where Paul concedes that he is an "amateur" (ἰδιώτης) in public speaking. Being an ἰδιώτης does not mean, however, that the person was not trained in rhetoric, but is related to financial earnings from rhetorical activity. In the context of 2 Cor 11, what Paul says about his being ἰδιώτης means that he was not receiving the salary that teachers of rhetoric would normally expect.[46] This becomes evident when we consider how Isocrates, one of the better known rhetoricians of the day, uses the word ἰδιώτης. He refers to some of his students as ἰδιῶται who chose not to become professional orators or teachers of rhetoric.[47] It is obvious to see that those who were professionally trained in rhetoric could become ἰδιῶται, not making a living by practicing oratory or teaching it.[48] Weima also argues that Paul denies using any rhetorical skills in his preaching in 1 Cor 1-2. Recent studies have amply shown, however, that what Paul opposed was not rhetorical usage as a whole but a particular tradition, the sophistic school of rhetoric.[49] Weima also argues that since rhetorical

---

[44] Martin Hengel, *The Hellenization of Judea in the First Century After Christ* (Philadelphia: Trinity, 1989), 35-40. See further on Nicolaus of Damascus, Ben Z. Wacholder, *Nicolaus of Damascus* (Berkeley: University of California Press, 1962), 33-40, who convincingly shows that the leading Pharisees were studying Greek literature and rhetoric. Weima cites Gerald M. Philipps to support his argument that the Pharisees did not have Hellenistic training such as rhetoric but his articles ("The Place of Rhetoric in the Babylonian Talmud," *Quarterly Journal of Speech* 43 [1957]: 390-93 and "The Practice of Rhetoric at the Talmudic Academies," *Speech Monographs* 26 [1959]: 37-46) reflect on much later sources than the first century (Babylonian Talmud!) and are based on older assumptions.

[45] Ben Witherington, III, *The Paul Quest: The Renewed Search for the Jew of Tarsus* (Downers Grove, Ill.: InterVarsity, 1998), 98.

[46] See Peterson, *Eloquence and the Proclamation*, 109-110.

[47] Isocrates, *Antidosis*, 200-204.

[48] See also Sext. Emp. *Math.*, 2.76-83 for a similar usage of the word ἰδιώτης. See further Kennedy, *New Testament Interpretation*, 95; Pogoloff, *Logos and Sophia*, 148-53; Dale Martin, *The Corinthian Body* (New Haven: Yale University Press, 1995), 48-49.

speeches were designed to address an "unknown or unfriendly audience" it is unlikely that Paul used rhetoric towards his audience with
whom he had a "close personal relationship" (467). This is completely
unfounded. Rhetorical handbooks frequently mention that the rhetor
should design his/her speech in accordance with the disposition of the
audience, whether well- or little-known, so that the speech should suit
the need of the moment. Finally, if Paul was the apostle to the Gentiles, whose main mission field was the urban areas of the Greco-
Roman world, was it not more appropriate for him to use rhetorical
skills to win them?[50] After all, he is the one who says

> For though I am free with respect to all, I have made myself a slave
> to all, so that I might win more of them. To the Jews I became as a
> Jew, in order to win Jews. To those under the law I became as one
> under the law (though I myself am not under the law) so that I might
> win those under the law. To those outside the law I became as one
> outside the law (though I am not free from God's law but am under
> Christ's law) so that I might win those outside the law. To the weak
> I became weak, so that I might win the weak. I have become all
> things to all people, that I might by all means save some. I do it all

---

[49] See Duane Litfin, *St. Paul's Theology of Proclamation: 1 Corinthians 1-4
and Greco-Roman Rhetoric,* STNSMS 79 (Cambridge: Cambridge University
Press, 1994); Pogoloff, *Logos and Sophia*; Michael A. Bullmore, *St. Paul's Theology of Rhetorical Style: An Examination of 1 Corinthians 2:1-5 in the Light of First
Century Graeco-Roman Culture* (San Francisco: International Scholars Publications, 1995); and especially Bruce W. Winter, *Philo and Paul among the Sophists,*
SNTSMS 96 (Cambridge: Cambridge University Press, 1997). Weima also refers
to these works in support of his thesis (except Winter's) but the statement like
"Paul rejects not rhetoric, but the cultural values wedded to it" (Pogoloff, *Logos
and Sophia,* 121) persuades me that Weima misreads them. Take a note also that
Weima quotes (p. 466) Bruce Winter's article ("Is Paul among the Sophists?" *Reformed Theological Review* 53 [1994]: 35) out of context: "Paul, as a matter of
principle, did not 'display his speeches rhetorically or according to the received
form of *the sophists*' (*On Rhetoric* 2.139, II)" (my emphasis). It is clear to me that
Winter argues that Paul refuses the use of rhetoric in the tradition of the sophists
but Weima makes Winter say that Paul rejected rhetoric as a whole. See also another article of Winter ("The Entries and Ethics of Orators and Paul [1 Thessalonians 2:1-12]," *TynBul* 44 [1993]: 55-74), which was also misused by Weima; Winter
argues that Paul does not approach the Thessalonians like "the virtuoso rhetors
known as 'sophists'" (p. 55) but Weima quotes (p. 466) Winter's conclusion out of
context and gives the impression that Winter believes that Paul rejected rhetoric
completely.

[50] On the literacy level as well as education of Paul's audience, see the apt
discussion of Witherington, *Paul Quest,* 90-4, and references there.

for the sake of the gospel, so that I may share in its blessings (1 Cor 9:19-23).[51]

I would simply echo the words of J.-N. Aletti:

> Ceux qui refusent à Paul d'avoir pu étudier la rhétorique, même de façon rudimentaire, feraient d'ailleurs bien de se demander ce que signifierait, pour un homme qui se prétend l'apôtre des païens, de ne pouvoir entrer dans les modes de raisonner et d'argumenter de ceux à qui il s'adresse![52]

What does Aristotle have to do with Paul? Πολὺ κατὰ πάντα τρόπον!

III. THE THEORY OF *STASIS*

The origin of the Greek term στάσις stems from Aristotelian physics, in which it has the meaning of "a standing still."[53] It refers to the pause between opposite or contrary movements, an immobility before a change in direction.[54] The ancient rhetoricians adapted and used the term to refer to the pause between movements of the argument, and later developed a complicated rhetorical theory of *stasis*. It is generally known that Hermagoras of Temnos first systematized the theory in the second century BC, but even in the fourth century BC, similar reflections on the theory can be found in legal oratory.[55] Hermagoras' work was lost,[56] however, and we can only depend on the fragments that sur-

---

[51] On this passage, see the seminal essay of Abraham J. Malherbe, "Determinism and Free Will in Paul: The Argument of 1 Corinthians 8 and 9," in *Paul in Hellenistic Context*, ed. Troels Engberg-Pedersen (Minneapolis: Fortress, 1995), 231-55, esp. 251-55. For the larger issue of Paul's adaptability in the Hellenistic context, see Clarence E. Glad, *Paul and Philodemus : Adaptability in Epicurean and Early Christian Psychagogy*, NovTSup 81 (Leiden: Brill, 1995). Otherwise noted, all biblical quotations are from NRSV.

[52] Aletti, "La présence," 4.

[53] O. A. L. Dieter, "Stasis," *Speech Monographs* 17 (1950): 349-50; Troy Martin, "Apostasy to Paganism: The Rhetorical Stasis of the Galatian Controversy," *JBL* 114 (1995): 438.

[54] Dieter, "Stasis," 349-51; Omar Swartz, "Hermagoras," in *Encyclopedia of Rhetoric and Composition*, ed. Theresa Enos (New York: Garland, 1996): 315-6.

[55] Ar. *Rhet.* 1373b-1374a, 1416b; Quint. 3.6.49; *Rhet. Ad Alex.* 1427a; Heath, *Hermogenes*, 19.

[56] For attempts of reconstruction of his lost text, see Dieter Matthes, "Hermagoras von Temnos, 1904-1955," *Lustrum* 3 (1958): 58-214 and Karl Barwick,

vived primarily in the writings of Cicero and the anonymous author of
Rhetorica ad Herennium.[57] The apostle Paul's contemporary, Quintilian, pays close attention to the theory of *stasis*[58] but it was Hermogenes
of Tarsus (!) in the second century AD who brought the theory to full
maturity.[59]

The theory of *stasis* is not easy to understand.[60] The major difficulty is the complexity and confusion of the terms that are used in ex-
plaining the theory. Even its name is variously called: "στάσις" (Cic.
Top. 25.93; Quint. 3.6.3); "*constitutio*" (*Ad. Her.* 1.11.18; Cic. *Inv.*
1.8.10; 1.10.13, 14; 2.14.15; Quint. 3.6.2); "*status*" (Cic. *Top.* 25.93,
95; Quint. 3.6.1)[61]; and "*quaestio*" (Quint. 3.6.2). As Quintilian explains: "That which I call the *basis* [*status*] some style the *constitution,*
others the *question,* and others again *that which may be inferred from
the question,*... These different names, however, all mean the same the
thing."[62] Furthermore, other terms related to the theory are even more
confused when translated into English from Latin and Greek.[63] Actually, even the terms in Latin and Greek that are involved with the theory were understood and used differently by ancient rhetoricians. For
example, crucial terms such as ζήτημα, αἴτιον, συνέχον were all understood and defined variously by Cicero, Quintilian and other rhetori-

---

"Zur Rekonstruktion der Rhetorik des Hermagoras von Temnos," *Philogus* 109
(1965): 186-218.

[57] Cic. *Inv.* 1.10-19, 2.12-59.178; *Ad. Her.* 1.18-27, 2.2-26. Their systems,
however, are markedly different from each other. See Malcom Heath, "The Substructure of *Stasis*-Theory From Hermagoras to Hermogenes," *Classical Quarterly*
44 (1994): 117-21.

[58] Quintilian surveys different views of the theory in Quint. 3.6.1-104 and
his own treatment can be found in Quint. 7.2-10.

[59] Heath, *Hermogenes,* 20.

[60] Malcom Heath laments that even scholars in the ancient rhetorical field do
not have a good grasp of it! (ibid., ix).

[61] The translator of Quintilian's *Institutio Oratoria* in the LCL, H. E. Butler,
alternates between "basis" and "issue" when he translates the Latin *status,* which is
also quite confusing.

[62] Quint. 3.6.2. (Butler's translation).

[63] We will use Malcom Heath's terminology in the course of this study. The
reason to follow his system is that his translation and study are most recent (his
translation of Hermogenes' περὶ τῶν στάσεων was published in 1995 and therefore, he takes advantage of recent studies and therefore provides far superior rendering than R. Nadeau's 1964 translation and commentary) and more importantly
he provides a glossary of terms that he uses in his book so that it is quite clear what
he means by his translation. He also provides a short biographical note on the Hellenistic and later rhetoricians (*Hermogenes,* 237-47). His glossary is found in pp.
249-60.

cians. Thus a decision about whose or which system to follow in this analysis needs to be made; here, Malcolm Heath's has been adopted.[64] Probably the best translation of *stasis* should be "issue" since the theory deals with the issues that arise from the argumentation between the parties.

Now let us examine the theory of *stasis* briefly. The most common setting in which *stasis* occurs is the court room. In the simplest model of *stasis* theory, when an accusation (κατάφασις) is countered by a response (ἀπόφασις), a *stasis* arises.[65] In this model, the *stasis* is the proposition of the defense, which is the position of Hermagoras according to Cicero.[66] There are, however, other variations on this position. The anonymous author of *Rhetorica ad Herennium* proposes that "*stasis* is the conflict of the initial propositions of prosecution and defense."[67] In this position, the *stasis* is not solely a property of the defense but of the prosecution as well. Quintilian's position is yet different from these positions: "It [*stasis*] is... the kind of question which arises from the first conflict, which we may represent as follows. 'You did it,' 'I did not,' 'Did he do it?,' or 'You did this,' 'I did not do this,' 'What did he do?'"[68] He focuses on "the question" that arises from the conflict between the accusation and the defense, shifting the attention from the accusation and the defense to the judge, so to speak. He rejects the idea that *stasis* is the proposition of the defense because in some cases the prosecution determines the *stasis*.[69] Also, he rejects the

---

[64] The weakness of recent applications of the *stasis* theory by New Testament scholars generally lie in their oversimplification of the theory. See Peterson, *Eloquence and the Proclamation*, 36-38.

[65] Nadeau, "Classical Systems," 54; Martin, "Apostasy," 438.

[66] Cic. *Inv.* 1.13: "placet autem ipsi constitutionem intentionis esse depulsionem."

[67] *Ad. Her.* 1.18: "constitutio est prima deprecatio defensoris cum accusationis insimulatione coniuncta." The quotation is a paraphrase by Heath, "*Stasis*-Theory Substructure," 116.

[68] Quint. 3.6.5.

[69] Indeed, the stasis theory is construed in the perspective of the prosecutor in the system of Minucianus, a rhetorician who was a contemporary of Hermogenes (Gertrud Lindberg, "Hermogenes of Tarsus," *ANRW* II 34.3 [1997]: 1990). See also Quint. 3.6.13-19. Does this mean that Quintilian rejects and departs from Hermagoras' system? Quintilian himself denies this and professes to adhere to Hermagoras' system. He insists that it is Cicero who misunderstood some aspects of Hermagoras' doctrines (3.6.58-60). Heath's contention that Quintilian had an independent source for Hermagoras' doctrines is not logical ("*Stasis*-Theory Substructure," 119). What Quintilian contests is differences in understanding and interpretation of Hermagoras' doctrines, not the sources.

position insisted on by *Rhetorica ad Herennium,* in which the *stasis* is the conflict between the initial propositions of prosecution and defense because it is not the first conflict but the question that arises from the first conflict.[70]

In Qunitilian's scheme, the phrase "You did it" represents the initial accusation (*intentio*=κατάφασις), which reveals the cause (*ratio*=αἴτιον) of the dispute, while the phrase "I did not" is the initial response (*infitatio*=ἀπόφασις), which informs the containment (*continens* or *firmamentum*=συνέχον) of the dispute.[71] One of the most crucial components in Quintilian's scheme, "the question" (*quaestio*=ζήτημα) can then be defined. One important aspect of all these explanations should be kept in mind—the point of view that the *stasis* theory takes is that of the defendant in the court room.[72] The defendant works hard to persuade the judge or the jury to make τὸ κρινόμενον (*iudicatio*)[73] for his or her advantage. Quintilian contends that ζήτημα and κρινόμενον are identical, which the jury must pronounce at the end of deliberation.[74] The *stasis* as "the kind of question which arises from the first conflict" clarifies many unclear notions regarding the theory itself and will be adopted to analyze Rom 9-11.[75] Quintilian's system is especially useful because it helps identify "the question" surrounding Paul's argument in these chapters. Identifying the kind of question that Paul deals with can point back to the argumentative strategy that he employs to address the specific rhetorical problem.

---

[70] Quint. 3.6.4-6. The reason for the modifications of the original theory of Hermagoras seems obvious: the prosecution's role in forming the *stasis* is clearly ignored in this definition. Cf. Heath, "*Stasis*-Theory Substructure," 116 and see also n. 9.

[71] Nadeau, "Classical Systems," 54; Martin, "Apostasy," 439.

[72] Of course, the same scheme can be reconstructed from the point of view of the accuser or the prosecutor but the main concern of the rhetorical handbooks remains that of the defendant.

[73] Nadeau translates this term as "the point-for-adjudication" ("Classical Systems," 55). See also the discussion of Antoine Braet ("The Classical Doctrine of *status* and the Rhetorical Theory of Argumentation," *Philosophy and Rhetoric* 20 [1987]: 81-2) and his own rendering as "that which-by the audience-is judged" (ibid., 84).

[74] Quint. 3.11.16-7.

[75] For a comprehensive survey of developments and variations of Hermagoras' system from Cicero to Syrianus, see Heath, "*Stasis*-Theory Substructure," 116-29.

There are four kinds of *stasis* at work in the theories of the ancient rhetoricians: Conjecture, Definition, Quality, and Objection.[76] These are taken up briefly now. (1) The *stasis* of "Conjecture" (*constitutio coniecturalis,* στοχασμός) arises when the defendant denies the facts of the case. A certain action can be denied or a person in the event of dispute can be denied.[77] If the facts of the case are not denied, but categorization of the facts is disputed, then it is (2) the *stasis* of "Definition" (*constitutio definitiva* or *proprietas,* ὅρος).[78] Quintilian says that "Definition is the statement of the fact called in question in appropriate, clear and concise language."[79] It is possible that the definition of a certain term or word is in question which calls for the rhetor to define the term for his or her advantage.[80] If the categorization of the facts in the case is not disputed, but the interpretation of the significance of the event is in question, then it is (3) the *stasis* of "Quality" (*constitutio qualitas* or *generalis,* ποιότης).[81] When the issue is none other than the previous three, and the procedure of the certain legal action is in question, then it is (4) the *stasis* of "Objection" (*constitutio translatio,* μετάληψις).[82] The *stasis* of Objection is the last resort that the defendant can take, as it were, when every other option has been failed.[83]

---

[76] A traditional structure for *stasis* theory mentioned in the works of Cicero (*Or.* 45; *De Or.* 2.104-13) and Quintilian (3.6.44, 56) is based on the three *stases* (Conjecture, Definition, and Quality). It was Hermagoras who added the fourth one (Objection) and made it canonical (Cic. *Inv.* 1.16; Quint. 3.6.68-85) (Heath, *Hermogenes,* 70-1).

[77] Cic. *Inv.* 1.8.10; Quint. 7.2; Hermog. *Stat.* 36-43 (the page number of Hermogenes' work is based on Heath' translation in his book); Lausberg, *Handbook,* §§ 99-103; Martin, *Antike Rhtorik,* 30-32.

[78] Cic. *Inv.* 1.8.10-11; 2.17.52-18.56; Quint. 3.5.56, 7.3; Hermog. *Stat.* 43-6; Lausberg, *Handbook,* §§ 104-22; Martin, *Antike Rhetorik,* 32-36.

[79] Quint. 7.3.2.: "Finitio igitur est rei propositae propria et dilucida et breviter comprehensa verbis enuntiatio."

[80] "For sometimes ... there is a question as to what includes, or ... no agreement as to the term to be applied to it" (Quint. 7.3.4). We will see whether this has direct relevance to Rom 9:6b where Paul disputes what is included in the term "Israel."

[81] Cic. *Inv.* 1.8.10; 1.9.12-11.15; 2.21.62-39.115; *De Or.* 2.25.106; *Part. Or.* 9.33; 12.42-43; 37.129-31; *Top.* 21.82; 22.84-85; 23.89-90; 24.92; Quint. 3.6.10; 7.4; Lausberg, *Handbook,* §§ 123-30; and Martin, *Antike Rhetorik,* 36-41. We will discuss this in detail later.

[82] Cic. *Inv.* 1.8.10; 1.11.16; 2.19.57-20.61; Lausberg, *Handbook,* §§ 131-33; Martin, *Antike Rhetorik,* 42-44.

[83] It is quite interesting to see that "the technical defense," so popular and effective in the modern times (especially in the American legal system), was

Of these four *stases,* the third one, the *stasis* of Quality was developed most by the ancient rhetoricians. Let us examine first how
Hermagoras' system developed in the writings of Cicero and more sub-
stantially in Quintilian. Cicero criticizes Hermagoras for dividing the
genus of *stasis* of Quality into four species: deliberative, epideictic, equitable and legal.[84] He argues that since "deliberative and epideictic
are genera of argument," they cannot be regarded as species of any one
genus of argument.[85] Further, "deliberative and epideictic speeches are
not an issue or a sub-head of an issue," because they are not an answer
to an accusation.[86] Therefore, for Cicero, there are only two kinds of
stasis of Quality: equitable and legal.[87] The equitable *stasis,* according
to Cicero, is that "in which there is a question about the nature of justice and right or the reasonableness of reward or punishment" while the
legal *stasis* is concerned with the nature of the law.[88] In Cicero's system, the equitable *stasis* is divided into two parts, the absolute and the
assumption. The absolute equitable *stasis* concerns the question of
right and wrong done. The assumptive equitable *stasis* does not provide a basis for a counter plea, but "seeks some defence from extraneous circumstances."[89] It is divided into four parts, which are *concessio*
(confession and avoidance), *remotio criminis* (shifting the charge), *re-
latio criminis* (retort of the accusation), and *comparatio* (comparison).[90]

Qunitilian's system of *stasis* of Quality is much more sophisticated in my view.[91] He clarifies many aspects by systematizing the *sta-*

---

viewed as the last resort by the ancients. Cf. Braet, "Classical Doctrine," 83. For
an interesting attempt to compare the *stasis* theory and the modern legal system
(German), see Franz Horak, "Die rhetorische Statuslehre und der moderne Aufbau
des Verbrechensbegriffs," in *Festgabe für Arnold Herdlitczka,* ed. Franz Horak and
W. Waldstein (München/Salzburg, 1972), 121-42.

[84] Cic. *Inv.* 1.9.12.
[85] Ibid.
[86] Cic. *Inv.* 1.10.13.
[87] Cic. *Inv.* 1.11.14.
[88] Ibid.
[89] Ibid.
[90] Cicero explains further each of these four parts but we will not spend
more time on his explanation because they are all comparable to Quintilian's system, which we will deal with shortly.
[91] The difference between Quintilian and Cicero is great, especially in the
clarity of explanation. Cicero's reconstruction of Hermagoras' system of *stasis*
leaves many aspects unclear while Quintilian clarifies many issues. According to
Quintilian, "[s]uch faults" should be blamed on Cicero's instructor because his *De
Inventione* is "simply a collection of school-notes on rhetoric which he worked up
into this treatise while quite a young man" (Quint. 3.6.59. Cf. 3.5.15).

ses from the strongest to the weakest. Quintilian starts with the strong-est possible defense, which can be called "Counterplea" (ἀντίληψις), in which the defendant does not admit any wrong done in the charge he/she faces, but in fact, acted honorably.[92] When the wrong is admit-ted by the defendant, then the defense should take another form, which is called "Counterposition" (ἀντίθεσις), in which the defense is sought on other grounds.[93] Again, Quintilian arranges four subtypes of this *stasis* in the order of strength they can assume. The strongest defense that Counterposition can take is "Counteraccusation" (ἀντέγκλημα), in which the defendant argues that the victim deserved the act. Quintil-ian's example includes a robber who was killed—It is true that the per-son was killed, but he was a robber that deserved death.[94] Still another form of Counterposition is called "Counterstatement" (ἀντίστασις), in which the defendant argues that "the act in question prevented the oc-currence of something worse."[95] Therefore, the result of such an act, even though it was not in itself a good thing to commit, is the lesser evil "in a comparison of evils."[96] So far, Quintilian lays out the meth-ods of defense in which an act could be defended. If the defense of the act is not possible, Quintilian urges, the next best course would be to shift the charge to another. This is called "Transference" (μετάστασις), in which the blame can be placed on another person or thing.[97] If none of these methods are available, the last resort would be "Mitigation" (συγγνώμη), essentially "making excuses."[98] There may be many other forms of excuses that the defense could use, such as ignorance and ac-cident, but when no other excuse is available for the defense, it should start pleading for mercy.[99]

In Hermagoras' system of *stasis,* the stases are coordinated, not subordinated. Thus, Hermagoras seems to give equal weight to each *stasis.*[100] Later, it was Hermogenes of Tarsus who was credited with

---

[92] Quint. 7.4.4. Quintilian's example is the case of a man who is disinher-ited because he went on military service and stood for office without his father's consent. In this case, the action committed is in fact honorable and is defensible. In Cicero's system it is called "absolute *stasis.*"

[93] Quint. 7.4.7. In Cicero's system, it is "*stasis* of assumption."

[94] Quint. 7.4.8.

[95] Quint. 7.4.12.

[96] Ibid.

[97] Quint. 7.4.13-14.

[98] Quint. 7.4.14.

[99] Quint. 7.4.17.

[100] Nadeau, "Classical Systems of Stases," 67.

introducing a subordinate system.[101] Already in the system of Quintilian, however, the *stases* are organized in the order of strength of defensibility. Therefore, Quintilian's system is a kind of transitional bridge
between Hermagoras and Hermogenes from a coordinate system to a
subordinate system. Quintilian's system of *stasis* is summed up and
presented in the following table:

(1) Conjecture	
(2) Definition	
(3) Quality ──┬──(4) Counterplea └──(5) Counterposition ──┬── (6) Counteraccusation ├── (7) Counterstatement ├──(8) Transference └──(9) Mitigation	
(10) Objection	

In sum, the ancient rhetorical theory of *stasis* has been grossly
neglected in the study of Paul's letters. This study will demonstrate
that it holds the key to understanding Paul's argumentation properly.
The theory developed and summarized by Quintilian appears to be
most applicable to an analysis of Rom 9-11. The theory of *stasis* will
be used to determine "the issue" of Paul's argumentation by dissecting
the way Paul structures his argumentation in Rom 9-11.

---

[101] Ibid.; for Hermogenes' subordinate system aptly explained, see Heath,
Hermogenes, 71-3.

CHAPTER TWO

THE HISTORICAL SITUATION AND THE
RHETORICAL SITUATION

I. HISTORICAL CRITICISM AND RHETORICAL CRITICISM

Historical criticism aims to discover "what actually happened" by scrutinizing a "corpus of ascertained fact" in the Bible.[1] The task of a historical critic of the New Testament is that of a historian who critically examines the sources in order to reach the facts behind the text. The final stage of this critical process is to pay close "attention to the historical situation."[2] In the historical-critical method, the historical situation is the backbone of exegesis; but in many cases the text itself is lost in the process of delineating the historical situation of the text. Preoccupied by getting "behind the text," many exegetes do not even come close to the text itself. Clearly, there are inadequacies in the application of the historical-critical method.

I am convinced that rhetorical criticism can help correct this problem since rhetorical criticism pays full attention to the text itself.[3] The rhetorical criticism used here is a historically "informed"

---

[1] E. Krentz, *The Historical-Critical Method* (Philadelphia: Fortress, 1975), 35; I. H. Marshall, "Historical Criticism," in *New Testament Interpretation: Essays on Principles and Methods*, ed. I. H. Marshall (Grand Rapids: Eerdmans, 1977), 126.

[2] John Reumann, "Methods in Studying the Biblical Text Today," *Concordia Theological Monthly* 40 (1969): 665 (cited by Krentz, *The Historical-Critical Method*, 51).

[3] Cf. Kennedy, *New Testament Interpretation*, 4.

methodology different from literary criticism. Kennedy states that
the goal of rhetorical criticism is to read

> the Bible as it would be read by an early Christian, by an inhabi-
> tant of the Greek-speaking world in which rhetoric was the core
> subject of formal education and in which even those without for-
> mal education necessarily developed cultural preconceptions
> about appropriate discourse.[4]

Thus, what is attempted in this study is a historical task. In her rhetorical critical work on 1 Corinthians, M. M. Mitchell emphasizes
that her rhetorical critical work, like mine, is a thoroughly historical
undertaking.[5] For her, rhetorical criticism is "one of the panoply of
tools which bear the name 'historical-critical method.'"[6] Therefore,
she says, "The present study is an historical rhetorical analysis of 1
Corinthians in the light of the literary/rhetorical conventions operative in the first century."[7]

There are nevertheless some scholars who think that rhetorical
criticism should be differentiated from historical criticism. For example, Dennis L. Stamps argues that these two criticisms should
have different interpretive goals and methods. He argues that rhetorical criticism should get out of the "historical paradigm" which
dominates the guild of New Testament studies.[8] He insists that rhetorical critical method is merely used by scholars who are preoccupied with recovering and reconstructing the historical scene of the
New Testament texts, which then becomes "the determinate basis" to
explain the text.[9] Therefore, he argues that "the practice of rhetorical
criticism is assimilated into the well entrenched historical paradigm
which governs New Testament studies" (Stamps alleges that New
Testament scholarly guild wants to protect itself by assigning a

---

[4] Ibid., 5.

[5] Mitchell, *Paul and the Rhetoric of Reconciliation*, 6.

[6] Ibid., 6. Martin Hengel warns against the danger of speaking of "*the*
historical-critical" method (*Acts and the History of Earliest Christianity* [Phila-
delphia: Fortress, 1979], 129). He points out "... the 'historical-critical method'
simply represents a necessary collection of the 'tools' for opening up past
events; that is, it is not a single, clearly defined procedure, but rather a mixture
of sometimes very different methods of working" (Ibid., 54).

[7] Mitchell, *Paul and the Rhetoric of Reconciliation*, 8.

[8] D. L. Stamps, "Rhetorical Criticism and the Rhetoric of New Testament," *LT* 6 (1992): 272.

[9] Ibid.

smaller role for rhetorical criticism).[10]   He then proposes his own rhetorical critical model which emphasizes textuality. To him, rhetorical criticism should be one of the literary criticisms rather than *a* historical criticism. He describes his understanding of rhetorical criticism this way:

> It [rhetorical criticism] is the attempt to analyse, interpret, read a literary unit (text if you please) by analyzing the text in terms of the three relationships of the *aptum*[11] set within the context of a defined rhetorical situation, variously conceived, in order to un-cover the argumentative or persuasive effect a text creates. Simply put, it examines the way discourses are constructed and the way they operate to create certain effects.[12]

Several questions are formed in response to Stamps' attacks on historical criticism and its practitioners. The first obvious question is why rhetorical criticism of the New Testament should belong only to literary criticism. Granted, the New Testament is literature, but is it not also a historical document? While many historical critics have been unduly preoccupied with digging for historical background and failed to explain the text, the problem is not in the method itself but with the ones who practice it. Stamps' allegation of selfish and domineering behaviors in the guild of New Testament studies is unfair; furthermore, it is not clear why he believes that there is a "war" going on between historical criticism and literary criticism.[13]

---

[10] Ibid. Stamps quotes several scholars for his examples, and here is one of them by Jan Lambrecht:

Whether rhetorical criticism should be presented as an independent, self-sufficient method must be rightly doubted. Perhaps one better sees the new rhetoric as an enriching segment of the larger and more encompassing historical-critical method ("Rhetorical Criticism and the New Testament," *Bijdragen* 50 [1989]: 248).

[11] Stamps borrows this term from H. Lausberg's *Handbuch der Literarischen Rhetorik: Eine Grundlegung der Literaturwissenschaft* (Stuttgart: Franz Steiner, 1960), I, 54-8 and 258. It "concerns the relationships which exist between the speaker, the speech, and the audience, for which one can substitute the figures author, text, and reader" ("Rhetorical Criticism," 275).

[12] Ibid., 276.

[13] In Stamps' words: "For one side the war is left undeclared, assimilation is the apparent strategy. For the other side, the war goes on, and the simple refusal by the other side to consider the issues raised by the nature and scope of rhetoric in texts only prolongs the battle" (Ibid., 277). We will discuss Stamps' understanding of the rhetorical situation shortly. For his more elaborate evaluation of rhetorical criticism of the New Testament, see idem, "Rhetorical Criticism of the New Testament: Ancient and Modern Evaluations of Argumenta-

Rhetorical criticism rightly belongs to the realm of historical criticism because "even the most adamantly ahistorical brands of rhetorical criticism are themselves historically conditioned."[14] Simply, since the New Testament documents are historical documents themselves, we cannot help but deal with them historically, in one way or another.[15]

Historical criticism and rhetorical criticism can complement each other by providing checks and balances. It is true that "we can no longer take a simple approach to historical reconstruction, as if we were somehow exempt from the subjectivity of socio-linguistic worlds, or as if the meaning of a text lies in the ashes of the past."[16] At the same time, we cannot approach the New Testament text as if it were a timeless document which transcends time and space to be an "argumentation." Historically balanced rhetorical criticism can offer a powerful interpretive strategy which encompasses seemingly competitive approaches.[17] C. Clifton Black believes that the presupposition of historical and rhetorical criticism comes from the same "model of communication" that delineates "(1) the intent of an author (2) the formulation of a text (3) or that forms or informs a reader."[18] Black correctly argues that it is impossible for a good rhetorical analysis to ignore historical characteristics and assumptions.[19]

---

tion," in *Approaches to New Testament Study,* ed. Stanley E. Porter and David Tombs, JSNTSup 120 (Sheffield: Sheffield Academic, 1995), 129-69.

[14] C. C. Black, "Rhetorical Criticism," in *Hearing the New Testament: Strategies for Interpretation,* ed. Joel B. Green (Grand Rapids: Eerdmans, 1995), 275.

[15] See further C. C. Black, "Rhetorical Questions: The New Testament, Classical Rhetoric, and Current Interpretation," *Dialog* 29 (1990): 62-70 and Pieter F. Craffert, "Relationships between Social-Scientific, Literary, and Rhetorical Interpretation of Texts," *BTB* 26 (1996): 45-55.

[16] Pogoloff, *Logos and Sophia,* 71.

[17] Ibid.

[18] Black, "Rhetorical Criticism," 275.

[19] Ibid., 275. In a similar vein, some narrative critics argue that their methodology is neither antihistorical nor nonhistorical and even that narrative criticism can make contributions to historical understanding. See Mark A. Powell, *What Is Narrative Criticism?*, Guides to Biblical Scholarship, ed. Dan O. Via (Minneapolis: Fortress, 1990), 96-7. Cf. Jack D. Kingsbury, "Reflections on 'the Reader' of Matthew's Gospel," *NTS* 34 (1988): 459, who suggests that the story world of the Gospels may serve as an "index" of the real world. For a positive assessment of narrative critical method from a historical-critical point of view, see Martinus C. de Boer, "Narrative Criticism, Historical Criticism, and the Gospel of John," *JSNT* 47 (1992): 35-48.

The recent dissertation of Brian Peterson takes a similar position, approaching rhetorical criticism with history in mind.[20]   Like Mitchell, Peterson believes that "the study of these ancient texts is first of all an historical task" but he also points out that Mitchell's refusal to use modern categories such as the rhetorical situation is "too rigid."[21]   Yet Peterson himself struggles to justify his use of imported modern concepts such as the rhetorical situation or "exigence"; he simply refers to Kennedy and Pogoloff whose approach, he asserts, is more "cogent" than Mitchell's. It is true that ancient rhetorical handbooks do not use terms such as "rhetorical unit," "rhetorical situation" or "exigence." That does not mean, however, that the *concepts* these terms refer to are absent in their works. For example, Quintilian emphasizes the adaptation of the ornaments of style in this way:

> For since the ornaments of style are varied and manifold and suited for different purposes, they will, unless adapted to the matter and the persons concerned, not merely fail to give our style distinction, but will even destroy its effect and produce a result quite the reverse of that which our matter should produce.[22]

His idea of the adaptation to "the matter and the persons concerned" exactly corresponds to the conceptual elements of the rhetorical situation advocated by Bitzer and Kennedy: namely, constraints, exigence, and audience. Quintilian lays a stronger emphasis on the adaptation of the rhetor to certain circumstances a little later: "For all ornament derives its effect not from its own qualities so much as from the circumstances in which it is applied, and the occasion chosen for saying anything is at least as important a consideration as what is actually said."[23]   Furthermore, he teaches the importance of the rhetor's adaptability in different circumstances:

> If the whole of rhetoric could be thus embodied in one compact code, it would be an easy task of little compass: but most rules are liable to be altered by the nature of the case, circumstances of time and place, and by hard necessity itself. Consequently *the*

---

[20] Peterson, *Eloquence and the Proclamation.*

[21] Ibid., 49-50.

[22] Quint. 11.1.2. The text and the translation used here are from H. E. Butler, ed., *The Institutio Oratoria of Quintilian,* vol. IV (LCL; Cambridge: Harvard University Press, 1922).

[23] Quint. 11.1.7. Cf. *Ad. Her.,* 3.9.16.

> *all-important gift for an orator is a wise adaptability since he is*
> *called upon to meet the most varied emergencies.*[24]

The most important similarity between ancient rhetorical theories and the modern application of their categories is the theory of
stasis, which is claimed to be "at the heart of ancient rhetoric in its
mature form."[25] We will pay close attention to this theory in our
analysis of rhetoric in Romans 9-11 later in this study.[26]

---

[24] Quint. 2.13.2 (my emphasis). I suspect Paul has this gift of adaptability in his use of rhetoric. Cf. also Malcom Heath, *Hermogenes* On Issues:
Strategies of Argument in Later Greek Rhetoric (Oxford: Clarendon, 1995), 4,
who says:

> Rhetoric deals with matters that are contingent and occasion-
> dependent; the answer to a rhetorical problem will vary according
> to the circumstances. Since concrete situations are infinitely vari-
> able it is not possible to anticipate and prescribe for every possi-
> ble situation; therefore no system of rhetoric can be exhaustive...
> The rhetorical theorist is concerned with general principles, *but*
> *the speaker is always concerned in the last analysis with what is*
> *appropriate in the particular situation* (my emphasis).

[25] Ibid., 2. See also Antoine Braet, "The Classical Doctrine of *status* and
the Rhetorical Theory of Argumentation," *Philosophy and Rhetoric* 20 (1987):
79-93. Peterson is quite correct to call attention to this much-neglected theory
in his study (*Eloquence and the Proclamation*, 50) and does an excellent job in
applying this theory in his analysis of rhetoric in 2 Corinthians 10-13. Insawn
Saw (*Paul's Rhetoric in 1 Corinthians 15: An Analysis Utilizing the Theories of
Classical Rhetoric* [Lewiston: Mellen, 1995]) also pays close attention to the
theory of *stasis.* But he refuses to use the concept of rhetorical situation simply
because it is foreign to classical rhetoric (p. 76). He also says that the last step
of Kennedy's method—evaluation of the overall effectiveness of the rhetoric in
meeting the exigence of the rhetorical situation—is "outside of the realm of
classical rhetorical theory" and therefore it should be rejected and rather focus
on the speaker, "for rhetorical handbooks were written for the training of good
orators" (p. 77). This kind of rigid adherence to the terms of the classical rhetorical traditions does not help advance our understanding of the rhetoric of the
New Testament. The same kind of problem plagues Mitchell's approach. She is
rightly criticized by A. C. Wire for not determining "the historical rhetorical
situation" of Corinth based on her excellent work (*JBL* 112 [1993]: 539-40).
Had she utilized the concept of rhetorical situation advocated by Kennedy, this
problem could have been avoided. Her insistence on adhering only to the ancient rhetorical categories prevents her from using any modern concepts in her
rhetorical analysis which could have otherwise furthered our understanding of
the historical situation of Corinth, which was indeed one of the goals of her
work.

[26] See the discussion of the theory in chapter 1.

EXCURSUS

THE SURVIVAL OF HISTORICAL CRITICISM

It was more than 25 years ago when Walter Wink declared that "historical biblical criticism is bankrupt."[27] Wink's declaration sprang from the method's inability "to interpret the Scriptures so that the past becomes alive and illumines our present with new possibilities for personal and social transformation."[28] The historical-critical method tends to remove the student far from the text. This so-called "distancing effect" drives the student of the Bible farther and farther from the text and its subject-matter.[29] Further, the methodology itself is not adequate for serving the community of faith because it fosters skepticism rather than conviction.[30] Must we, then, abandon the method itself?[31] Not really, argues Lee Keck in his stimulating 1980 essay.[32] Keck points out that even though the promise of historical criticism[33] has not been fulfilled, the survival of both the historical-method and the Bible as the canon of the community are critically

---

[27] Walter Wink, *The Bible in Human Transformation: Toward a New Paradigm for Biblical Study* (Philadelphia: Fortress, 1973), 1.

[28] Ibid., 2. But when did the historical-critical method promise to transform persons and society? Was not the original goal of the historical-method to free exegetes from dogmatic Christendom? (cf. Anthony C. Thiselton, "New Testament Interpretation in Historical Perspective," in *Hearing the New Testament: Strategies for Interpretation*, 10-13).

[29] Peter Stuhlmacher, *Historical Criticism and Theological Interpretation of Scripture: Toward a Hermeneutics of Consent*, trans. Roy A. Harrisville (Philadelphia: Fortress, 1977), 62; Archie L. Nations, "Historical Criticism and the Current Methodological Crisis," *SJT* 36 (1983): 61. Nations identifies twelve discrete problems of historical-critical method raised by various scholars (pp. 61-63).

[30] Ibid., 61-62.

[31] This is what some ultra-conservative scholars have attempted to do. For example, see Gerhard Maier, *The End of the Historical-Critical Method*, trans. Edwin W. Leverenz and Rudolph F. Norden (St. Louis: Concordia Publishing House, 1974) and Eta Linnemann, *Historical Criticism of the Bible: Methodology or Ideology?* (Grand Rapids: Baker Book House, 1990); also see Peter Stuhlmacher's devastating criticism of Maier's book in Stuhlmacher, *Historical Criticism*, 66-71.

[32] Leander E. Keck, "Will the Historical-Critical Method Survive? Some Observations," in *Orientation by Disorientation: Studies in Literary Criticism and Biblical Literary Criticism: Presented in Honor of William A. Beardslee*, ed. Richard A. Spencer (Pittsburgh: Pickwick, 1980), 115-27.

[33] "[I]t would explain the Bible, both as a whole and in all its parts, by anchoring it in historical circumstances" (ibid., 115-16).

connected. The reason is simple—precisely because historical criticism is "historical."[34] Without historical criticism, communities of faith lose alertness to the fact that the past brings "analogues" to the present. The discernment that historical criticism/reconstruction brings is also vital to the life of the community itself because it helps it "to come to terms with its own past—precisely in relation to its canon."[35] Keck is surely correct when he says: "In short, what is at stake in the survival of historical criticism as a vital factor in the study of the Bible is its capacity to help the community take responsibility for its past."[36]

II. THE HISTORICAL SITUATION

We turn our attention now to the crucial meeting points of both methodologies: namely, the historical situation and the rhetorical situation. Clarifying the relationship between the two will be paramount for our understanding of rhetorical critical methodology. Let us first look briefly at the historical situation.

How do we define the historical situation? It is based on the understanding of history as "systematic knowledge of the past" which includes human beings' activities in "time, space, and society, expressed in a coherent report (usually written)."[37] History is best told by narrative rather than statistical or sociological reporting.[38] Not merely a display of things of the past, history is also an interpretation of the past. Thus, historical narrative already involves some rhetorical situation of the author and the reader. Traditionally, the historical situation has been synonymous with the *Sitz im Leben*, a term developed in form criticism.[39] It includes various factors surrounding history such as persons, events, and relations that consti-

---

[34] Ibid., 123.

[35] Ibid., 124.

[36] Ibid.; see also his recent essay, "The Premodern Bible in the Postmodern World," *Int* 50 (1996): 130-41.

[37] Krentz, *The Historical-Critical Method*, 34.

[38] Jack Hester, *Doing History* (Bloomington & London: Indiana University Press, 1971), 27-39.

[39] When Kennedy likens the rhetorical situation to the *Sitz im Leben*, it is quite ironic, since the address of James Muilenburg ("Form Criticism and Beyond," 1-18) called for biblical scholars to go *beyond* form criticism to the way ahead provided by rhetorical criticism.

tuted a situation which existed in time and space.[40] Thus, historians only deal with the facts and information available to themselves, but these facts and information do not necessarily encompass every historical fact that exists. Further, it is true that every "fact" cannot be recovered—some selectivity is essential in a historian's reconstruction if narrative is to take less time to tell than the events took to occur. Thus, historical narrative is always a historian's story, whose point of view should clearly be distinguished from "historical facts." There simply cannot be a historical reconstruction that is equal to "historical facts." It is always *a* reconstruction of "historical facts" by a particular historian.[41] Thus, the historical situation always occurs in the narrative (story) of the one who reports history. We will now examine the concept of the rhetorical situation in detail.

III. THE RHETORICAL SITUATION

Lloyd F. Bitzer's Theory

George Kennedy utilizes Lloyd F. Bitzer's programmatic article, "The Rhetorical Situation,"[42] in his program of rhetorical criticism.[43] In his article, Bitzer begins his discussion by stating that "the rhetorical situation is the context in which speakers or writers create rhetorical discourse."[44] To him, "rhetoric is a mode of altering reality."[45] The alteration of reality is brought by "the creation of discourse which changes reality through the mediation of thought and action."[46] The strategy of the rhetor is molded by his or her need to persuade the audience to become engaged in thought and action so that it becomes a mediator of change.[47] Further, Bitzer argues that all rhetorical discourse is situational. What he means is that since a work of rhetoric "comes into existence for the sake of something be-

---

[40] Jan Botha, *Subject to Whose Authority? Multiple Readings of Romans 13*, Emory Studies in Early Christianity 5 (Atlanta: Scholars, 1994), 141.

[41] Cf. ibid., 141.

[42] *Philosophy and Rhetoric* 1 (1968): 1-14.

[43] *New Testament Interpretation*, 34-36.

[44] Bitzer, "The Rhetorical Situation," 1.

[45] Ibid., 4.

[46] Ibid.

[47] Ibid.

yond itself," rhetoric "functions ultimately to produce action or change in the world."[48] He defines "rhetorical situation" as

> a complex of persons, events, objects, and relations presenting an actual or potential exigence which can be completely or partially removed if discourse, introduced into the situation, can so constrain human decision or action as to bring about the significant modification of the exigence.[49]

There are three constituents that comprise this rhetorical situation. The first of these is "exigence." "Exigence" is "an imperfection marked by urgency; it is a defect, an obstacle, something waiting to be done, a thing which is other than it should be."[50] Only exigence that can be modified by discourse is considered rhetorical; that is, situations that cannot be altered by any means, for example, death, winter, and natural disasters, are not rhetorical exigences. Bitzer also notes that an exigence is not rhetorical when it can be modified only by means other than discourse. The second constituent, the audience, is rhetorical when it consists "only of those persons who are capable of being influenced by discourse and of being mediators of change."[51] This is a very important aspect of rhetorical criticism, especially in relation to historical criticism. The rhetorical audience can be identical with the historical audience, but they may differ; e.g., the rhetorical audience of Paul's letter to the Romans can be different from the historical makeup of the Roman church. In other words, identifying the persons or groups that Paul, the rhetor, aims to influence and persuade through the discourse of his letter is a different question from asking what kinds of people were present in the Roman church historically. This question will be explored in detail shortly.

The third constituent of the rhetorical situation is a set of constraints which are made up of persons, events, objects, relations, time, and place. These are important parts of the situation because "they have the power to constrain decision and action needed to modify the exigence."[52] These constraints include "beliefs, attitudes, documents, facts, traditions, images, interests, motives and the

---

[48] Ibid., 3-4.

[49] Ibid., 6.

[50] Ibid.

[51] Ibid., 8.

[52] Ibid.

like."[53] Bitzer sees two main classes of constraints: "(1) those origi-
nated or managed by the rhetor and his method and (2) those other
constraints, in the situation, which may be operative."[54] One of the
constraints, for example, for Paul as he was writing his letter to the
Romans was surely classical rhetoric, since he and his audience lived
in a culture so saturated with rhetorical practices.[55]

The Rhetorical Situation Debate

An ongoing debate on various aspects of rhetorical situation
theory has continued since Bitzer's article was published in 1968.
The first response came from Arthur B. Miller,[56] who takes on the
problem of rhetorical exigence. He argues that "the ultimate character of an exigence is a conclusion in the mind of its perceiver."[57]
What he means is that either the speaker's or the hearer's exigence is
determined by constraints that they experience. They may be different; but when hearers realize that they have essentially common constraints with the speaker, there forms "a meaning basis for identification between hearer and speaker."[58] Therefore, "the rhetor must
know the constraints of his hearers before he exercises any option in
attempting to harmonize his and the hearers' constraints." Then, the
rhetor can choose the topic of communication best suited to persuading the audience.[59] This clarifies Bitzer's theory of exigence in the
way that the rhetor elects his or her selection of topics (*topoi*) in creating discourse fitting to the specific rhetorical situation. Richard E.
Vatz's[60] response was more negative than Miller's. He argues that
Bitzer's understanding of rhetoric and "situation" requires a "realist"
philosophy of meaning.[61] He alleges that Bitzer's views come from

---

[53] Ibid.

[54] Ibid.

[55] Kennnedy, *New Testament Interpretation,* 160, relates the rhetorical
constraints to the historical constraints identified by A. E. Harvey in his book,
Jesus and the Constraints of History (Philadelphia: Westminster, 1982); so Pogoloff, *Logos and Sophia,* 78.

[56] Arthur B. Miller, "Rhetorical Exigence," *Philosophy and Rhetoric* 5
(1972): 111-18.

[57] Ibid., 112.

[58] Ibid., 117.

[59] Ibid., 118.

[60] Richard E. Vatz, "The Myth of the Rhetorical Situation," *Philosophy
and Rhetoric* 6 (1973): 154-61.

[61] Ibid., 154.

his Platonist *Weltanschauung.* He believes that this kind of philosophy is not compatible with rhetoric because "meaning is not intrinsic in events, facts, people, or 'situations' nor are facts 'publicly observable.'"[62] Furthermore, he argues that Bitzer's views are even dangerous because the ethical implications of his perspective of rhetoric and situation are those of irresponsibility. Vatz argues that the rhetor *creates* reality or salience by his or her rhetoric rather than simply reflecting on it. He believes that his view increases the rhetor's moral responsibility. Thus, "the rhetor is responsible for what he chooses to make salient."[63] In conclusion, he adopts a perspective diametrically opposed to Bitzer's:

> I would not say "rhetoric is situational," but situations are rhetorical; not "... exigence strongly invites utterance," but utterance strongly invites exigence; not "the situation controls the rhetorical response..." but the rhetoric controls the situational response; not "... rhetorical discourse ... does not obtain its character-as-rhetorical from the situation which surrounds them or creates them.[64]

Is Bitzer's theory really deterministic as Vatz claims? John H. Patton points out that this kind of claim results from a misunderstanding of Bitzer's theory based on a fatalistic theory of knowledge and action.[65] Bitzer certainly gives flexibility to the rhetor who decides to employ a particular line of argument, to use particular examples, and to shape his or her argument to suit the certain features of a given audience. All these features are not "*predetermined* by the universally controlling nature of rhetorical situations."[66] Therefore, Vatz's claim that rhetorical situations are fatalistic should be rejected. Further, Vatz's allegation against Bitzer that his views are ethically irresponsible is not true. The effect of rhetoric or rhetorical power is well recognized by Bitzer in that he believes it "alters reality," but he does not attribute ethical values to it because the subject matter of his discussion is completely different from that of Vatz.

---

[62] Ibid., 156.

[63] Ibid., 158.

[64] Ibid., 159.

[65] J. H. Patton, "Causation and Creativity in Rhetorical Situations: Distinctions and Implications," *Quarterly Journal of Speech* 65 (1979): 39. For the theory of "determinism," see Gerald Dworkin, ed., *Determinism, Free Will, and Moral Responsibility* (Englewood Cliffs, N.J.: Prentice-Hall, 1970).

[66] Patton, "Causation and Creativity," 38-39.

Vatz's theory, however, has important implications for New Testament interpretation. It is true that the rhetoric of the New Testament creates a rhetorical situation, even millennia later. The powerful rhetoric of Paul should have created its rhetorical situation in the Roman congregation through his letter. However, we only have scanty evidence for how his rhetoric worked among the Roman believers.[67]

In 1974, there was another response to Bitzer's article by Scott Consigny.[68] Consigny argues that the rhetorical situation is "an indeterminate context marked by troublesome disorder which the rhetor must structure so as to disclose and formulate problems."[69] Therefore, he agrees with Vatz that the problem of Bitzer's definition of the rhetorical situation is that he construes the situation as determinate and predetermining a "fitting" response. At the same time he faults Vatz in that the rhetor can freely create his own exigences and select his subject matter in a manner of "pure arbitration." He then proposes a solution to this antinomy between two theories by utilizing an ancient rhetorical theory known as "topics" in his understanding of rhetoric as "art."[70] He insists that

> [u]sing topics, the rhetor has universal devices which allow him to engage in particular situations, maintaining an "integrity" but yet being receptive to the heteronomies of each case. The real question in rhetorical theory is not whether the situation or the rhetor is "dominant," but the extent, in each case, to which the rhetor can discover and control indeterminate matter, using his art of topics to make sense of what would otherwise remain simply absurd.[71]

---

[67] See James D. G. Dunn, *The Theology of Paul the Apostle* (Grand Rapids: Eerdmans, 1998), 531-32, who believes that what Paul attempted in Rom 9-11 failed because the early church evidence shows that what Paul wanted to transform—namely, the shifting of discussion from a "Jewish-Gentile" confrontation to "Israel" by redefining "Israel" as the called of God—did not achieve its goal. This will be discussed further later.

[68] Scott Consigny, "Rhetoric and Its Situations," *Philosophy and Rhetoric* 7 (1974): 175-86.

[69] Ibid., 178.

[70] Ibid., 181-83. He draws on Aristotle (*The "Art" of Rhetoric, Rhetorica*), Cicero (*Topica*), and Vico.

[71] Ibid., 185.

Thus, the rhetorical situation is not determinate as Bitzer argues, but indeterminate and flexible. It is the rhetor's task to make his or her rhetoric a "fitting" response to the situation.

David M. Hunsaker and Craig R. Smith criticize Consigny's view for being exclusively speaker-oriented with the result that the audience is not accounted for in his theory. Further, they believe that the classical system of topics that Consigny proposes as an alternative to Bitzer's and Vatz's theories fails to encompass all aspects of the rhetorical situation.[72] Instead, they propose that another ancient theory, *stasis*, should be used to analyze the rhetorical situation because it usefully strikes a balance between situation, speaker, and message.[73] Hunsaker and Smith offer perceptive discussions on audience and speaker in the rhetorical situation. They distinguish actual and rhetorical audiences, in which an actual audience is the object of a speaker in rhetorical discourse. This actual audience becomes a rhetorical audience when the perceptions of the rhetorical exigence of the speaker and audience match well and are congruent. If the speaker misperceives the nature of the situation and the audience, the audience may not be a rhetorical one.[74] The speaker, in turn, is normally included in the rhetorical audience. "How, then, does the speaker step forth from the situational audience, out of his role as auditor and into the role of rhetor?"[75] This is done by the exigence itself which determines the character of a rhetor. In this aspect, they agree with Bitzer. But "[t]he potential rhetor must have the capability of speaking persuasively to an audience in order to be the actual rhetor."[76] Then, Hunsaker and Smith emphasize the commonality between the rhetor and the audience which exists in the perceptions of the speaker and the audience in the rhetorical situation. When this commonality exists in the rhetorical situation, issues are generated in the minds of the speaker and the audience, and the situation constrains decision and action by both. They assert: "[t]he goal of rhetorical discourse is *consensus,* the transformation of issue perceptions, bringing about a realignment and reconciliation between

---

[72] David M. Hunsaker and Craig R. Smith, "The Nature of Issues: A Constructive Approach to Situational Rhetoric," *Western Speech Communication* 40 (1976): 144-45.

[73] Ibid., 151-52.

[74] Ibid., 151.

[75] Ibid., 152.

[76] Ibid., 152.

perceptual disparities, and thus the resolution of conflict created by such disparities."[77]

John Patton reaches a similar conclusion but in a more perceptive way:

> the situational theory offers a way to explain and evaluate perceptions in terms of the accuracy and clarity with which they reflect observable, historical features of situations and the constructive potential of the responses to which they may lead for the solution of genuine problems.[78]

Certainly, in Bitzer's theory the rhetorical situation is grounded in history, or observable sets of circumstances. Patton correctly understands that in Bitzer's theory, "the underlying assumption is that rhetoric is essentially *historical,* i.e., in keeping with its origin in the classical period as a pragmatic art, its purpose is to alter real events and experiences" [79] In Bitzer's own words, "the exigence and the complex of persons, objects, events and relations which generate rhetorical discourse are located in reality, are objective and publicly observable historic facts in the world we experience."[80] Patton agrees with Bitzer that "[h]istorical realities remain the focal point for rhetorical activity."[81]

That the rhetorical situation is grounded in the historical situation gives rise to enormous implications for the interpreters of the New Testament who view rhetorical criticism as an integral part of

---

[77] Ibid., 156 (their emphasis). Cf. Kenneth Burke, *A Rhetoric of Motives* (Berkeley: University of California Press, 1969), 22-23.

[78] Patton, "Causation and Creativity," 54-55.

[79] Ibid., 44 (emphasis added).

[80] Bitzer, "Rhetorical Situation," 11. He reasserts this point later: "Genuine rhetorical situation, as opposed to sophistical and spurious ones, are real in the sense that the situational constituents—exigence, audience, and constraints—are present in the historic environment" (Lloyd F. Bitzer, "Functional Communication: A Situational Perspective," in *Rhetoric in Transition: Studies in the Nature and Uses of Rhetoric*, ed. Eugene E. White [University Park: The Pennsylvania State University Press, 1980], 24.).

[81] P. K. Tompkins, J. H. Patton and Lloyd F. Bitzer, "The Forum: Tompkins on Patton and Bitzer, Patton on Tompkins, and Bitzer on Tompkins (and Patton)," *Quarterly Journal of Speech* 66 (1980): 89; cited by Duane F. Watson, "The Contributions and Limitations of Greco-Roman Rhetorical Theory for Constructing the Rhetorical and Historical Situations of a Pauline Letter" (Paper presented at the Malibu Conference of Rhetoric and Religion, Pepperdine University, Malibu, Calif., 1996), 5. My sincere thanks to Prof. Watson who generously and promptly made available to me a copy of his paper.

historical criticism. If "[t]he rhetorical situation and historical situation are not divorced from one another, only separated by the act of
writing and reading,"[82] then what is the relationship between the
two?

III. THE RHETORICAL SITUATION IN NEW TESTAMENT
RHETORICAL CRITICISM

When George Kennedy introduced Bitzer's theory in his program of rhetorical criticism for New Testament interpretation, he
based his model on Bitzer's 1968 article. Strangely, the subsequent
debate on the theory of the rhetorical situation has been almost completely ignored.[83] As a result, the application of the theory in New
Testament rhetorical criticism has been problematic because the theory has not been properly understood and the rhetorical situation has
often been simply confused with the historical situation. We will
take a brief look at how New Testament interpreters have used the
theory of the rhetorical situation in their practices of rhetorical criticism of New Testament texts.

The Rhetorical Situation as the Historical Situation

When Kennedy says the rhetorical situation "*roughly* corresponds to the *Sitz im Leben* of form criticism,"[84] the seed for misunderstanding is sown. What he apparently intended to do was to relate
the concept of the rhetorical situation to the one familiar to New Testament exegetes from form criticism. Many studies following Kennedy's model have thus confused the rhetorical situation with the historical situation.[85] For example, in one of his several works on Ro-

---

[82] Ibid., 5.

[83] The complaint by Vorster (J. N. Vorster, "The Context of the Letter to
the Romans: A Critique on the Present State of Research," *Neot* 28 [1994]: 138)
about this phenomenon is justified. But now see Botha, *Whose Authority?* 144-
48 and Watson, "The Contributions and Limitations," 2-5 for responses from
New Testament critics.

[84] Kennedy, *New Testament Interpretation*, 34 (my emphasis).

[85] See M. L. Reid, "A Rhetorical Analysis of Romans 1:1-5:21 with At-
tention Given to the Rhetorical Function of 5:1-21," *Perspectives in Religious
Studies* 19 (1992): 258-60; N. Elliott, *The Rhetoric of Romans: Argumentative
Constraint and Strategy and Paul's Dialogue with Judaism*, JSNTSup 45 (Shef-

mans, Marty Reid describes the rhetorical situation of Romans in terms of history:

> Historically, we can reconstruct the return of Jewish-Christians (and Jews) to Rome during Nero's accession to the throne in A.D. 54. Upon their return, they soon discovered that the character of the Christian community had radically altered with the infusion of non-Jews..... We can *hypothesize* that the situation at Rome at the time of Paul's writing was one of *distrust* and *intolerance*.[86]

Even from a purely historical-critical point of view, this is bad history. There is no historical evidence for such a reconstruction[87] but more importantly there is no warrant in the *text* of Romans for such a hypothesis. Where in the text of Romans can one find that the Christians in Rome *distrust* each other or have the problem of *intolerance*? He also argues that "the weak" that Paul refers to in Romans 14:1-15:7 are "Jewish-Christians" because "the letter was directed primarily to a gentile audience."[88] The logic of this sentence escapes re-

---

field: Sheffield Academic, 1990), 9-94; Jeffery A. Crafton, "Paul's Rhetorical Vision and the Purpose of Romans: Toward a New Understanding," *NovT* 32 (1990): 317-39; idem, *The Agency of the Apostle: A Dramatic Analysis of Paul's Responses to Conflict in 2 Corinthians,* JSNTSup 51 (Sheffield: Sheffield Academic, 1991), 59, 103-4, 137-8.

[86] Reid, "Romans 1:1-5:21," 259 (emphasis added). Andrew Lincoln has almost the same understanding of the situation in Rome: "As Paul understands their situation, harmony among the Christians in Rome is threatened, because these Gentile Christians are experiencing tensions with Jewish Christians, ..." ("From Wrath to Justification: Tradition, Gospel, and Audience in the Theology of Romans 1:18-4:25," in *Pauline Theology, Volume III: Romans,* ed. David M. Hay and E. Elizabeth Johnson [Minneapolis: Fortress, 1995], 132). Lincoln claims that he reads this information from Paul's exhortations in Rom 14:1-15:13 but there is no warranty that "the strong" and "the weak" refer to the Gentile Christians and the Jewish Christians, respectively. The more serious flaw of his paper is that he fails to show how this rhetorical situation works out in 1:18-4:25, the passage that he interpreted. His paper does not even attempt to relate his understanding of the rhetorical situation to the text. See also his article, "Abraham Goes to Rome: Paul's Treatment of Abraham in Romans 4," in *Worship, Theology and Ministry in the Early Church: Essays in Honor of Ralph P. Martin,* ed. M. Wilkins and T. Paige, JSNTSup 87 (Sheffield: JSOT Press, 1992), 163-79, where he also says that Paul's goal of writing the letter is "to unify the Gentile Christians and the Jewish Christians... so that they accept one another..." (p. 168).

[87] Of course, it is obvious that he is alluding to the Suetonius' *Claudius 25.4* but that this cannot be used for the historical reconstruction of the Roman church has been well argued many times. See below.

[88] Reid, "Romans 1:1-5:21," 259.

peated readings. If a letter is mainly addressed to a certain group, then does the other group necessarily become "the weak"? Since these two groups have such a difficult time together, "[a]pparently, strained Jewish-gentile relations existed, which fostered a lack of mutual acceptance and tolerance." Again, where is the textual basis for such a claim? This is a clear example of importing unwarranted historical speculations in the name of the rhetorical situation. Indeed, he later argues that the rhetoric of Paul in Romans is the "rhetoric of mutuality" "to address the various divisions among his audience."[89] Apart from the impression that this resembles more the situation in Corinth, it is impossible to find these notions in Romans unless one imagines things outside the text of Romans itself. It is quite clear that the confusion between the rhetorical situation and the historical situation is the reason for the mistake.

The Rhetorical Situation against the Historical Situation

An increasing number of scholars holds that the rhetorical situation should be distinguished from the historical situation. The foremost advocate of this position is Dennis L. Stamps.[90] He points out that the rhetorical-critical method of Kennedy has the goal of recovering "real" history and thus his method is still within the realm of historical-critical method.[91] He likewise argues that even though E. Schüssler Fiorenza's theory[92] utilizes reader-response criticism in her program of rhetorical method, "her actual application... to 1 Corinthians ends up being very much a historically conditioned reconstruction of the rhetorical situation."[93] Then, building upon W.

---

[89] Idem, "A Consideration of the Function of Rom 1:8-15 in Light of Greco-Roman Rhetoric," *JETS* 38 (1995): 184; See also the somewhat modified view in idem, "Paul's Rhetoric of Mutuality: A Rhetorical Reading of Romans," in *SBL 1995 Seminar Papers*, ed. Eugene H. Lovering, Jr. (Atlanta: Scholars, 1995), 138-39.

[90] D. L. Stamps, "Rethinking the Rhetorical Situation: The Entextualization of the Situation in New Testament Epistles," in *Rhetoric and the New Testament: Essays From the 1992 Heidelberg Conference*, ed. Stanley E. Porter and Thomas H. Olbricht, JSNTSup 90 (Sheffield: JSOT Press, 1993), 193-210; idem, "Rhetorical Criticism of the New Testament," 129-69.

[91] Stamps, "Rethinking," 195-96.

[92] E. Schüssler Fiorenza, "Rhetorical Situation and Historical Reconstruction in 1 Corinthians," *NTS* 33 (1987): 386-403.

[93] Stamps, "Rethinking," 197.

Wuellner[94] and Schüssler Fiorenza, Stamps presents his own "entextualized" rhetorical situation theory. While acknowledging the value of 'historically oriented' rhetorical criticism, he believes that it is limited because it is essentially a type of 'rhetorical' form criticism. He insists that the limitation of this kind of rhetorical criticism stems from its complete dependence upon classical rhetoric. His understanding of the rhetorical situation is the situation embedded in the text ("entextualization"). Thus his model departs from the historical understanding of the situation completely and moves into the realm of literature ("the rhetorical situation exists as a textual or literary presentation within the text or discourse as a whole," 199). He believes that "a text presents a selected, limited and crafted entextualization of the situation" and that that kind of rhetorical situation should be used in rhetorical-critical interpretation of the New Testament texts.

The rhetorical situation should certainly be distinguished from the historical situation, as Stamps argues. However, the rhetorical situation is still grounded in history. The letters of Paul were written to the actual (historical) situation and to the actual people whom Paul attempted to persuade.[95] Thus, it seems impossible to depart from history when we deal with historical documents like the Pauline epistles.

The Rhetorical Situation with the Historical Situation

Other scholars who apply the concept of the rhetorical situation in their studies seem to struggle in an effort to strike a balance between the historical situation and the rhetorical situation.[96] What

---

[94] Wilhelm Wuellner, "Where Is Rhetorical Criticism Taking Us?" *CBQ* 49 (1987): 448-63.

[95] Stamps' method requires him to turn the text of the letter into a narrative text. In order to do this, he utilizes Norman Petersen's theory in his book *Rediscovering Paul: Philemon and the Sociology of Paul's Narrative World* (Philadelphia: Fortress, 1985). However, Petersen's theory of the narrative nature of Pauline letters really aims to expose the sociological relationship between the letter parties by extracting the story of the relationship between the sender and the receivers. Certainly, Petersen has a completely different thing in mind when he develops his theory, and Stamps' application of this theory in his reconstruction of the "entextualized" rhetorical situation stands on shaky ground.

[96] We may mention Pogoloff, *Logos and Sophia*, 71-95; Botha, *Whose Authority?*, 140-50; Karl A. Plank, *Paul and the Irony of Affliction*, SBLSS (At-

then is the relationship between the two? How can we approach the
rhetorical situation of historical documents like Paul's letters? W.
Wuellner, in his programmatic essay in 1987,[97] argues that the difference between the rhetorical situation and the historical situation is
that "the premises of a text" as appeal or argument occupy the foremost interest for the rhetorical critic.[98] Also, what distinguishes literary analysis from rhetorical analysis is that in rhetorical criticism
"a text must reveal its context."[99] What Wuellner means by "context" here is the rhetorical situation which is more than the historical
situation or generic *Sitz im Leben.* However, Wuellner does not explain in detail how the rhetorical situation is "more than" the historical situation.

Lauri Thurén also agrees that the rhetorical situation is essentially different from the historical situation.[100] He provides this definition: "The rhetorical situation consists of the picture of the audience which the author seems to presuppose, of the audience's premises and expectations, and as a result thereof, of the intended effects
of the text."[101] Like Wuellner, Thurén emphasizes the premises of
the text as the primary criteria for the reconstruction of the rhetorical
situation. Yet he concerns himself with the historical situation of 1
Peter also because he believes that "rhetorical criticism takes historical information seriously, but instead of being descriptive it seeks to
penetrate the intention of the text, e.g. which general knowledge or
values in the historical situation are helpful for the argument."[102]
Through this, he insists that we can overcome the defects inherent in
historical information. The "real" historical situation is always
somewhat different from the written form of history,[103] and the text

---

lanta: Scholars, 1987), 11-31; Khiok-Khng Yeo, *Rhetorical Interaction in 1 Co-
rinthians 8 and 10: A Formal Analysis with Preliminary Suggestions for a Chi-
nese, Cross-Cultural Hermeneutic,* Biblical Interpretation Series 9 (Leiden: E. J.
Brill, 1995), 70-74; J. N. Vorster, "Toward an Interactional Model for the
Analysis of Letters," *Neot* 24 (1990), 118-26; idem, "Context of the Letter to the
Romans," 127-45.

[97] Wuellner, "Rhetorical Criticism."

[98] Ibid., 455-56.

[99] *The New Encyclopaedia Britannica.* (1975), s.v. "Rhetoric: Rhetoric in
Literature," by T. O. Sloan, 798-99; cited by Wuellner, "Rhetorical Criticism,"
450.

[100] Lauri Thurén, *The Rhetorical Strategy of 1 Peter: With Special Regard to Ambiguous Expressions* (Åbo: Åbo Academy Press, 1990), 71.

[101] Ibid., 70-71.

[102] Ibid., 55.

[103] See W. J. Ong, *Orality and Literacy: The Technologizing of the Word*

itself creates its own situation because some situation is always presupposed in the text. Yet Thurén argues that "external, historical information" can deepen our understanding of the real situation.[104]
Thurén's understanding of the rhetorical situation is still based on the
historical situation, but he clearly distinguishes them.

The Historical Situation Through the Rhetorical Situation

In her work on the women prophets in Corinth, A. C. Wire reconstructs their portraits through Paul's use of rhetoric in his letter to
the Corinthians. She asks, "If Paul's intent is to persuade rather than
to describe the Corinthians, can Paul's rhetoric lead to the people he
is trying to persuade?"[105] She believes that the way Paul argues for
his own position can yield clues which lead to the real people in Corinth (especially, the women prophets, who are the focus of her study)
because Paul would have tailored his argument to best suit the situation in Corinth. She charges that rhetoricians have evaded the question of the possibility of reconstruction of historical situations
through rhetorical analysis "by limiting themselves to reconstructing
the rhetorical situation and disclaiming any interest in history."[106]
She argues that historians cannot ignore the fact that Paul's letters
are "as close to history as writing can get" because his letters serve
as "a proxy for his presence in a specific historical context."[107] Yet
history is not "a monolithic reality set in a determined past outside
the literary creation," but "a piecing together of fragile textual and
material remains."[108] Thus, through gathering the "textual and material remains" that can be found in the Corinthian correspondence,
Wire reconstructs the rhetorical situation and then the historical
situation of the Corinthian women prophets. Her basic concept is
sound, but one may be leery of using "The New Rhetoric" exclusively as she does in constructing the rhetorical situation of first century Corinth. If she is interested in history, would it not be more
adequate to use Greco-Roman rhetorical categories and tools in her
study?

(New York: Methuen, 1982).

[104] Thurén, *Rhetorical Strategy*, 55, n. 59.

[105] A. C. Wire, *The Corinthians Women Prophets: A Reconstruction Through Paul's Rhetoric* (Minneapolis: Fortress, 1990), 1.

[106] Ibid., 4.

[107] Ibid.

[108] Ibid.

Elizabeth Schüssler Fiorenza's article, published in 1987,[109] sets out a specific program for reconstructing the historical situation through the rhetorical situation. She argues that "the concept of 'rhetorical situation' developed in rhetorical criticism might help us to gain access to the historical communicative situation of New Testament writings."[110] She proposes that a rhetorical critical analysis should move through four stages: 1. Identification of the rhetorical interests and models of contemporary interpretation. 2. Delineation of the rhetorical arrangement, interests, and modifications. 3. Elucidation and establishment of the rhetorical situation. 4. Reconstruction of the common historical situation and symbolic universe of the writer/speaker and the recipients/audience. Still, she acknowledges that "such a rhetorical reconstruction of the social-historical situation is still narrative-laden and can only be constituted as a 'sub-text' to Paul's text."[111] The whole basis of her program hinges on her understanding of rhetoric itself:

> … in the rhetorical act speakers/writers seek to convey an image of themselves as well as to define the rhetorical problem and situation in such a way that both 'fit' to each other so that the audience/reader will be moved to their standpoint by participating in their construction of the world.[112]

Thus, to Schüssler Fiorenza, the rhetorical act of Paul, who is the implied author of 1 Corinthians, serves as a window to the actual world of the Corinthians community, because the 'sub-text' of Paul is not simply his story, but "the story of the Corinthian church to which Paul's rhetoric is to be understood as an active response."[113]

This is an illuminating thesis. If the rhetorical situation is rooted in the historical situation, then the rhetorical situation should

---

[109] Schüssler Fiorenza, "Rhetorical Situation." See also idem, "The Rhetoricity of Historical Knowledge: Pauline Discourse and Its Contextuality," in *Religious Propaganda and Missionary Competition in the New Testament World: Essays Honoring Dieter Georgi*, ed. Lukas Bormann, *et al.* (Leiden: E. J. Brill, 1994), 443-69.

[110] Schüssler Fiorenza, "Rhetorical Situation," 387.

[111] Ibid., 388.

[112] Ibid.

[113] Ibid.; cf. Dale B. Martin, *Slavery As Salvation: The Metaphor of Slavery in Pauline Christianity* (New Haven: Yale University Press, 1990), 147, who states that Paul's way of using some rhetorical strategies "sheds much light on the historical reconstruction of the Corinthian letters and the role of those letters in the conflicts within the church at Corinth."

reflect the reality of that actual situation. Jan Botha correctly states that "any situation is of necessity embedded within an historical situation."[114] Yet rhetorical criticism's ultimate goal is not to go behind the text and see the historical situation as if the rhetorical analysis can show us the actual world, e.g., the Roman congregation through Paul's letter to the Romans. The aim is to see the historical information of the *text* for the sake of argumentation. Thus, the premises of the investigation are the text itself. In this study, then, we will not ignore the historical aspect of a text, yet we will not depend on it completely.[115]

Finally, Duane F. Watson's recent attempt to clarify the issues surrounding the rhetorical situation and the historical situation merit a detailed discussion. He claims that historical-critical methodologies are not adequate to construct the historical situation of a Pauline epistle.[116] He then argues that rhetorical analysis can provide a much needed corrective to this situation by utilizing Greco-Roman rhetorical theory.[117] He believes that "the rhetorical situation is an evaluative construction derived from and seeking to change the facts of the historical situation."[118] The rhetor's goal is to change the historical situation by communicating the exigence to an audience. Such exigence is indicative of the way the rhetor communicates because the rhetor wants to adapt it to be a "fitting" response to a certain historical situation. Therefore, he concludes that "the rhetorical situation and the historical situation are not divorced from one another, only separated by the act of writing and reading."[119] Yet he emphasizes that "the rhetorical situation is not equated with the historical situation." What then is the difference? He seems to say that the rhetori-

---

[114] Botha, *Whose Authority?* 149.

[115] Cf. Ibid., 149-150.

[116] Watson, "The Contributions and Limitations," 1.

[117] Ibid. He quotes Perelman and Olbrechts-Tyteca, who serve as the basis for his thesis:

Every social circle or milieu is distinguishable in terms of its dominant opinions and unquestioned beliefs, of the premises that it takes for granted without hesitation: these views form an integral part of its culture, and *an orator wishing to persuade a particular audience must of necessity adapt himself to it.* Thus the particular culture of a given audience shows so strongly through the speeches addressed to it that we feel we can rely on them to a considerable extent for our knowledge of the character of past civilizations (*The New Rhetoric*, 20-21; emphasis added).

[118] Ibid., 5.

[119] Ibid.

cal situation is a part of a larger historical situation that encompasses the historical, cultural, and social dimensions of the Greco-Roman world. He asserts that "the end result of the rhetorical study of a text" is "hypothetical construction of the historical situation based on the rhetor's construction of the rhetorical situation and perception of the audience."[120]

The strength of Watson's presentation is that for the first time, he has described the procedure of moving from the rhetorical situation to the historical situation in detail, integrating features from Greco-Roman rhetorical handbooks.[121] He shows how a rhetorical analysis can be used to lead one to the historical situation, by analyzing the species of rhetoric, the *stasis* of the argument, invention, arrangement, and style. For example, from the invention that Paul employs, one can trace back to the situation of the audience. Paul's use of Old Testament examples, for instance, can be categorized as an inartificial proof which Paul uses to establish the authority of his argument on the basis of outside sources with his audience. We can infer that Paul needed to establish a kind of authority with his audience because either the audience has some suspicion about his authority or he wants to verify his argument. When this is combined with an analysis of Paul's use of *ethos* in his letters, we can infer further what kind of status he enjoys or does not enjoy with the particular audience. When he depends on insinuation or proof, we may assume that he is on poor terms with the audience.[122]

IV. CONCLUSIONS

It has now become clear that the rhetorical situation and the historical situation should not be equated. What, then, are the differences? First of all, the rhetorical situation describes "rhetorical activity" that takes place between the text and the audience while the historical situation describes the situation in which the audience is placed. The historical situation primarily concentrates on the description of persons, objects, events and others as they existed in the past so that they may be helpful background for the interpretation of

---

[120] Ibid., 7.

[121] Ibid., 7-27.

[122] Ibid., 10-11.

the text. For example, in describing the historical situation of Romans, the historical makeup of the Roman congregation is of crucial importance,[123] whether they were primarily Jewish, Gentile, or both. In establishing the rhetorical situation, however, the historical makeup is of secondary importance, but the speaker's intended audience, i.e., the audience on which the rhetor aims to exert force for change, is of primary importance. In the case of Romans, we will seek to determine what kind of audience Paul (the rhetor) wants to persuade in order to bring about a change in the situation.

Second, the potentiality of change in the audience's thoughts and/or actions is an important criterion in establishing the rhetorical situation. In the rhetorical situation, we seek to find what the rhetor perceives as "imperfection" or exigence in the situation of the audience. Identifying the interests of the rhetor in changing the situation is the main focus of the description of the rhetorical situation. Of course, this situation is clearly rooted in the historical situation. In a way, establishing the rhetorical situation requires an eclectic method of sorting out historical situations in regard to the rhetor's argumentative strategy.

Third, the historical situation places more emphasis on the real situation of the audience or the point of view of the audience[124] while the rhetorical situation places more emphasis on the perspective of the rhetor, his or her own situation, and his or her response to the audience's situation, based on the text. The rhetorical situation is interested in finding the situation which surfaces on the text in the course of argumentation.[125]

Fourth, the rhetorical situation is not interested in finding "what actually happened," which is the expressed aim of the historical situation. The goal of establishing the rhetorical situation is not to describe the historical facts nor their possible referents. Yet the rhetorical criticism of the New Testament does not ignore the historical aspects of its text, because it is impossible to deal with a historical document such as the New Testament in a non-historical way. The text is used as a window to the reality of the historical situation

---

[123] Peter Lampe, *Die stadtrömischen Christen in den ersten beiden Jahrhunderten*, 2d ed., WUNT 2/18 (Tübingen: Mohr, 1989).

[124] For the problem of mirror-reading of a Pauline epistle, see John M. G. Barclay, "Mirror-Reading a Polemical Letter: Galatians As a Test Case," *JSNT* 31 (1987): 73-93.

[125] Cf. Thurén, *Rhetorical Strategy*, 55.

in many historical-critical works,[126] but in rhetorical criticism, the text is the focus of the attention.

EXCURSUS

CLAUDIUS 25.4 AND THE OCCASION OF ROMANS

Since the pioneering works of F. C. Baur in the last century,[127] the reasons why Paul wrote his letter to the Roman congregation have been a hotly debated subject. Baur's insistence that Romans should have been written to the concrete historical circumstances in the Roman church was his reaction to the dominant view that Romans was a *christianae religionis compendium*[128] written by Paul re-

---

[126] See W. S. Vorster, "The Historical Paradigm--Its Possibilities and Limitations," *Neot* 18 (1984): 104-23, esp., 117-19.

[127] "Über Zweck und Veranlassung des Römerbriefs und der damit zusammenhängenden Verältnisse der römischen Gemeinde," *Tübinger Zeitschrift für Theologie* 3 (1836): 59-178; *Paul the Apostle of Jesus Christ* (trans. from 2d German edition, ed. E. Zeller, rev. A. Menzies; London: Williams & Norgate, 1876), I, 308-65.

[128] This often quoted phrase of Philip Melanchthon occurs in his *Loci communes, 1521, Werke in Auswahl* 2.1, ed. R. Stupperich (Gütersloh: Bertelsmann, 1952), 7. It is not fair, however, to think that Melanchthon ignores the situation of the Roman congregation altogether when he interprets Romans. In his several works on Romans, he struggles with his assessment of the purpose of Romans and changes his position several times. Initially, he thought that Romans was written to refute Paul's opponents in Rome (thus, judicial rhetoric) but later saw its purpose as instruction for the church (thus, didactic rhetoric, which he adds to the traditional three [deliberative, demonstrative, and judicial]). Further, in his *Annotationes in epistolas Pauli ad Romanos et ad Corinthios,* he discusses the *status* of Romans, which is an application of ancient Greco-Roman *stasis* theory, and very similar to modern rhetorical situation theory. In his own words, the *status* "is a summary sentence concerning the point of contention and thus is a brief pronouncement or proposition containing the sum of the controversy to which all proofs and arguments are referred." (*Inst. Rhet.,* fol. 8ᵛ; translation by Timothy J. Wengert, "Philip Melanchthon's 1522 Annotations on Romans and the Lutheran Origins of Rhetorical Criticism," in *Biblical Interpretation in the Era of the Reformation: Essays Presented to David C. Steinmetz in Honor of His Sixtieth Birthday,* ed. Richard A. Muller and John L. Thompson [Grand Rapids: Eerdmans, 1996], 128-29). To Melanchthon, the *status* of Romans is "that we are justified by faith" (*Ann. Rom.,* fol. 3ᵛ). His rhetorical analysis of Romans shows striking similarities to George Kennedy's method. Indeed, Wengert claims that "[m]odern rhetorical criticism is merely

gardless of the situation in Rome since the Reformation. Baur's studies became a starting point for numerous attempts to delineate the specific situation of the Roman church but the opinions of scholars have varied widely.[129] The collection of essays in the volume *The Romans Debate*[130] amply shows the different approaches that scholars have taken over the years.[131] Not all, but many scholars agree that the historical situation in the Roman church holds the key to the proper understanding of the letter.[132] But it is true that the various historical reconstructions are based on scanty evidence and have been built on shaky ground. Leander Keck complains:

> [t]he resolutely historical-critical approach to our question, determined to read Romans as a letter thoroughly shaped by its historical context, appears to have placed us not so much on a clear path toward the goal but in a labyrinth—"an intricate combination of passages in which it is difficult to find one's way or an exit."[133]

One of the suggested clear paths to the reconstruction of the specific historical situation in Romans that actually led to a labyrinth is the widespread notion of the expulsion of the Jews by Claudius.[134]

---

reiterating arguments already investigated by Melanchthon and especially by his epigone, George Major" (Ibid., 127). This is an overstatement but it is true that Melanchthon was already doing many things in the sixteenth century that the twentieth century New Testament critics are doing.

[129] For a succinct survey of positions, see L. Ann Jervis, *The Purpose of Romans: A Comparative Letter Structure Investigation*, JSNTSup 55 (Sheffield: Sheffield Academic, 1991), 11-28.

[130] Karl P. Donfried, ed., Revised and Expanded Edition (Peabody: Hendrickson, 1991).

[131] It is not necessary to reiterate all the theories in the volume. I will deal with several representative approaches and rather concentrate on the works published after its edition in 1991. For a summary of issues in the voloume, see Donfried's competent survey in his introduction in *The Romans Debate,* xli-lxxii.

[132] Important exceptions include Nygren (Anders Nygren, *Commentary on Romans*, trans. C. C. Rasmussen [Philadelphia: Fortress, 1949]) and Barth (K. Barth, *The Epistle to the Romans* [Oxford: Oxford University Press, 1933]). See Beker's summary of scholars who are pointing to various historical occasions and purposes for Romans in *Paul the Apostle: The Triumph of God in Life and Thought* (Philadelphia: Fortress, 1980), 69, esp. 378-79 up to early 1980's.

[133] "What Makes Romans Tick?" in *Pauline Theology, volume III: Romans,* eds. David M. Hay and E. Elizabeth Johnson (Minneapolis: Fortress, 1995), 20. The quotation within the quotation comes from *Random House Dictionary of the English Language* (New York: Random House, 1966).

[134] It seems that the theory has gained almost universal acceptance in re-

Probably the most quoted single line of history for New Testament studies, "Since the Jews constantly made disturbances at the instigation of Chrestus, he [Claudius] expelled them from Rome,"[135] this report has served as concrete evidence for many interpreters to establish the situation in Rome.[136] An author reports that he can classify at least nine different positions using this evidence:

---

cent years. See recent publications such as Rainer Riesner, *Paul's Early Period: Chronology, Mission Strategy, Theology*, trans. Doug Stott (Grand Rapids: Eerdmans, 1998), 162-67; Luke T. Johnson, *Reading Romans: A Literary and Theological Commentary* (New York: The Crossroad Publishing Company, 1997), 4; Brendan Byrne, *Romans*, Sacred Pagina 6 (Collegeville, Minn.: The Liturgical Press, 1996), 11; Douglas Moo, *The Epistle to the Romans*, NICNT (Grand Rapids: Eerdmans, 1996), 4-5 (his reference to *Life of Claudius* 25.2 is wrong; it should be 25.4); Rudolf Brändle and Ekkehard W.Stegemann, "Die Entstehung der ersten 'christlichen Gemeinde' Roms im Kontext der jüdischen Gemeinden," *NTS* 42 (1996): 1-11; Traugott Holtz, "Die historischen und theologischen Bedingungen des Römerbriefes," in *Evangelium-Schriftauslegung-Kirche: Festschrift für Peter Stuhlmacher zum 65. Geburtstag*, ed. Jostein Ådna, Scott J. Hafemann and Otfried Hofius (Göttingen: Vandenhoeck & Ruprecht, 1997), 238-54. There are several scholars, however, who question the validity of this approach: Paul J. Achtemeier, "Unsearchable Judgments and Inscrutable Ways: Reflections on the Discussion of Romans," in *Pauline Theology, Volume IV: Looking Back, Pressing on*, ed. E. Elizabeth Johnson and David M. Hay (Atlanta: Scholars, 1997), 5-8; Leander E. Keck, "Searchable Judgments and Scrutable Ways: A Response to Paul J. Achtemeier," in *Pauline Theology, Volume IV*, 22-24; Dixon Slingerland, "Suetonius *Claudius* 25.4, Acts 18, and Paulus Orosius' *Historiarum Adversum Paganos Libri VII*: Dating the Claudian Expulsion(s) of Roman Jews," *JQR* 83 (1992): 127-44; idem, "Chrestus: Chritus?," in *New Perspectives on Ancient Judaism*, ed. Alan J. Avery-Peck, The Literature of Early Rabbinic Judaism: Issues in Talmudic Redaction and Interpretation (Lanham: University Press of America, 1989), 4:133-44; idem, "Suetonius *Claudius* 25.4 and the Account in Cassius Dio," *JQR* 79 (1989): 305-22; Mark D. Nanos, *The Mystery of Romans: The Jewish Context of Paul's Letter* (Minneapolis: Fortress, 1996), 372-87.

[135] *de Vita Claudii* 25.4: "Iudaeos impulsore Chresto assidue tumultuantes Roma expulit." The text and translation used here are from LCL edition (Suetonius, *The Lives of the Caesars*, trans. and edited by J. C. Rolfe [LCL; Cambridge, Mass.: Harvard University Press, 1914]).

[136] E.g., the comment by Simon Marcel, "[a] study of the edict of Claudius ca. 49 and its consequences is a logical beginning point for reconstructing the situation of Roman Christianity when Paul wrote" (*Verus Israel: A Study of the Relations between Christians and Jews in the Roman Empire, 135-425*, trans. H. McKeating [Oxford: Oxford University Press, 1986], 98; cited by James C. Walters, *Ethnic Issues in Paul's Letter to the Romans: Changing Self-Definitions in Earliest Roman Christianity* [Valley Forge, Pa.: Trinity Press International, 1993], 57). Walters' book is indeed entirely built upon this hypothesis.

Claudius restricted Roman Jewish worship and expelled rioters;[137] he closed one synagogue and expelled some of its members;[138] he closed some synagogues and expelled rioters;[139] he closed all synagogues but expelled no one;[140] he closed all synagogues and threatened expulsion;[141] he closed all synagogues, threatened expulsion, and some Jews did leave or were expelled;[142] he closed all synagogues, and religious Jews left the city;[143] he closed synagogues and expelled rioters;[144] he closed synagogues and expelled all Jews;[145] all Jews were simply expelled.[146]

---

[137] V. M. Scramuzza, *The Emperor Claudius* (Cambridge, Mass.: Harvard University Press, 1940), 151; idem, "The Policy of the Early Roman Emperors towards Judaism," in *The Beginnings of Christianity*, ed. F. J. Foakes Jackson and Kirsopp Lake (London: MacMillan, 1920-33), 296.

[138] R. Penna, "Les Juifs à Rome au temps de l'Apôtre Paul," *NTS* 28 (1982): 331; G. Luedemann, *Paul, Apostle to the Gentiles* (Philadelphia: Fortress, 1984), 166.

[139] E. Haenchen, *Die Apostelgeschichte* (MeyerK 3; 5th ed.; Göttingen: Vandenhoeck & Ruprecht, 1965), 58.

[140] J. Juster, *Les Juifs dans l'Empire Romain* (Pairs: Paul Geuthner, 1914), 1:411; S. Guterman, *Religious Toleration and Persecution in Ancient Rome* (London: Aiglon Press, 1951), 150.

[141] A. Harnack, *The Mission and Expansion of Christianity in the First Three Centuries* (2d ed.; New York: Putnam, 1908), 1:5.

[142] M. Stern, "The Jewish Diaspora," in *The Jewish People in the First Century*. ed. S. Safrai and M. Stern in co-operation with D. Flusser and W. C. van Unnik (Philadelphia: Fortress, 1974), 1:182; idem, *Greek and Latin Authors on Jews and Judaism* (Jerusalem: Israel Academy of Sciences and Humanities, 1974-1984), 2:116.

[143] F. F. Bruce, *Commentary on the Book of Acts* (Grand Rapids: Eerdmans, 1966), 368; E. Schürer, *The History of the Jewish People in the Age of Jesus Christ*, ed. G. Vermes and F. Millar (Edinburgh: T.&T. Clark, 1973), 3:77; H. Vogelstein and P. Rieger, *Geschichte der Juden in Rom* (Berlin: Mayer & Müller, 1895-96), 1:20; A. Suhl, *Paulus und seine Briefe* (SNT 11; Gütersloh: Gütersloher Verlagshaus Mohn, 1975), 326.

[144] H. Leon, *The Jews of Ancient Rome* (Philadelphia: The Jewish Publication Society of America, 1960), 24f.; A. Berliner, *Geschichte der Juden in Rom von der ältesten Zeit bis zur Gegenwart* (Frankfurt: Kauffmann, 1893), 1:25-26; R. O. Hoeber, "The Decree of Claudius in Acts 18:2," *CTM* 31 (1960): 691-92; G. May, "La politique religieuse de l'empereur Claude," *Revue historique de droit français et étranger*, 4th ser., 17 (1938): 43.

[145] S. Benko, "The Edict of Claudius of A.D. 49 and the Instigator Chrestus," *TZ* 25 (1969): 407 and 413; E. M. Smallwood, "Jews and Romans in the Early Empire," *History Today* 15 (1965): 236.

[146] T. Zielinski, "L'empereur Claude et l'idée de la domination mondiale des Juifs," *Revue de l'Universite de Bruxelles* 32 (1926-27): 143-44; H. Janne, "Impulsore Chresto," *Annuaire de l'Institut de philologie et d'histoire orientales* 2 (1934): 533-35; M. Borg, "A New Context for Romans XIII," *NTS* 19 (1972-

The confusing array of these positions is a clear indication of the highly conjectural nature of the historical reconstruction of the Roman church at the time. These various positions have resulted from the attempts to harmonize the so-called edict of Claudius with Acts 18:2 and the Roman historian Dio Cassius' third century record:[147]

> As for the Jews, who had again increased so greatly that by reason of their multitude it would have been hard without raising a tumult to bar them from the city, he [Claudius] did not drive them out, but ordered them, while continuing their traditional mode of life, not to hold meetings.[148]

This statement is in direct conflict with the statement of Suetonius. First of all, in this report, Claudius did not expel the Jews but simply prohibited their meetings. The reason for the prohibition was not clearly stated.[149]

Luke's reference in Acts 18:2 to Claudius' expulsion of all Jews[150] seems to add credibility to Suetonius' account but it does not prove anything because Luke does not disclose why they were ordered to leave Rome. Furthermore, there is no evidence that Priscilla and Aquila were Christian Jews at the time that they met Paul. Certainly, Luke does not report this nor does he suggest that the expul-

---

73): 211, n.2; one can perhaps add some more items in recent studies here but they largely fall into one of these categories. The quotation comes from D. Slingerland, "Suetonius *Claudius* 25.4 and the Account in Cassius Dio," *JQR* 79 (1989): 321.

[147] Many scholars (most recently Fitzmyer, *Romans,* 31-32; Brändle and Stegemann, "Die Entstehung," 9) also appeal to the fifth century Christian historian Orosius for the exact date of Claudius' expulsion since he reports that there is a reference in Josephus that this expulsion happened in the ninth regnal year of Claudius (January 25, 49 C.E. to January 24, 50 C.E.). This reference, however, can nowhere be found (Achtemeier, "Unsearchable Judgments," 5-6).

[148] *Historae Romanae* 60.6.6-7. The translation is quoted from *Roman History,* trans. and edited by E. Cary (LCL; Cambridge, Mass.: Harvard University Press, 1924).

[149] R. Penna argues that Dio Cassius intentionally omits anything concerning Christianity in his book; thus, the instigation of Chrestus should have been related to the Christians (*Paul the Apostle: Jew and Greek Alike: A Theological and Exegetical Study,* vol. 1, trans. T. P. Wahl [Collegeville, Minn.: The Liturgical Press, 1996], 36).

[150] "There he found a Jew named Aquila, a native of Pontus, who had recently come from Italy with his wife Priscilla, because Claudius had ordered all Jews to leave Rome." (NRSV)

sion was due to the Christian matters as many scholars have con-
tended.[151] The most decisive evidence that Suetonius' account of the
expulsion of Jews does not have anything to do with Christianity or
Christ[152] also comes from Luke in Acts 28:21-22:

> They replied, "We have received no letters from Judea about you,
> and none of the brothers coming here has reported or spoken any-
> thing evil about you. But we would like to hear from you what
> you think, for with regard to this sect we know that everywhere it
> is spoken against."

These are the words of the local Jewish leaders in Rome after they
heard Paul's explanation that his imprisonment was for "the sake of
the hope of Israel" according to Luke (Acts 28:17-20). This rather
neutral response, if not friendly, does not seem to square with the
presumed conflict and hostility harbored between Christians and
Jews that resulted in the complete expulsion of the Jews from the city
only a few years previously (Paul's arrival is assumed ca. 58-62 C.E.
and the expulsion in 49 C.E. and their return after the death of
Claudius in 54 C.E. in most reconstructions).[153] In a typical reconstruction, the Jews (including Christian Jews [the "weak" in Rom
14:1-15:3] and sometimes God-fearing gentiles) who were expelled
in 49 C.E. (for some even in 41 C.E.[154]) returned to Rome in 54 C.E.
only to find that their leadership roles had been transferred to now
predominantly gentile believers (the "strong"). Furthermore, the
gatherings were not being held in the synagogues any longer but in
the newly formed house churches which had became the centers of
Roman Christianity. They (the "strong") became hostile to Jewish
Law and customs and even showed their "anti-Judaic" sentiments.[155]

If Paul had been writing to the people in this kind of situation
several years prior to his visit to Rome, how could the Jewish leaders
appear to be unfamiliar with "this sect"? If the edict of Claudius was
as horrible as the complete expulsion of all Jews from the city be-

---

[151] Benko, "Edict," 413; Nanos, *The Mystery of Romans*, 376-77.

[152] For a convincing argument that the name "Chrestus" could not mean
"Christus" with ample evidence, see Slingerland, "Chrestus: Christus?" 133-44.
For an opposing view that Chrestus was indeed a misspelling of Christus, see
Fitzmyer, *Romans*, 31.

[153] Nanos, *The Mystery of Romans*, 372-73.

[154] See Achtemeier, "Unscrutable Judgments," 6-7.

[155] On this issue of the origin and development of the first Roman Christianity, see esp., Nanos, *The Mystery of Romans*, 85-165.

cause of "this sect," and the conflict and hostility so prevalent among
their people that Paul had to write to them to correct the situation
only a few years earlier, how could the Jewish leaders have forgotten
it?[156] Or from Luke's point of view, why does Paul

> not build on the irreconcilable animosity of the Jewish commu-
> nity(s) toward the Christian message..., or at least, why doesn't
> Luke make the logical connection between their *firsthand, exten-*
> *sive, and extremely negative* knowledge of the gospel and its pro-
> claimers and the situation in Rome upon Paul's arrival?[157]

Furthermore, is it not strange that Luke does not report in Acts 18:2
the reason for the expulsion of all Jews if the incident was caused by
Jewish-Christian conflict?[158]

Therefore, it is my conclusion that Suetonius' *Claudius* 25.4
should not be used for a reconstruction of the historical situation of
Romans, let alone its rhetorical situation.

---

[156] Of course, the logic can go in the opposite direction. That is, one can
argue that Luke's account is not historical because it contradicts historical data.
Penna (*Paul the Apostle*, 20) is the clearest example among many: "Luke's narrative is not historical in the strict sense. That is confirmed even in 28:22....
This profession of ignorance contradicts at least two *historical data*" (my emphasis). But what kind of *historical data* does he mean? Penna assumes that the
expulsion of all Jews as a result of conflict with Christians is "the fact" (his language) and criticizes Luke. But this criticism of Luke is not fair since the incident described in *Claudius* 25.4 cannot be established as "the historical fact"
concerning the relationship between Christians and Jews. There is simply no
concrete evidence for that. Furthermore, Penna does not explain why then Luke
omits such important *historical data.*

[157] Nanos, *The Mystery of Romans*, 375 (author's emphasis).

[158] Cf. Nanos' comment on this point: "Following the modern scholars'
development of the programmatic nature of Luke's intentions in constructing
Acts, one must surely ask why Luke would not use this for all its worth, setting
up the Jewish community in Rome as already rejecting, or at least predisposed
to reject, on the basis of its own experience, the Pauline gospel" (Ibid., 376). It
is quite interesting to note that Riesner's book is built strongly upon the complete trust on Acts in its historicity yet he does not consider the accounts of Acts
seriously in his acceptance of *Claudius* 25.4 as the trustworthy evidence for the
historical reconstruction of the situation of Romans (*Paul's Early Period*, 162-
67).

CHAPTER THREE

THE RHETORICAL SITUATION OF ROMANS

Before we can discuss the rhetorical situation of Romans 9-11, we need to set it in the framework of the rhetorical situation of Romans as a whole, even if only briefly. The rhetorical situation of Romans 9-11 is, of course, a part of the rhetorical situation of the whole letter, and therefore, not independent of it. Thus, it is dangerous to isolate a particular rhetorical situation of a rhetorical unit from the larger whole because such a rhetorical situation can be out of context and misleading. The strength of a literary or rhetorical reading of a text is to see the whole picture and interpret certain passages in the context in which such a text is located. Karl Plank puts this matter well:

> Over against the legacy of piecemeal reading—habits of interpretation that sever given bits of text from their relationship with other portions of a common text—the literary or the rhetorical critic emphasizes the vital role of textual context in discerning the meaning of any given passage. No portion of text bears meaning in general, but only in terms of some context in which a text becomes perceptible and particular.... The interaction between that whole and part reveals the underlying values of the world which the text creates. It maps the textual foreground and obligates the critical reader to take seriously the full dimensions of literary context.[1]

Isolating a rhetorical situation from a larger context is still practiced by many interpreters.[2] A. H. Snyman's article well illustrates such a dan-

---

[1] Plank, *Paul and the Irony of Affliction*, 11.

[2] See e. g., Snyman, "Style and the Rhetorical Situation of Romans 8:31-39," *NTS* 34 (1988): 218-31; Anders Eriksson, "'Women Tongue Speakers, Be

ger involved in isolating the rhetorical situation of a certain passage. He says that Romans 8:31-39 is a *peroratio* of the rhetorical unit Romans 5-8 and then declares that it is epideictic in terms of the three species of rhetoric.[3] This conclusion is drawn from his analysis of the rhetorical situation of Romans 8:31-39. He does not even attempt to define the rhetorical situation of Romans 5-8, let alone that of Romans as a whole, but just defines the rhetorical situation of 8:31-39. This is impossible. How can one pericope or a few verses have a specific species of rhetoric? Further, if the passage is a *peroratio* as he argues, is it not natural for it to be epideictic in nature?[4]

Therefore, it is imperative that we examine the rhetorical situation of Romans as a whole before we proceed to concentrate on the rhetorical situation of Romans 9-11.

I. THE FUNCTIONS OF *EXORDIUM* AND *PERORATIO* IN GRECO-ROMAN RHETORIC

The task of defining the rhetorical situation of the whole letter of Romans is not a small task. Indeed, it could be a whole dissertation.[5] What we need here, however, is a framework that we can build upon and that will anchor our investigation of the rhetorical situation of Romans 9-11.[6] I believe this framework can be established by concen-

---

Silent': A Reconstruction Through Paul's Rhetoric," *Biblical Interpretation* 6 (1998): 83-4; and The Bible and Culture Collective, "Rhetorical Criticism," in *The Postmodern Bible*, ed. Elizabeth A. Castelli, *et al.* (New Haven: Yale University Press, 1995), 151-52.

[3] Snyman, "Romans 8:31-39," 227-28.

[4] N. Elliott accuses Kennedy of misleading New Testament critics to think that a rhetorical situation can be established for segments of a text (*The Rhetoric of Romans: Argumentative Constraint and Strategy and Paul's Dialogue with Judaism*, JSNTSup 45 [Sheffield: Sheffield Academic, 1990], n. 95). Cf. Kennedy, *New Testament Interpretation*, 34-5. Anderson, *Ancient Rhetorical Theory and Paul*, 173, agrees on this point.

[5] Cf. J. N. Vorster, "The Rhetorical Situation of the Letter to the Romans—an Interactional Approach," unpublished DD dissertation, University of Pretoria, 1991.

[6] The ideal way of delineating the rhetorical situation of Romans is 1. to work out a framework first (e.g., *exordium* and *peroratio*), 2. to gather each argumentative unit's situation (e.g., 1:14-4:25; 5:1-8:39; 9-11; 12-15:13), and 3. to determine the overarching situation. The task, however, is beyond the scope of this study and will be treated in the future.

trating on the opening (1:1-13, 15) and closing (15:14-16:27) of the letter because they function as *exordium* and *peroratio* in the rhetorical structure of Romans. We will briefly look at the functions of *exordium* and *peroratio* in Greco-Roman rhetorical theories and then evaluate the feasibility of applying their theories to our texts.

The *Exordium*

The function of the *exordium*[7] in ancient rhetoric is, first of all, to prepare the hearer's mind to be "well-disposed, attentive, and receptive (*benivolum, attentum, docilem*)."[8] Cicero advises that in order to achieve this, the rhetor should make a careful study of the case that he/she has to present.[9] Quintilian puts this emphatically: "the sole purpose of the *exordium* is to prepare our audience in such a way that they will be disposed to lend a ready ear to the rest of our speech."[10]

There are two ways to structure the *exordium* for this end: *principium* or προοίμιον ("Direct Opening") and *insinuatio* or ἔφοδος ("Subtle Approach").[11] The rhetor can use the *principium* when the audience has a positive assessment of the rhetor or when the topic that one argues is an honorable[12] case. In this situation, the rhetor must use direct and plain language to win the good-will of the audience.[13] But if the audience is hostile toward the rhetor, he/she has to "have recourse to the insinuation,"[14] which is "an address which by dissimulation and indirection unobtrusively steals into the mind of the auditor."[15] Cicero explains that the hostility from the audience can

---

[7] For discussions of the *exordium*, see Pl. *Phdr.* 51.266D; Ar. *Rhet.* 3.14-15; *Rhet. Ad Alex.* 29, 35; *Ad. Her.* 1.3.5-7.11; Cic. *Inv.* 1.14.19-18.26; Cic. *De Or.* 1.31.143, 2.42.178, 2.43.182-84; Cic. *Part. Or.* 8.28-30; Cic. *Or.* 15.50, 35.122, 124; Cic. *Top.* 26.79; Quint. 4.1.1-79. Also, see Lausberg, *Handbuch,* 1:150-63 (§§ 263-88); Josef Martin, *Antike Rhetorik: Technik und Methode*, Handbuch Der Altertumswissenschaft II/3 (München: Beck, 1974), 60-75.

[8] Cic. *Inv.,* 1.15.20; unless otherwise noted, all translations and the original texts follow LCL editions.

[9] Ibid; *Ad. Her.* 1.3.5; Quint. 4.1.40.

[10] Quint. 4.1.5.

[11] *Ad. Her.* 1.4.6-6.10; Cic. *Inv.* 1.15.20-17.23; Quint. 4.1.42-51.

[12] A case is honorable when the defense or attack seems to be universally recognized. See *Ad. Her.* 1.3.5. Also see Bruce J. Malina and Jerome H. Neyrey, *Portraits of Paul: An Archaeology of Ancient Personality* (Louisville: Westminster John Knox, 1996), 65-67, for an apt summary of five types of cases.

[13] Cic. *Inv.* 1.15.20.

[14] Ibid., 1.15.21.

[15] Ibid., 1.15.20.

arise principally from three causes: if the case is scandalous; if the opponents have already convinced the audience; or the audience is tired
of listening.[16]

Perhaps the most important object of any rhetor is to establish
the proper *ethos* in the *exordium*. Since the *exordium* sets the tone of
the entire speech, it is of the utmost importance for the rhetor, especially when not well known to the audience, to achieve a good *ethos* so
that the audience might be disposed to receive the speech well. D. A.
Russell's explanation of the importance of *ethos* is to the point: (1) the
speaker needs to "project a sympathetic image of himself" so that he
might be seen to be "likable and—even more important—
trustworthy"; (2) he has to "identify and study the specific qualities of
his audience," especially "qualities of character," so that when a plea is
made he would know how the audience would react.[17] In the case of
Romans, we assume that Paul studied his audience carefully before
writing his letter, so that we can infer the character of his audience
from his writing. William Brandt also emphasizes the importance of
establishing *ethos* in the *exordium* of a speech: "the writer in his introduction must define himself and he must define his problem."[18] In reference to Aristotle's *Rhetoric,* Book II, Brandt also says that "the
writer of argumentation must establish a kind of presence at the beginning of an argument"[19] that "whatever ethos the speaker or writer attempts to create, it must be established before a sympathetic response
can be hoped for."[20] We will examine whether Paul's main concern in
writing his *exordium* is focused on establishing the proper *ethos*. In
our examination of the *exordium* of Romans, we will see what kind of
exordium Paul uses and the implication of it for the rhetorical situation
of Romans.

---

[16] Cic. *Inv.* 1.17.24.
[17] D. A. Russell, *Greek Declamation* (Cambridge: Cambridge University
Press, 1983), 87. Russell lists one more item in his explanation, the importance of
representing the characters of opponents and other people appearing in the story so
that the speaker's narrative seem plausible.
[18] William J. Brandt, *The Rhetoric of Argumentation* (Indianapolis: Bobbs-
Merrill, 1970), 51.
[19] Ibid., 52.
[20] Ibid., 53.

The *Peroratio*

Let us briefly consider the functions of *peroratio*. The *peroratio* (ἐπίλογος/*conclusio*) is the end and conclusion of the whole speech[21] but it can also be used in other places such as in an *exordium* after the strongest argument.[22] Quintilian divides *peroratio* into two parts: *repetitio* and *amplificatio* (*adfectus*/αὔξησις).[23] The *repetitio* is recapitulation or summing up of the argument that the rhetor has advanced in the *probatio* to refresh the audience's memory.[24] The *amplificatio*, on the other hand, is the central feature of the *peroratio* because with this the rhetor strengthens his thesis or weakens the opposition's.[25] The *amplificatio* deals mainly with emotional aspects of the case.[26] The rhetor stirs the emotion of the audience to fortify his case and to weaken the position of the opponents.[27]

Good rhetoric should relate the *exordium* to the *peroratio* at the end of a speech. Quintilian disagrees with some of his contemporary rhetoricians who teach that the *exordium* should deal with the past and the *peroratio* the future, and therefore should be distinguished in content.[28] He rather teaches that the two parts of the speech should be closely related in content and that certain things require fuller treatment in the *peroratio* than in the *exordium*, where the rhetor can simply outline them.[29] The ancient audience who was familiar with rhe-

---

[21] *Ad. Her.* 1.3.4.

[22] *Rhet. Ad Alex.* 36.1444b.22-24; *Ad. Her.* 2.30.47.

[23] Quint. 6.1.1. Cicero's division uses three parts: *enumeratio, indignatio,* and *conquestio* (*Inv.* 1.52.98). In other place, however, he uses two divisions: *enumeratio* and *amplificatio* (*Part. Or.* 15.52-17.60).

[24] *Ad. Her.* 2.30.47. See also Ar. *Rhet.* 3.19.4.1419b; *Rhet. Ad Alex.* 20; Cic. *Inv.* 1.52.98-100; Cic. *Part. Or.* 17.59; Quint. 6.1.1-8.

[25] Quint. 6.1.52.

[26] Quint. 6.1.9-55, 6.2, 3.

[27] For a good summary of *amplificatio,* see Duane F. Watson, *Invention, Arrangement, and Style: Rhetorical Criticism of Jude and 2 Peter,* SBLDS 104 (Atlanta: Scholars, 1988), 26-8. For more details, see Ar. *Rhet.* 1.9.1368a.38-40; Cic. *De Or.* 3.26.104-27.107; Cic. *Part. Or.* 15.52-17.58; Long. *Subl.* 11.1-12.2; Quint. 8.4; Lausberg, *Handbuch,* 1:220-27 (§§ 400-403); Martin, *Antike Rhetorik,* 153-58, 208-10.

[28] Quint. 4.1.28. One may argue that Paul pays attention to his past (apologetically) in his *exordium* and focuses on the future in the *peroratio*. But both the *exordium* and *peroratio* include reference to Paul's past and future; it is more reasonable to see connections between these sections of the letter, not in a temporal sense but thematically.

[29] Quint. 6.1.12; 4.1.5.

torical practices would naturally expect the rhetor to come back to the matters the rhetor introduced briefly in the *exordium*.[30] We will see whether Paul consciously reiterates the points that he outlines in the *exordium* when he reaches his *peroratio*.

With this understanding of the functions and relationship of *exordium* and *peroratio* we will now examine the *exordium* and the *peroratio* of Romans in order to establish the entire letter's rhetorical situation. After a brief analysis of each passage, we will concentrate on delineating the exigence (or *causa*[31]), and two other components of the rhetorical situation, namely, the speaker and the audience.

II. THE *EXORDIUM* AND THE *PERORATIO* OF ROMANS

The Limits of the *Exordium* and the *Peroratio* in Romans

The *Exordium*. It is true that scholars do not agree which verses form the *exordium* (or epistolary prescript) and *peroratio* (or epistolary postscript) in Romans. Let us consider the opening of the letter first. In his formal rhetorical analysis of Romans, Robert Jewett takes 1:1-12 as the *exordium*[32] while N. Elliott takes 1:1-17[33] and W. Wuellner, 1:1-15.[34] David Aune argues that 1:1-15 is not an *exordium* but an epistolary prescript,[35] in viewing Romans as a protreptic letter. Samuel Byr-

---

[30] So Samuel Byrskog, "Epistolography, Rhetoric, and Letter Prescript: Romans 1.1-7 As a Test Case," *JSNT* 65 (1997): 43. Cf. A. B. du Toit's chart in his article, "Persuasion in Romans 1:1-17," *BZ* 33 (1989): 199-200. Du Toit's approach does not draw from Greco-Roman rhetorical theories but it is worthwhile to consider because he conveniently illustrates the "verbal and contentual overlapping" between Rom 1:1-17 and 15:14-33.

[31] Cf. H. Lausberg, *Elemente der literarischen Rhetorik* (Munich: Hueber, 1967), 21-23, who discusses *Situationsfrage*.

[32] Robert Jewett, "Following the Argument of Romans," in *The Romans Debate: Revised and Expanded Edition*, ed. Karl P. Donfried (Peabody: Hendrickson, 1991), 265-77.

[33] Elliott, *The Rhetoric of Romans*, 70-86.

[34] Wilhelm Wuellner, "Paul's Rhetoric of Argumentation in Romans: An Alternative to the Donfried-Karris Debate Over Romans," in *The Romans Debate*, 128-46.

[35] David E. Aune, "Romans As a Logos Protreptikos in the Context of Ancient Religious and Philosophical Propaganda," in *Paulus und das antike Judentum*, ed. Martin Hengel and Ulrich Heckel, WUNT 58 (Tübingen: Mohr, 1991), 91-124.

skog is correct when he says that 1:1-7 forms the epistolary prescript[36] while it is included in the rhetorical *exordium* which runs through v. 13. Grammatically, it is plain to see that v. 14 begins a new section which is connected with γάρ through vv. 16-18, and then διότι (v. 19), again γάρ (v. 20) and διότι again (v. 21).[37] In understanding this structure, v. 15 seems to be a hindrance because it connects with vv. 11-12 regarding Paul's desire to visit Rome. But v. 15 appears more as a parenthetical digression that Paul makes immediately after embarking on the major section of the letter.[38] Therefore, I take v. 15 as belonging together with 1:1-13, a part of the *exordium*. Most commentators, in their desire to designate 1:16-17 as the theme of the letter, usually see 1:1-15 as an introduction to the letter, in which Paul casually states an introduction of himself and some trivial matter of his desire to come to them before stating the truly important theological theme of the letter.[39] What most ignores is that v. 14 clearly begins a new block of Paul's argumentation, within which vv. 16-17 are embedded in a larger argument.[40] Further, recent studies have shown that vv. 16-17 do not qualify as an overarching theme of the letter even in chapters 1-11, not to mention the whole letter.[41] The epistolary prescript (1:1-7) is not

---

[36] Byrskog, "Epistolography," 27-46.

[37] See Paul J. Achtemeier, *Romans,* IBC (Atlanta: John Knox, 1985), 35-36, for a translation and explanation of this point. See also idem, "Unsearchable Judgments," 13.

[38] Ibid., 13, n. 28. Cf. NRSV, which also understands 1:15 as a parenthetical statement: "—hence my eagerness to proclaim the gospel to you also who are in Rome."

[39] But see Cranfield, *Romans,* I, 73-4, who includes v. 16a in the introduction.

[40] Moo argues that "grammatically subordinate clauses frequently stand out in importance by virtue of their content—especially in Greek, with its love of subordinate clauses (hypotaxis)." In this view, Achtemeier's argument based on grammar should be rejected (*Romans,* 64). Moo, however, does not provide any evidence or example for his argument but simply asserts his point. Further, he states earlier in his commentary that the theme of the whole letter is "the gospel" which encompasses diverse topics in Romans (p. 29-30). If "the gospel" is the theme of the letter as he argues, why, then, cannot the other occurrences of the term in the letter, concentrated in the *exordium* and the *peroratio* (1:1, 9, 15; 15:16, 19), be taken as the thematic statement? Why should only 1:16-17 be the theme, especially when the term appears only in the middle of Paul's exposition of his indebtedness to the Gentiles in terms of preaching it and it is surrounded by other important terms like "righteousness," "salvation," and "faith"?

[41] Ross Wagner recently proposes that 15:7-13 should be considered "as a summation of the themes of the letter as a whole" and "the theological center of Romans" ("The Christ, Servant of Jew and Gentile: A Fresh Approach to Romans

technically an *exordium* but functions as an *exordium* in both inform-
ing and disposing the reader/hearer to be receptive to the subject matter.[42] Thus, we will look at 1:1-13 and 15 in our investigation.[43]

The *Peroratio*. The next passage that we will examine is Romans 15:14-16:27. Most scholars agree that Romans 15:14 starts the
letter closing or *peroratio* but do not agree where the closing ends.
Elliott treats only 15:14-33 as the letter closing and ignores chapter 16
without any explanation.[44] Wuellner[45] takes 15:14-16:23 while Jewett[46] takes 15:14-16:27 as the *peroratio*. Aune takes 15:14-16:27 as
the epistolary postscript in his structure.[47] I believe that taking 15:14-
16:27 as the *peroratio* of Romans is most reasonable even with its textual problems, and thus, we will examine these verses in our discussion.[48]

15:8-9," *JBL* 116 [1997]: 473). N. T. Wright also suggests that Rom 15:7-13 can
be the seen as the climax of the entire epistle (*Climax of the Covenant: Christ and
the Law in Pauline Theology* [Minneapolis: Fortress, 1991], 235).

[42] Duane Watson calls the epistolary prescript a "*quasi*-exordium" in his
analysis of the epistle of Jude (Watson, *Invention, Arrangement, and Style*, 40-1).
In our discussion, we will closely examine whether these verses in the prescript
(1:1-7) fulfill this expectation.

[43] Cf. Hans Hübner who sees that 1:8-15 as *exordium* in his analysis ("Die
Rhetorik und die Theologie: Der Römerbrief und die rhetorische Kompetenz des
Paulus," in *Die Macht des Wortes: Aspekte gegenwärtiger Rhetorikforschung*, Ars
Rhetorica 4, ed. Carl Joachim and Heinz-Joachim Müllenbrock [Marbug: Hitze-
roth, 1992], 169). But he later changes his mind and characterizes 1:8-15 as a *nar-
ratio* (*Biblische Theologie des Neuen Testaments, Band 2: Die Theologie des Pau-
lus und ihre neutestamentaliche Wirkungsgeschichte* [Göttingen: Vandenhoeck &
Ruprecht, 1993], 239).

[44] He also says that the *peroratio* of Romans is 15:14-*32*! What happens to
15:33 he does not once again explain (Elliott, *The Rhetoric of Romans*, 86-104).
His confusion and neglect of Romans 16 bear some serious interpretive consequences. See below.

[45] Wuellner, "Paul's Rhetoric of Argumentation," 136-41.

[46] Jewett, "Following the Argument of Romans," 274.

[47] Aune, "Romans as a Logos Protreptikos," 91-124. Aune's efforts to
maintain the letter structure with rhetorical features of the letter result in Romans
as simply a letter rather than the protreptic speech for which he argues. Cf.
Stanley E. Porter, "Paul of Tarsus and His Letters," in *Handbook of Classical
Rhetoric in the Hellenistic Period 330 B.C.-A.D. 400*, ed. Stanley E. Porter (Leiden; New York; Köln: Brill, 1997), 560.

[48] The problem of applying rhetorical categories into the Pauline letters has
been extensively debated. For a summary of this discussion, see Porter, "Paul of
Tarsus," 562-67. For a bibliography of the issue, see Watson and Hauser, eds.,
Rhetorical Criticism, 160-61. To the list, I would add Hermann Probst, *Paulus*

Romans 1:1-13, 15

First, we will examine 1:1-13, 15 as the *exordium* of Romans. Paul's expansion of the usual Greco-Roman epistolary convention in 1:1-7 is concentrated on the part of the sender himself. This expansion may imply that one of the purposes of Romans is the introduction of the sender to the Roman congregation,[49] or can mean something much more than that. We need to examine the expansion in some detail. The structure of this passage can be shown more clearly when it is diagrammed as follows:

1.1 Παῦλος
    δοῦλος Χριστοῦ Ἰησοῦ,
    κλητὸς ἀπόστολος
    ἀφωρισμένος
        εἰς εὐαγγέλιον θεοῦ,
        2 ὃ προεπηγγείλατο
            διὰ τῶν προφητῶν αὐτοῦ
            ἐν γραφαῖς ἁγίαις
        3 περὶ τοῦ υἱοῦ αὐτοῦ
            τοῦ γενομένου
                ἐκ σπέρματος Δαυὶδ
                κατὰ σάρκα,
        4 τοῦ ὁρισθέντος υἱοῦ θεοῦ ἐν δυνάμει

und der Brief: Die Rhetorik des antiken Briefes als Form der paulinischen Korin-therkorrespondenz (1 Kor 8--10), WUNT 2/45 (Tübingen: Mohr, 1991), 99-107; Stanley E. Porter, "The Theoretical Justification for Application of Rhetorical Categories to Pauline Epistolary Literature," in *Rhetoric and the New Testament: Essays From the 1992 Heidelberg Conference*, ed. Stanley E. Porter and Thomas H. Olbricht, JSNTSup 90 (Sheffield: JSOT, 1993),100-22; Jeffrey T. Reed, "Using Ancient Rhetorical Categories to Interpret Paul's Letters: A Question of Genre," in *Rhetoric and the New Testament*, 292-324; John L. White, "Apostolic Mission and Apostolic Message: Congruence in Paul's Epistolary Rhetoric, Structure and Imagery," in *Origins and Method: Towards a New Understanding of Judaism and Christianity: Essays in Honour of John C. Hurd*, ed. Bradley H. McLean (Sheffield: Sheffield Academic, 1993), 145-61; D. L. Stamps, "Rhetorical Criticism of the New Testament," 141-47; Peterson, "Eloquence and the Proclamation," 25-35; Byrskog, "Epistolography," 27-46; and Duane F. Watson, "The Integration of Epistolary and Rhetorical Analysis of Philippians," in *The Rhetorical Analysis of Scripture: Essays From the 1995 London Conference*, ed. Stanley E. Porter and Thomas H. Olbricht, JSNTSup 146 (Sheffield: Sheffield Academic, 1997), 398-426.

[49] Johnson, *Reading Romans*, 20.

κατὰ πνεῦμα ἁγιωσύνης
ἐξ ἀναστάσεως νεκρῶν,
Ἰησοῦ Χριστοῦ τοῦ κυρίου ἡμῶν,
5 δι' οὗ ἐλάβομεν χάριν καὶ ἀποστολὴν
εἰς ὑπακοὴν πίστεως
ἐν πᾶσιν τοῖς ἔθνεσιν
ὑπὲρ τοῦ ὀνόματος αὐτοῦ,
6 ἐν οἷς ἐστε καὶ ὑμεῖς κλητοὶ Ἰησοῦ Χριστοῦ,
7 πᾶσιν τοῖς οὖσιν ἐν ' Ρώμῃ ἀγαπητοῖς θεοῦ,
κλητοῖς ἁγίοις,
χάρις ὑμῖν καὶ εἰρήνη
ἀπὸ θεοῦ πατρὸς ἡμῶν καὶ κυρίου Ἰησοῦ Χριστοῦ.[50]

First, the three qualifications of Paul in the beginning (δοῦλος Χριστοῦ Ἰησοῦ, κλητὸς ἀπόστολος, and ἀφωρισμένος) are clearly rhetorical paronomasia (παρονομασία, παρήχησις, annominatio) on Παῦλος, which are plays on words which have similar but not identical sounds.[51] With successive words ending with the same sounds, we see that this prescript is carefully crafted by Paul. Paul's first designation of himself as δοῦλος Χριστοῦ Ἰησοῦ reminds his audience that the source of his authority[52] and the destination of his commitment and submission is the Messiah Jesus.[53] When Paul identi-

---

[50] Cf. Byrskog, "Epistolography," 29; J. P. Louw, *Semantics of New Testament Greek,* SBLSS (Philadelphia; Chico: Fortress; Scholars, 1982), 143.

[51] For the theory and use of paronomasia see Lausberg, *Handbuch,* 322-23 (§ 637); *Ad. Her.* 4.22.29; Cic. *De Or.* 2.63.256; Galen O. Rowe, "Style," in *Handbook of Classical Rhetoric in the Hellenistic Period 330 B.C.-A.D. 400,* ed. Stanley E. Porter (Leiden: Brill, 1997), 132.

[52] See Dale B. Martin, *Slavery As Salvation: The Metaphor of Slavery in Pauline Christianity* (New Haven: Yale University Press, 1990). A. B. du Toit argues that Paul calls himself δοῦλος ahead of ἀπόστολος in order to relativize and qualify "what could be experienced as peremptory connotations of the latter title" (du Toit, "Persuasion in Romans 1:1-17," 204) but in the light of Martin's study, the effect of calling oneself a δοῦλος of someone in an authoritative position (in this case, the Messiah Jesus) hardly achieves what du Toit argues for. However, I am in agreement with du Toit on the point that Paul is very careful to assert his authority as an apostle to the Romans throughout the passage (Romans 1:1-15).

[53] Johnson, *Reading Romans,* 20-21. In the Old Testament, δοῦλος κυρίου/θεοῦ is used as a title of honor for Moses, Joshua, David and the prophets (cf. Josh. 14:7; 24:29; Judg. 2:8; 2 Kg. 17:23; Ps. 89:3). Paul's adaptation of this title with Χριστοῦ Ἰησοῦ instead of κυρίου or θεοῦ clearly shows Jesus the Messiah is already honored as God (cf. Ἰησοῦ Χριστοῦ τοῦ κυρίου ἡμῶν in 4d) (James M. Scott, *Adoption as Sons of God: an Exegetical Investigation into the*

fies himself as κλητὸς ἀπόστολος, he not only refers to his personal experience of calling on the Damascus road (Acts 9:1-9; cf. Gal 1:15-16) but also associates himself with the audience because he calls his audience κλητοὶ Ἰησοῦ Χριστοῦ (v.6) and κλητοῖς ἁγίοις (v.7). Especially, by calling his audience "κλητοὶ Ἰησοῦ Χριστοῦ," Paul creates a strong bond between himself and them, since both have received the calling from the same person, Jesus Christ himself.[54]

The third qualification on Παῦλος is a participial phrase, ἀφωρισμένος εἰς εὐαγγέλιον θεοῦ.[55] Paul's use of ἀφωρίζω clearly indicates that his understanding of apostleship is derived from his Jewish background, since the whole phrase reminds one of Isa 49:1 and Jer 1:5 (cf. *As. Mos.* 1:14) where the Old Testament prophets received their call and commission.[56] The purpose of Paul's being "set apart" as an apostle is for the gospel of God, which Paul describes with a relative clause in v. 2. Paul says that the gospel of God "has been promised beforehand through his prophets" in the "holy writings," which obviously are meant to be the scriptures of Israel.[57] Paul's appeal to the scriptures of Israel for the gospel of God he preaches in the *exordium* prepares his audience for his quotations and allusions to the scriptures of Israel throughout the letter, especially in chapters 9-11.[58] Indeed, Romans contains at least fifty-one quotations from the Old Testament[59], and if all the allusions to the Old Testament are included,

---

Background of ΥΙΟΘΕΣΙΑ *in the Pauline Corpus*, WUNT 2/48 [Tübingen: Mohr, 1992], 224-25).

[54] See A. Satake, "Apostolat und Gnade bei Paulus," *NTS* 15 (1968-69): 96-107.

[55] The substantive participial phrase is used only once in the identification of the sender unit and is therefore unique in the section (L. Ann Jervis, *The Purpose of Romans: A Comparative Letter Structure Investigation*, JSNTSup 55 [Sheffield: Sheffield Academic, 1991], 73).

[56] See further K. H. Rengstorf, "ἀπόστολος," *TDNT,* I, 407-47. For the possibility of allusion of the word to Paul's past as a "Pharisee," see M. Hengel, *The Pre-Christian Paul* (Philadelphia: Trinity Press International, 1991), 40-53. It is of little importance for our purpose because it is very difficult to imagine that Paul's audience would catch such an allusion to his past even if he had intended one.

[57] James D. G. Dunn, *Romans 1-8*, WBC 38a (Dallas: Word, 1988), 11.

[58] There is a clear connection of 1:2 to 9:6a (Οὐκ οἷον δὲ ὅτι ἐκπέπτωκεν ὁ λόγος τοῦ θεοῦ). It will be explored fully in the next chapter.

[59] Dietrich-Alex Koch, *Die Schrift als Zeuge des Evangliums: Untersuchungen zur Verwendung und zum Verständnis der Schrift bei Paulus*, BHT 69 (Tübingen: Mohr, 1986), 21-4. Cf. E. E. Ellis, *Paul's Use of Old Testament* (Grand Rapids: Baker, 1957), 150-52, who found fifty-three quotations in Romans.

we find that the whole letter of Romans is saturated with the scriptures of Israel. This "heavy concentration of scriptural quotations and allusions" shows that "Paul is seeking to ground his exposition of the gospel in Israel's sacred texts."[60]   Rhetorically speaking, the fact that Paul appeals to the authority that his audience readily acknowledges throughout his argumentation in his letter gives us important clues to the rhetorical situation. It shows that Paul does not enjoy a firm authoritative position with his audience.[61] Further, Paul makes clear that what he is going to argue is not his own invention but something that has been promised and foretold by ancient authorities, which in this instance are the scriptures of Israel.[62]

Verses 3-4 have been hotly debated regarding whether Paul used the traditional confessional materials of the early church or not. Without really going into the debate here, I submit that we can never be sure about this, nor likewise the extent of Paul's redactions or the layers of tradition, and so forth. Rhetorical critics are tempted to see traditional materials that Paul incorporated here; if so, it would be easy to conclude that Paul consciously uses materials with which the Roman Christians are already familiar in order to create a strong bond and association with his audience. But doing so would indulge one of the weaknesses of historical criticism—playing highly conjectural guessing exercises that cannot ever be proved with confidence. What is available to us is the text itself, and we will concentrate on the text with the understanding that it is the fact that Paul wrote these verses, notwithstanding their origin. They could be purely Pauline or pre-Pauline, but one thing is clear—Paul uses them in his composition.[63]

---

[60] Richard B. Hays, *Echoes of Scripture in the Letters of Paul* (New Haven: Yale University, 1989), 34.

[61] Cf. Watson, "The Contributions and the Limitations," 15-6.

[62] We should ask ourselves why Paul would appeal to the ancient Jewish authority if he is persuading a Gentile audience. This question will be explored a little later.

[63] It is my suspicion that many interpreters have been so preoccupied with the origin of these materials or Pauline redactions that they have missed the importance of these verses' place in the argumentation of the letter. We will argue that they are included in the parts that make the thematic statements for the whole letter. Cf. Charles H. Giblin, "'As It Is Written…' A Basic Problem in Noematics," *CBQ* 20 (1958): 477-98, who argues that the phrase εὐαγγέλιον ὃ προεπηγγείλατο (1:1-2) contains the theme of Romans. His exposition (only on Rom 1-5), however, fails to show how the phrase functions as the thematic statement for the whole letter.

As our diagram shows, the phrase τοῦ υἱοῦ αὐτοῦ is qualified with two attributive participial phrases and it has been recognized by many commentators that here is a chiastic structure.[64] The first relative clause describes the origin of Jesus in the lineage of the house of David. Together with the use of the verb ὁρίζω,[65] Paul is clearly alluding to the promises of 2 Sam 7:12-14[66] and Psalm 2:7.[67] With κατὰ σάρκα, Jesus' earthly life is described, and the reference to σάρξ is not pejorative[68] but "theologically neutral."[69] That the Messiah Jesus came from the royal lineage of David in accordance with the promises of God through the Jewish prophets in the Jewish scriptures indeed sets the tone of the whole letter: The gospel of God is about the Jewish Messiah in the tradition of the Jewish religion and Jewish scriptures.

The Messiah Jesus was also declared (ὁρισθέντος) the Son of God with power (ἐν δυνάμει).[70] Then, the most difficult part in the description of Jesus in these verses is encountered: κατὰ πνεῦμα ἁγιωσύνης,[71] which has significance in Paul's overall argument in

---

[64] Among many, see particularly Jervis, *The Purpose of Romans,* 74, and Gordon D. Fee, *God's Empowering Presence: The Holy Spirit in the Letters of Paul* (Peabody, Mass.: Hendrickson, 1994), 479. Some commentators find parallelism (Semitic?) but not a chiasm here. See Dunn, *Romans 1-8,* 5, who also sees the antithetical relationship between the two relative clauses. Fee rightly points out that this is not necessarily so (Fee, *God's Empowering Presence,* 479, n. 18).

[65] L. C. Allen, "The Old Testament Background of (ΠΡΟ)ʹΟΡΙΖΕΙΝ in the New Testament," *NTS* 17 (1970-71): 104-8.

[66] So Scott, *Adoption as Sons of God,* 241-44. See his note 75 for references to the works that recognize this.

[67] See Peter Stuhlmacher, *Paul's Letter to the Romans,* trans. S. J. Hafemann (Louisville: Westminster/John Knox, 1994), 18-9 for further Old Testament references.

[68] *Contra* Dunn, *Romans 1-8,* 13, who argues for the negative connotation in Paul's usage on the ground that it is in an antithetical position to κατὰ πνεῦμα. But what he ignores is that the phrase that Paul contrasts is not κατὰ πνεῦμα only but the whole prepositional phrase, κατὰ πνεῦμα ἁγιωσύνης. Cf. Michael Theobald, "'Dem Juden zuerst und auch dem Heiden' Die paulinische Auslegung der Glaubensformel Röm 1,3f.," in *Kontinuität und Einheit für Franz Mussner,* ed. Paul-Gerhard Müller and Werner Stenger (Freiburg: Herder, 1981), 386-90.

[69] Fee, *God's Empowering Presence,* 480-81.

[70] I take the phrase ἐν δυνάμει to modify "Son of God," not ὁρισθέντος. So Byrskog, "Epistolography," 29, n.7.

[71] The phrase is a literal rendering of the Hebrew רוּחַ קָדְשׁ, which is consistently translated in the LXX as τὸ πνεῦμα τὸ ἅγιον. The phrase is incredibly rare in Greek literature and only occurs in *T. Levi* 18:11 ("καὶ πνεῦμα ἁγιωσύνης ἔσται ἐπ᾽ αὐτοῖς") and a Jewish amulet (see Erik Peterson, "Das Amulett von

Romans. There have been various proposals for understanding this phrase,[72] which can be summarized as follows: (1) the phrase refers to Christ's human spirit—his exceptional and transcendent Holiness;[73] or (2) Jesus' "spirit" similar in meaning to "attitude" or "disposition";[74] or (3) simply the Holy Spirit, the third person of the Trinity.[75] The recent suggestion by A. B. du Toit is worth considering.[76] He finds parallelism between ἐκ σπέρματος Δαυίδ and υἱοῦ θεοῦ ἐν δυνάμει, not ἐξ ἀναστάσεως νεκρῶν, insisting that "the balancing elements of a parallelism need not always contain a direct or full-blown semantic relationship to each other"[77] and also that the phrase is not a corresponding statement to κατὰ σάρκα.[78] He then argues that κατὰ πνεῦμα ἁγιωσύνης should be understood in a modal sense, resulting in a translation, "according to the spirit of holiness." Du Toit then proceeds to find the "mode of existence" that κατὰ πνεῦμα ἁγιωσύνης refers to by assuming that κατὰ σάρκα refers to Jesus' "physical (pre-resurrection) mode of existence."[79] He finds the support to his thesis in 1 Cor 15:35-49 and understands κατὰ πνεῦμα ἁγιωσύνης as referring to "Jesus' pneumatic mode of existence after his resurrection."[80] But at the same time, he says that the phrase also refers to the Holy Spirit because it is impossible to separate the human spirit from it when Paul refers to πνεῦμα in his letters. Therefore, "we

---

Acre," in *Frühkirche, Judentum und Gnosis: Studien und Untersuchungen* [Rome: Herder, 1959], 346-54).

[72] For the literature on the subject with good summaries, see Theoblad, "Röm 1:3f," 381-84 and Robert Jewett, "The Redaction and Use of an Early Christian Confession in Romans 1:3-4," in *The Living Text: Essays in Honor of Ernest W. Saunders*, ed. Dennis E. Groh and Robert Jewett (Lanham, Md.: University Press of America, 1985), 99-122. For more recent literature, see Fitzmyer, *Romans,* 239-42.

[73] W. Sanday and A. C. Headlam, *A Critical and Exegetical Commentary on the Epistle to the Romans,* ICC (New York: Charles Scribner's Sons, 1926), 9.

[74] NRSV, "according to the spirit of holiness."

[75] E.g., Scott, *Adoption as Sons of God,* 239-41. To make sense of his exegesis, Scott insists that the preposition κατὰ here is used in an "instrumental" sense. It is, however, not only improbable grammatically, but also not congruent in meaning when combined with the following phrase, ἐξ ἀναστάσεως νεκρῶν.

[76] "Romans 1,3-4 and the Gospel Tradition: A Reassessment of the Phrase *ΚΑΤΑ ΠΝΕΥΜΑ ΑΓΙΩΣΥΝΗΣ,*" in *The Four Gospels 1992: Festschrift Frans Neirynck, V. 1,* ed. F. van Segbroeck, *et al.* (Leuven: Leuven University Press, 1992), 249-56.

[77] Ibid., 252.

[78] Ibid., 253.

[79] Ibid., 254.

[80] Ibid.

have a double reference, one to Jesus' spirit, the other to the Holy Spirit, controlling Jesus' spiritual existence after his resurrection."[81]

Although this suggestion is interesting, du Toit's interpretation does not make much sense when examined closely. First, his alleged parallelism between ἐκ σπέρματος Δαυίδ and υἱοῦ θεοῦ ἐν δυνάμει is impossible grammatically, since the phrase υἱοῦ θεοῦ ἐν δυνάμει does not make any sense when it is separated from the articular participle, τοῦ ὁρισθέντος.[82] Second, his argument that we have a double reference is awkward because the two κατά-phrases make a contrast—why would Paul repeat the reference to Jesus' human aspect once again? Finally, it is most difficult to justify the modal sense of κατά + accusative, a construction which usually denotes a relationship of a specific element to something else, hence the meaning of "with respect to, in relation to, or with regard to."[83]

The better solution is provided by Gordon Fee in his monumental treatment of the use of the Holy Spirit in the Pauline corpus.[84] He views κατὰ σάρκα as referring to "the sphere of his human life," while the "Spirit" phrase refers to "the sphere of Spirit life."[85] Thus, these two phrases describe "the two expressions of existence,"[86] of which κατὰ σάρκα signifies the existence that is "truly human and belonging to the present age," while κατὰ πνεῦμα signifies the existence that is "belonging to the eschatological age inaugurated by the resurrection and the advent of the Spirit."[87] Fee takes πνεῦμα ἁγιωσύνης as referring to the Holy Spirit, with the genitive in a dynamic sense

---

[81] Ibid., 255.

[82] Du Toit himself acknowledges the difficulty by saying, "...it would be fair to say that a more direct and fuller correspondence would do *more justice* to the figure of parallelism" (ibid., 252). The reason for opting for his less justified alternative is that he could not find any correspondence between two ἐκ(ξ)-phrases. But this is a rather circular argument—what if we can find meaningful correspondence between these two phrases? Would that not be better?

[83] BAGD, II.6; Johannes P. Louw and Eugene A. Nida, ed., *Greek-English Lexicon of the New Testament: Based on Semantic Domains*, 2d ed. (New York : United Bible Societies, 1989), *s.v.*

[84] *God's Empowering Presence: The Holy Spirit in the Letters of Paul,* 1994.

[85] Fee, *God's Empowering Presence,* 481. Although Fee does not make reference, C. K. Barrett proposes a very similar translation: "in the sphere of the flesh,... in the sphere of the Holy Spirit,...." (*A Commentary on the Epistle to the Romans,* 2d ed. [Peabody, Mass.: Hendrickson, 1991], 20-21).

[86] So Barrett: "Christ belongs to two spheres or orders of existence" (*Romans,* 21).

[87] Fee, *God's Empowering Presence,* 481-82.

(=the Spirit who gives/supplies holiness),[88] anticipating "much of the argument of the rest of the letter,"[89] with which I strongly agree.[90]

Fee further argues that Jesus as "Son of God with power" should be understood in terms of the eschatological Spirit who is designated as "the Spirit who is holy in character and thus supplies holiness." Paul's intent by this designation is to mark off the concerns of the letter from the beginning.[91] The concerns that Fee thinks of are related to the lives of the believing community in Rome, Jew and Gentile together, in terms of their individual and corporate behavior. I wonder if much more is implied here. Paul later describes his missionary work among the Gentiles in terms of the powerful manifestation of the Holy Spirit in Rom 15:18-19. Indeed, he says that he won "the obedience" of the Gentiles "ἐν δυνάμει σημείων καὶ τεράτων, ἐν δυνάμει πνεύματος θεοῦ" (v.19). I am convinced that Paul's intent here is not only to show the content of the gospel of God but also to make clear that the gospel has the power which comes from the Holy Spirit even to make the dead alive, which happened not only to Jesus but also to the Gentiles who "obeyed" God. Thus, when this verse is read with the following verse, the subject matter of Paul's argument throughout the letter (at least in the *exordium* and the *peroratio*) is strongly stated in a compact way: the promise of the gospel (v.2), the content of the gospel (v.3), the power of the gospel (v.4), and the result of the gospel (v.5).[92]

The phrase Ἰησοῦ Χριστοῦ τοῦ κυρίου ἡμῶν stands like a pivot in the prescript. It not only forms an inclusio with περὶ τοῦ υἱοῦ

---

[88] So B. Schneider, "Κατὰ Πνεῦμα Ἁγιωσύνης (Romans 1,4)," *Bib* 48 (1967): 381.

[89] Fee especially points out the description of the Gentile believers in 15:16 (ἡγιασμένη ἐν πνεύματι ἁγίῳ). Grammatically, the feminine singular participle ἡγιασμένη cannot qualify the neuter plural τῶν ἐθνῶν, but later as Fee explains (p. 626), τῶν ἐθνῶν is in apposition with ἡ προσφορὰ, which is modified by ἡγιασμένη. Then, indeed the Gentile believers are "sanctified by the Holy Spirit."

[90] Cf. Achtemeier who says:

A more appropriate locus for such a theme would be at the beginning of the letter, and in that case 1:2-4 would be an admirable candidate, summarizing as it does the economy of salvation and leading into Paul's declaration of his own call to evangelize the gentiles ("Unsearchable Judgment," 13).

[91] Fee, *God's Empowering Presence*, 483-84.

[92] Cf. Schneider, "Κατὰ Πνεῦμα "Ἁγιωσύνης," 359-87, who argues that the description of the gospel of God in Rom 1:2-5 shows "an outline of salvation of history in three successive stages" (pp. 386-87).

αὐτοῦ,[93] but also functions as a kind of bridge to the following description of the purpose of his apostleship, which he received from God as a gift. By calling the Messiah Jesus τοῦ κυρίου ἡμῶν, Paul identifies himself with his audience, once again expressing his solidarity with them, in serving the same Lord. Paul here subtly affirms the fact that he believes in the same Lord with them (the Romans). Paul qualifies his apostleship for the second time, first with κλητὸς in v. 1 and here with a relative clause "δι᾽ οὗ ἐλάβομεν χάριν καὶ ἀποστολήν." That is, Paul makes it clear that he is not a self-designated apostle but the one who was "called" and received his apostleship from the Lord as a gift. The use of the first person plural in ἐλάβομεν is not simply an "epistolary plural"[94] (because Paul does not mention any co-senders in Romans unlike his other letters) but here Paul shows his audience that he wants to present himself not as the only apostle but as one of the apostles.[95] This rhetorical strategy is understandable because Paul had neither founded the church in Rome nor had he visited them (1:10, 13).

Now he specifies the purpose of his apostleship further with the phrase εἰς ὑπακοὴν πίστεως. Paul uses the preposition εἰς twice in the prescript and in both cases uses it in the sense of purpose.[96] Further, in both cases the preposition explains the purpose of Paul's apostleship. The first states that it is for εὐαγγέλιον θεοῦ and the second ὑπακοὴν πίστεως ἐν πᾶσιν τοῖς ἔθνεσιν. I am convinced that the latter explains the result of the former, that is, the result of the powerful manifestation of the gospel in winning the obedience of the Gentiles (cf. 15:18-19).[97] At this point we need to examine the meaning and content of the phrase in some detail. The key to understanding it is to decipher the heavily loaded phrase, ὑπακοὴν πίστεως.[98] Most of all,

---

[93] Hays is correct to see that the phrase περὶ τοῦ υἱοῦ αὐτοῦ should be connected with ἐν γραφαῖς ἁγίαις which immediately precedes it rather than εὐαγγέλιον θεοῦ (Hays, *Echoes of Scripture*, 85). *Contra* among many, Dunn, *Romans 1-8*, 11.

[94] See Samuel Byrskog, "Co-Senders, Co-Authors and Paul's Use of the First Person Plural," *ZNW* 87 (1996): 230-50.

[95] Du Toit, "Persuasion in Romans 1:1-17," 204.

[96] BAGD, 4.d, f. Cf. Cranfield's translation of εἰς: "for the purpose of bringing about" (Cranfield, *Romans*, I, 66).

[97] Further, it is connected to 1:9 and 1:16-17, where "the gospel" is explained in detail.

[98] The meaning of this phrase has been much debated. See D. B. Garlington, *Faith, Obedience, and Perseverance: Aspects of Paul's Letter to the Romans*,

it is striking to see the Jewishness of this phrase, even though there is
no evidence that the phrase has ever been used in any Jewish literature.[99] The word ὑπακόη, which was not a common word in the first
century, is derived from ἀκούω ("hear") and the verb ὑπακούω includes the meaning of "give ear to, answer, heed."[100] The important
fact is that LXX translates the Hebrew שָׁמַע ("hear") with ὑπακούω,
and there is no word "obey" in Hebrew.[101] Considering the Jewish
emphasis on "responding obediently to what one hears," which is the
central expression of the faith in the Shema, it is quite natural for the
LXX to translate it that way.[102] Further, the concept of hearing obediently is closely related to that of keeping the covenant: when Israel
hears God's words and obediently keeps them, she will be blessed
(Deut 4:1-14, 33, 36; 5:1-5, 22-27; 6:3-25; 7:12-14; 8:1-5; 11:13-27);
but when she fails to obey, the curse of destruction will follow (Deut
8:20; 9:23; 11:26-28).[103]

Paul seems to use the word πίστις with a thoroughly Jewish
connotation[104] here in conjunction with ὑπακόη. The Hebrew equivalent for πίστις is אמונה, which has the double meaning of "trust" and a

---

WUNT 79, ed. Martin Hengel and Otfried Hofius (Tübingen: Mohr, 1994), 10-31
for a summary of the issues and bibliography.

[99] idem, 'The Obedience of Faith': A Pauline Phrase in Historical Context,
WUNT 2/38, ed. Martin Hengel and Otfried Hofius (Tübingen: Mohr, 1991), 233.

[100] Dunn, Romans 1-8, 17.

[101] Garlington, Obedience of Faith, 11; Nanos, The Mystery of Romans,
222; Dunn, Romans 1-8, 17.

[102] Nanos, The Mystery of Romans, 222. F. W. Young's IDB article on
"obedience" makes this point clear:

> To really hear God's word inevitably involves one in an obedient
> response in action prompted by faithfulness to and faith in the God
> who is revealing himself in and through particular historical events.
> Not to respond in obedient action is tantamount to unbelief—and so
> the prophet chastises his people for their blind eyes and deaf ears
> (Isa 6:9-10), which betray their faithlessness. This inevitable con-
> sequence of failing to hear is rebellion or disobedience. But rebel-
> lion is not just the willful disobedience of one who has heard. Re-
> bellion is the sign that one has not really heard, since to hear im-
> plies a faith-obedience response (IDB 3.580; cited by Garlington,
> Faith, 18).

[103] Garlington, Obedience, 11-13; Nanos, The Mystery of Romans, 222-3.

[104] Garlington is right when he points out that Paul does not debate the
meaning of faith with his opponents in his letters. We can safely assume, then,
Paul and his Jewish counterpart share a common understanding regarding the
meaning of faith. The point of controversy was rather the object of that faith
(Faith, 18-9).

"commitment" (to the covenant) resulting from trust.[105] The two terms have almost the same meaning in their Jewish context. Garlington puts this aspect well: "In a real sense, then, to speak of faith *is* to speak of obedience."[106]

Now, when Paul coined the phrase ὑπακοὴ πίστεως, what did he mean? The genitival relationship between ὑπακοή and πίστις can be understood in various ways:

(1) Objective Genitive: "obedience to the faith" (i.e., to faith in the sense of *fides quae creditur,* the body of doctrine accepted); "obedience to faith" (i.e., to the authority of faith); "obedience to God's faithfulness attested in the gospel";

(2) Subjective Genitive or Genitive of Source: "obedience which faith works"; "the obedience required by faith"; "obedience that springs from faith";

(3) Adjectival Genitive: "believing obedience"; "faith's obedience";

(4) Genitive of Apposition: "the obedience which consists in faith" (faith as an act of obedience).[107]

Of these options, Cranfield chooses the genitive of apposition as the most probable because "Paul's preaching is aimed at obtaining from his hearers true obedience to God, the essence of which is a responding to His message of good news with faith."[108] Nanos, however, regards this option as weak because "while faith and obedience are parallel terms they do maintain some distinction that this conclusion fails to uphold."[109] He further asks, "Why bother with the phrase

---

[105] Garlington, *Faith,* 17. Garlington cites Edmund Perry in support of it: the Old Testament does not set trust and obedience in contrast to each other as separate ways of satisfying the demands of God. *'emuna* comprehends the totality of what we commonly mean in the familiar expression "faith and works." Obedience without trust (i.e. obedience not genetically generated from trust) is not the obedience God requires. Only the obedience of trust is reckoned to man as righteousness... (E. Perry, "The Meaning of *'emuna* in the Old Testament," *JBR* 21 [1953]: 255-56).

[106] Garlington, *Faith,* 18. So too H. W. Bartsch: "Faith and obedience are one action. Faith has to be proven by obedience" ("The Concept of Faith in Paul's Letter to the Romans," *BR* 13 [1968]: 51; cited by Garlington, *ibid.*). Cf. Victor P. Furnish, *Theology & Ethics in Paul* (Nashville: Abingdon, 1968), 182-87.

[107] Adapted from Cranfield, *Romans,* 1:66; Garlington, *Faith,* 14; Nanos, *The Mystery of Romans,* 224.

[108] Cranfield, *ibid.* Perhaps, this option has been most popular among commentaries including Barrett, Calvin, Murray, Käsemann, Ridderbos, Schlier, Sanday and Headlam, and Wilckens.

[109] Nanos, *The Mystery of Romans,* 224.

if Paul's point is the faith of the faith?"[110] He argues that "one's theological understanding of the contexts" is the real factor in determining one's grammatical conclusions.[111] Likewise, Garlington, while agreeing with Cranfield that the genitive of apposition covers basic points that Paul wants to make, still thinks that "contextual factors in Romans" should determine the meaning of the phrase.[112] Therefore, on the grammatical level, he opts for "adjectival genitive," in that πίστεως describes ὑπακοή "in a manner to be defined by the larger context and in keeping with the most pertinent exegetical data."[113] To him, the meaning of the phrase ὑπακοὴ πίστεως is: "the obedience which consists of faith, and the obedience which is the product of faith."[114] It is difficult, however, for me to find the difference from Cranfield's explanation.

A still better explanation is given by Nanos. He is right when he emphasizes the context of Romans in considering the meaning of the phrase. It is true that we cannot make many advances on a purely grammatical level. The context to which Nanos pays close attention is the context of audience. He points out that Paul did not intend to apply this phrase to *all* (including the Christian Jews) but to *Gentiles* who are Paul's intended audience.[115] Certainly, by the phrase ἐν πᾶσιν τοῖς ἔθνεσιν Paul means "among all the Gentiles," not "all the nations" including Jews.[116] It is so obvious that he does not include Jews ἐν πᾶσιν τοῖς ἔθνεσιν when he says "among whom you are" (1:6; also cf. 1:13c) because it would not make any sense to tell the Romans that they belong to the nations of the earth![117] For him, ὑπακοὴ πίστεως is directed towards "*Gentiles* who come to faith in Jesus Christ and highlights appropriate monotheistic behavior that accompanies such a con-

---

[110] Ibid., n. 164.

[111] Ibid.

[112] Garlington, *Faith,* 17.

[113] Ibid., 30.

[114] Ibid.

[115] Nanos extensively argues that the "implied audience" for Paul in Romans is Gentiles (*The Mystery of Romans,* 41-84). I do not know whether Nanos uses the term "implied audience" in a literary/narrative-critical sense or not. One regrets that he uses the term rather loosely, without explanation. However, it is clear that what Nanos intends to mean is that Gentiles are Paul's intended audience.

[116] So Dunn, *Romans 1-8,* 18; Cranfield, *Romans,* 67.

[117] Daniel Fraikin, "The Rhetorical Function of the Jews in Romans," in *Anti-Judaism in Early Christianity: Volume I: Paul and the Gospels,* Studies in Christianity and Judaism 2, ed. Peter Richardson (Waterloo, Ontario: Wilfrid Laurier University, 1986), 94.

fession."[118]   Dunn also points out that when Paul links the thought of
"obedience" to "the nations," Paul may have had in mind Ps 2:8 and
Isa 49:6-7, where the Gentile mission is described, and he more likely

> had in mind the importance of obedience within Jewish self-
> understanding—obedience as Israel's proper response to God's
> covenant grace (as particularly in Deut 26:17; 30:2; the Shema of
> course begins שְׁמַע יִשְׂרָאֵל, "Hear, O Israel" [Deut 6:4], though the
> LXX translates שְׁמַע here as ἄκουε). The point would then be that
> Paul intends his readers to understand the faith response of the *Gen-
> tiles* to the gospel as the fulfillment of God's covenant purpose
> through *Israel*.[119]

It is important to escape from a general theological understanding of
the phrase ὑπακοὴ πίστεως in our interpretation.[120]   Paul specifically
says that his apostolic calling is (to bring) "the obedience of faith
among all the Gentiles," which is certainly different from stating certain soteriological or theological enthymemes generally.   It is especially important to recognize this because Paul is here making a programmatic statement about his specific apostolic commission as "apostle to the Gentiles" (cf. Gal 2:8-9) which the Roman congregation may
or may not have known or acknowledged.   After all, Paul is introducing himself to an unknown congregation, but this congregation includes members for whom he was also called to minister (15:16).   Further, when the audience hears Paul describe his missionary activities
(to win) "obedience of the Gentiles (εἰς ὑπακοὴν ἐθνῶν)" (15:18-19),
it becomes clear that Paul epitomizes his apostleship in terms of "the
obedience of faith among the Gentiles."   Further, with the phrase
ὑπὲρ τοῦ ὀνόματος αὐτοῦ, Paul states the ultimate goal of his apostleship—it is to bring honor to God for bringing the Gentiles to God as
the sanctified offering honors God's name (15:18, 9; 9:17; cf. Acts
14:27; 15:3-4, 12; 21:19-20).

As pointed out already, Paul emphasizes that he was writing to
the Gentiles in v. 6, when he identifies the recipients within the "identification of the sender" unit of the opening formula.   This is a very

---

[118] Nanos, *The Mystery of Romans,* 225.

[119] Dunn, *Romans 1-8,* 18 (my emphasis).

[120] Garlington's otherwise fine study pays too much attention to its theological meaning, with the result that he generalizes the meaning of the phrase too
widely. Closer attention should have been paid to its immediate context, namely,
the following phrase, "among all the Gentiles." The same problem is detected in
the study of Glenn N. Davies (*Faith and Obedience in Romans: A Study in Romans 1-4,* JSNTSup 39 [Sheffield: JSOT, 1990], *passim*).

unusual feature among Pauline letters.[121] Paul makes clear that he is
speaking to the Gentile audience in the Roman congregation.[122] Another unusual aspect of the identification of the recipients in Romans is
that among all the undisputed letters of Paul, here is the only case
where Paul singles out the Gentiles as the addressees.[123] Therefore, it
is evident that the audience that Paul envisages here is the Gentiles, no
matter what the actual historical makeup of the congregation of the
Roman church.

In v. 6 Paul also emphasizes that they are included in his apostolic charge.[124] Therefore, he implies that he should bring the "obedience of faith" to them also but we know that they have already heard
the gospel. Yet, Paul expresses his desire to proclaim the gospel to
them in person (1:15) even though he has been prevented (1:13). But
he repeats that desire;[125] throughout Romans the theme of "obedience
of faith" recurs repeatedly.[126]

---

[121] Jervis points out that indeed this is the only case in Pauline letters in the
New Testament (*The Purpose of Romans,* 78).

[122] This is not to deny that there was a single Jew in the Roman congregation; all the evidence suggests that the congregation did include a Jewish popula-
tion (see among many works, Walters, *Ethnic Issues in Paul's Letter to the Romans,* 19-55). What is submitted here is that the audience on whom Paul intended
to make an impact is clearly Gentile, more specifically, Gentile Christians, as Paul
makes clear in v. 7 (see below).

[123] Fraikin, "The Rhetorical Function," 95. For a convenient comparison of
the introductory sections in other Pauline letters, see Jervis, *The Purpose of Romans,* 69-85. Jervis, in spite of her many other good observations, misses the
point when she says that "[t]hese different believers were both Gentile and Jewish
Christians" (p. 82).

[124] Jervis, *The Purpose of Romans,* 79.

[125] On the topic of the Greco-Roman letter as *parousia* of the sender, see
Nils A. Dahl, "Letter," *IDBSup,* 538-40; R. W. Funk, "The Apostolic 'Parousia':
Form and Significance," in *Christian History and Interpretation: Studies Pre-
sented to John Knox,* ed. W. R. Farmer, C. F. D. Moule and R. R. Niebuhr, 249-68
(Cambridge: Cambridge University Press, 1967); and H. Koskenniemi, *Studien zur
Idee und Phraseologie des griechischen Briefes bis 400 n. Chr.* (Helsinki:
Akateeminen Kirjakauppa, 1956). Elliott also argues that Paul achieves his intention of "evangelizing" the Romans "between chs. 1 and 15, that is, *by the letter
itself*" (*The Rhetoric of Romans,* 87). It is interesting to note that in light of 2 Cor
10:10-11 where Paul seems to agree with his adversaries that his letters are weightier and stronger than his personal presence, the sending of his letter prior to his
visit was intentional or at least beneficial for Paul's purposes (cf. Brendan Byrne,
S.J., "Rather Boldly [Rom 15:15]: Paul's Prophetic Bid to Win the Allegiance of
the Christians in Rome," *Bib* 74 [1993]: 87).

[126] "Paul develops the theme of the obedience that must characterize the
faith of those he is addressing in Rome, not in opposition to the faith of Israel, but

V. 7a at last identifies the audience specifically as all (πᾶσιν) who are in Rome. Paul calls them as ἀγαπητοῖς θεοῦ and κλητοῖς ἁγίοις. We have already mentioned that by calling his audience "called" (twice) Paul creates a strong bonding between himself and the audience. The word ἅγιοι is a Jewish term, used to describe a community or nation as set apart to God.[127] It echoes ἁγίαις (v.2) and ἁγιωσύνης (v.4) within the prescript. Dunn points out that "holiness" is closely related to faithful law-keeping, which separated the Israelites from the nations (Lev 20:22-26).[128] To call the Gentiles "the called" and "the saints" signifies that they are clearly recognized as the people of God. This becomes clearer in the phrase ἀγαπητοῖς θεοῦ, which is another Jewish term used to call Israel in many places in the Jewish tradition (Deut 32:15 [LXX]; 33:26 [LXX]; Ps 60:5 [LXX 59:7]; 108:6 [LXX 107:7]; Isa 43:4; 44:2 [LXX; ἠγαπημένος Ισραελ]; Hos 3:1; 14:4; Wis 16:26; Bar 3:36; 3 Macc 6:11).[129] Therefore, with ἀγαπητοῖς θεοῦ and κλητοῖς ἁγίοις, Paul identifies his Gentile audience in the same way that Jews would identify themselves as "a chosen and distinctive people."[130] Therefore, we can assume that the audience Paul envisages here is Gentiles who have already accepted the gospel of God and have become "the people of God." Finally, v. 7b contains a conventional greeting formula of Paul, a standard form that Paul usually uses.[131]

Rom 1:8-13 contains Paul's epistolary thanksgiving clause (vv. 8-12) with a disclosure statement (v.13). Paul adapts the conventional liturgical εὐχαριστῶ-formula to reinforce the positive relationship he had already established with his audience in the prescript.[132] Paul's

---

rather in direct continuity with and even in the service of Israel" (Nanos, *The Mystery of Romans*, 226). See also Davies, *Faith and Obedience*, 35-174, for the recurrence of this theme specifically in Rom 1-4.

[127] Dunn, *Romans 1-8*, 20.

[128] Ibid.

[129] For further references, see O. Wischmeyer, "Das Adjective ΑΓΑΠΗΤΟΣ in den paulinischen Breifen. Eine traditionsgeschichtliche Miszelle," *NTS* 32 (1986): 477.

[130] Garlington, *Obedience*, 242.

[131] Jervis, *The Purpose of Romans*, 84: "The Romans 'greeting unit'… is entirely standard. It functions… to affirm the faith Paul shares in common with his readers, to (re)establish the common bond they have in Christ, and to remind them of his apostolic hopes for them."

[132] Du Toit, "Persuasion," 206. Elliott is correct to point out that Paul's commendation does not reflect a "delicate" situation (Dahl) or the apostle's "insecure" feelings (Käsemann) but is "the sort of expression of good will" in order to predispose one's audience (*The Rhetoric of Romans*, 77).

language in the thanksgiving section is marked by his careful approach to the audience, well designed to win a sympathetic hearing from them and also to prepare them for what he is going to present to them. What Paul says in vv. 8-12, however, cannot be regarded as a half-true affirmation of the faith of the Roman Christians. Indeed, Dunn argues that the style of Rom 1:8-15 owes "more to Paul's sincerity and awkwardness than to *conscious* rhetorical art."[133] I agree with Dunn inasmuch as Paul was in an awkward position when he wrote his letter to the Romans and that he was sincere when he approached them through his letter. But precisely because he was in an awkward situation and because he wanted to approach them with utmost sincerity, without losing a fair hearing for that which he wanted to present to them and by which to persuade them, he used a highly sophisticated and well-crafted rhetoric in introducing himself and his letter.[134] It is also important to see that in the thanksgiving section Paul continues the themes of faith, the gospel, and the Gentiles which he developed in the letter prescript (vv. 1-7), which immediately precedes it.[135] This observation confirms the fact that 1:8-13, 15 belong together with 1:1-7 to form a rhetorical *exordium*, even though they are separated in the formal structure of the letter.

Paul recognizes that their faith (ἡ πίστις ὑμῶν) is proclaimed in the entire world (1:8; cf. 1 Thess 1:7). It is true that he does not hint at any deficiency or need of correction on the part of the Roman Christians (cf. 1 Cor 1:4-9),[136] but it is also true that his thanksgiving is notably brief and simple.[137] At this point, we should point out that Paul is certainly using *insinuatio* rather than *principium*, that his statements about the Roman Christians' faith should be evaluated carefully. Paul

---

[133] Dunn, *Romans 1-8*, 27 (my emphasis).

[134] The chief problem I can detect in Dunn's remark is that he still regards rhetoric and rhetorical practice as an "insincere and pretentious" way of communication (*American Heritage Dctionary*, 3rd edition) or a "deceitful" play of words.

[135] So Dunn, *Romans 1-8*, 27 (In Dunn's words: they are Paul's "chief concerns"). He also points out that Paul leads them into the letter's thematic statement (vv. 16-17). Although I don't agree with him that vv. 16-17 form the theme of the letter, I see the same connection starting from vv. 1-7. Again, this confirms that 1:2-6 should be seen as the theme of the letter because 1:16-17 only repeats what Paul already firmly established as the theme of the letter in the *exordium*.

[136] Johnson, *Reading Romans*, 23.

[137] Du Toit, "Persuasion," 206. Du Toit also argues that the reason for the brevity could be the result of either Paul's lack of information on them or his desire to refrain from criticizing them. But there is no way for us to be sure about this.

soon would express his desire to impart (μεταδιδόναι) to them some spiritual gifts (v. 11). Of course, this does not show explicitly that they lack any gift or are deficient in their faith, yet as the apostle who is responsible for their spiritual well-being, he would remind them of the things that they could improve (cf. 15:14-15).

But then Paul quickly corrects himself by saying "or rather so that we may be mutually encouraged by each other's faith, both yours and mine" (v.12).[138] With v.11, this is quite an interesting form of *correctio*,[139] which is a rhetorical device used to attain *aptum*.[140] The speaker uses the social *correctio* to gain the social *aptum,* which is between the speech delivered (with words and matters) and the audience.[141] This is usually achieved "with the cautious moderation of expression."[142] Lausberg says that the speaker uses "the trope signal" to indicate the use of *correctio,* and the "signal" may be *inartificiale* or *artificiale.*[143] When Paul says "τοῦτο δέ ἐστιν" in the beginning of v. 12, he is clearly making an "artificial" signal to tone down his remark in v. 11.[144] Certainly, one can surmise that Paul regretted what he just said in the light of the Roman church's reputation (v. 8) and origin (not being a Pauline church) and so he retracted what he had just uttered.[145]

---

[138] Cf. Barrett's translation: "or rather, what I wish is..." (*Romans,* 26). But Barrett thinks that Paul's "embarrassment" caused him to make "the loose and inaccurate construction" in vv.11-12 (ibid., 25).

[139] For a full description of *correctio,* see H. Lausberg, *Handbook of Literary Rhetoric: A Foundation for Literary Study,* ed. David E. Orton and R. Dean Anderson, trans. Matthew T. Bliss, Annemiek Jansen and David E. Orton (Leiden: Brill, 1998), 346-49, §§ 784-86. Cf. du Toit "Persuasion," 207; J. Paul Sampley, "Romans in a Different Light: A Response to Robert Jewett," in *Pauline Theology III: Romans,* ed. David M. Hay and E. Elizabeth Johnson (Minneapolis: Fortress, 1995), 120.

[140] See chapter 2.

[141] According to Lausberg, there are two kinds of *correctio,* the other being semantic-onomasiological *correctio,* which is used to attain the semantic-onomasiological *aptum* between the word and the intended matter. In this kind of *correctio*, the speaker rejects an expression that was used a moment before, and replaces it with another expression that is *stronger* than the former (*Handbook, §* 785). Certainly, we are not dealing with this kind of *correctio.*

[142] Ibid., § 784.

[143] The reason for using a "signal" is to safeguard the success of the orator's serious "*voluntas*" since the intentional change of the object of designation is not conducive to such success. Therefore, "the 'signal' corrects the (voluntary) 'error' of the first linguistic *signum*" (Lausberg, *Handbook,* 789, § 1244 "tropus" [III]).

[144] For several examples of such *correctio,* see Lausberg, *Handbook,* p. 349 § 786 (2).

[145] So Barrett, *Romans,* 26.

However, we should not forget that Paul not only wants to achieve a positive image of himself in the *exordium,* but also that he is presenting himself as an authoritative figure, namely the apostle to the Gentiles, whose sphere of ministry includes the Romans. In order to achieve these two objectives without overpowering them or looking weak in presenting himself, Paul uses a *correctio.* To the modern readers his remark may be "lame-sounding"[146] or "an apologetic defensive"[147] but to the Romans who were familiar with rhetorical practices it should have sounded understandable.

Paul concludes his *exordium* with the so-called "disclosure formula," οὐ θέλω δὲ ὑμᾶς ἀγνοεῖν (v.13). This is used by Paul frequently to introduce important information, always accompanied by the vocative ἀδελφοί (cf. 11:25; 1 Cor 10:1; 12:1; 2 Cor 1:8; 1 Thess 4:13).[148] The fact that Paul had desired to come to Rome often is important for the Romans to know, especially in connection with chapter 15 where he will ask them to participate in his missionary project in Spain. In this sentence, Paul once again includes his audience among the Gentiles ("καὶ ἐν καθὼς καὶ ἐν τοῖς λοιποῖς ἔθνεσιν").

Rom 15:14-16:27

Now let us turn our attention to the *peroratio* of Romans. As we compare Rom 1:1-13, 15 with 15:14-16:27, we are struck by the repetition and parallels. We have already mentioned that good rhetoric in the *peroratio* would capsulize and expand the themes that the rhetor began in the *exordium.* It is plain that Romans is a good example of this practice. Paul, in his conclusion, returns repeatedly to the themes which he stated in his introduction. And this development is done with such skill and craft that it is absurd to assume that it happened by accident. We can summarize the overlappings in the following way:

Parallel/Allusion	1:1-13, 15	15:14-16:27
1. The prophetic writings	1:2 διὰ τῶν προφητῶν αὐτοῦ ἐν γραφαῖς ἁγίαις	16:26 διά τε γραφῶν προφητικῶν
2. Obedience of faith to the Gentiles	1:5 εἰς ὑπακοὴν πίστεως	16:26 εἰς ὑπακοὴν

---

[146] Dunn, *Romans 1-8,* 27.

[147] Käsemann, *Romans,* 19.

[148] Cranfield, *Romans,* I, 81.

	ἐν πᾶσιν τοῖς ἔθνεσιν	πίστεως εἰς πάντα τὰ ἔθνη 15:18 εἰς ὑπακοὴν ἐθνῶν, λόγῳ καὶ ἔργῳ
3. Praise for his audience	1:8	15:14
4. Paul's ministry for the gospel as cultic service	1:9 ὁ θεός, ᾧ λατρεύω... ἐν τῷ εὐαγγελίῳ τοῦ υἱοῦ αὐτοῦ	15:16 εἰς τὸ εἶναί με λειτουργὸν Χριστοῦ Ἰησοῦ εἰς τὰ ἔθνη, ἱερουργοῦντα τὸ εὐαγγέλιον τοῦ θεοῦ
5. Grace and apostleship "I am your apostle-- that's why I can remind you (preach the gospel to you)."	1:5 δι᾽ οὗ ἐλάβομεν χάριν καὶ ἀποστολὴν	15:15 διὰ τὴν χάριν τὴν δοθεῖσάν μοι ὑπὸ τοῦ θεοῦ
6. Reference to power	1:4 ἐν δυνάμει	15:19 (twice)
7. Reference to prayer	1:9-10	15:30-32
8. Hindrance in coming	1:13a	15:22
9. Reference to harvest	1:13 καρπός	15:28
10. Intention to visit	1:10, 11, 13, 15 (esp. ἔρχομαι, ὁράω)	15:22, 23, 24, 28, 29, 32 (esp. ἔρχομαι)
11. Bringing them a spiritual blessing	1:11 χάρισμα πνευματκόν	15:29 εὐλογία
12. Dependence on God's will	1:10 θέλημα τοῦ θεοῦ	15:32 θέλημα θεοῦ
13. Language of	1:13	15:22

prevention	κωλύω	ἐγκόπτω
14. Gospel/Preaching the Gospel	1:1, 9 εὐαγγέλιον 1:15 εὐαγγελίσασθαι	15:16, 19 εὐαγγέλιον 15:20 εὐαγγελίζεσθ- αι
15. Sanctified	1:4 κατὰ πνεῦμα ἁγιωσύνης 1:7 κλητοὶ ἅγιοι	15:16 ἡγιασμένη ἐν πνεύματι ἁγίῳ

In 15:14-33, Paul begins his *peroratio* with an expression of confidence in and praise for his audience, smoothly recapitulating what he has written so far: "I have written to you *rather boldly*" (15:15). There is certainly an apologetic tone in Paul's use of the word τολμηρότερον. Paul makes sure that he did not write his long theological argument as if he were evangelizing for the first time but "by way of reminder (ὡς ἐπαναμιμνῄσκων)" (15:15a). At the same time, however, he is giving the reason why he was able to do so: "because of the grace given me by God" (15:15b). This reminds us immediately of his allusion to the "grace and apostleship" received in 1:5. There, grace and apostleship are linked epexegetically, "almost a hendiadys."[149] It is reasonable, then, to understand here that Paul is alluding to his apostleship—in other words, he is saying, "I am able to remind you of certain things that you should remember because I am your apostle."[150] Once again, we see that Paul is very careful in asserting his authority as apostle to them as we observed in the previous section. Paul continues to describe his apostleship in terms of his ministry for the gospel as cultic service in 15:16, which echoes his earlier description in 1:9, and the purpose of his ministry as the acceptance of "the offering of the Gentiles," which is "sanctified by the Holy Spirit (ἡγιασμένη ἐν πνεύματι ἁγίῳ)." Again, there is a connection to the designation of his recipients as "κλητοὶ ἅγιοι" (1:7) as well as "κατὰ πνεῦμα ἁγιωσύνης" (1:4), as mentioned earlier. Paul's under-

---

[149] Käsemann, *Romans,* 14.

[150] Peter Müller also points out that Paul's language here reminds one of 1 Cor 3:10, where Paul equates his apostleship with grace when he says that "according to the grace of God given to me" he laid the foundation of the church in Corinth ("Grundlinien paulinischer Theologie [Röm 15,14-33]," *KD* 35 [1989]: 219).

standing of his apostleship is not limited to an initial preaching of the gospel for the conversion of the Gentiles but his concern is also for their holy living as new people of God. And it will be seen shortly that their holy living is closely connected to participation in the missionary endeavor for the evangelization of the world where the name of Christ has never been preached.

Paul goes on to testify that the incredible success of his apostolic ministry among the Gentiles is the basis of his "boasting" (καύχησιν) in Christ Jesus (15:17).[151] What Jesus Christ accomplished through Paul's ministry he "dare[s] to say" (τολμήσω... λαλεῖν, connection to τολμηρότερον in 15:15) is, literally, "for the obedience of the Gentiles" (εἰς ὑπακοὴν ἐθνῶν) which forms an obvious parallel to 1:5 and 16:26.[152]

We also discover through Rom 15:19-33 that Paul was at a crucial juncture in his missionary career when he wrote Romans. He was probably in the city of Corinth (Rom 16:23; cf. 1 Cor 1:14), waiting to go to Jerusalem with the collection gathered from the Gentile churches of Macedonia and Achaia (Rom 15:25-26). He testifies that "from Jerusalem as far around Illyricum" (ἀπὸ Ἰερουσαλὴμ καὶ κύκλῳ μέχρι τοῦ Ἰλλυρικοῦ) the gospel of Christ has been fulfilled (πεπληρωκέναι τὸ εὐαγγέλιον τοῦ Χριστοῦ, 15:19). What does Paul mean by "fulfilling" the gospel of Christ? Paul Sampley's explanation hits the mark:

> His [Paul's] calling is not just to *preach* the gospel to the Gentiles, not just, for example, to carry the message to a city or a province or an area; that is indeed part of his calling, but it would inadequately reflect his broader sense of mission. Paul's "fulfilling the gospel" involves also the inculcating of new ways of walking within his churches, the healing of schisms within those communities, and the calling for growth and mutual upbuilding among the believers, wherever Gentiles are a part of the body of Christ.... In this light, his letter to the Romans is also a part of his total effort to "fulfill the gospel"—in this case his fulfilling the gospel requires him to urge upon believers who never heard him preach the gospel the call to a fuller and more unified life. So Romans is not merely or even primarily written "for the sake of mission"; *it is mission* at work![153]

---

[151] For Paul's use of this important word, καύκησις, in Romans, see a particularly good discussion by Luke Johnson in his *Reading Romans,* 80, 210.

[152] For the implication of the parallel, see above.

[153] Sampley, "Romans in a Different Light," 114-15 (author's emphasis). In this light, the problem that W. Schmithals raised two decades ago in his book, *Der Römerbrief as historisches Problem* (SNT 9; Gütersloh: Mohn, 1975), namely, the

Paul's desire to proclaim the gospel among the believers in Rome is not simply for the sake of evangelism, because they are already believers, but to "fulfill" the gospel as he states in 15:19. In 1:15, he specifically says that he wants to proclaim the gospel "among you who are in Rome (καὶ ὑμῖν τοῖς ἐν Ῥώμη)," clearly meaning the Gentile believers in Rome. In other words, Paul is speaking of the proclamation of the gospel in more pastoral terms. For Paul, to preach the gospel to the Gentiles means to secure their obedience.[154] In the light of 1:5 and 15:18, what Paul wants to do in Rome by preaching the gospel (1:15) is to encourage and strengthen the faith of the Romans so they may "obey" God.[155] The specific meaning of "the obedience of faith" in the situation of the Roman Christians, especially the Gentile Christians in the Roman church, should be understood in their missionary context. Their participation in the missionary project of Paul is tantamount to their "obedience" to God who "called" them by grace to be his people. As newly called "people of God," they are to support and cooperate with Paul in his future missionary projects in the

---

contradiction between Romans 15:20 and 1:13-15 that in one place (15:20) Paul says that he does not want to proclaim the gospel (εὐαγγελίζεσθαι) where Christ has already been named but in another place (1:13-15) he expresses his desire to go to Rome to proclaim the gospel (εὐαγγελίσασθαι) so that he may reap some harvest among them although Christ's name had been obviously named there (p. 169) can be solved reasonably. For a good review of Schmithals' fascinating book, see A.J.M. Wedderburn, "The Purpose and Occasion of Romans Again," in *The Romans Debate*, 195-202. For a critique of Schmithals' now almost universally rejected proposal to dissect the letter into several different ones, see Keck, "What Makes Romans Tick?" 9-10. We are advised by Richard Hays not to waste our time on the subject because this kind of attempt is one of "the idiosyncratic musings" that "belong in a museum of exegetical curiosities" ("Adam, Israel, Christ: The Question of Covenant in the Theology of Romans: A Response to Leander E. Keck and N. T. Wright," in *Pauline Theology III: Romans*, 76). See also Beker, *Paul the Apostle*, 60-61, who raises a similar issue.

[154] So Elliott, *The Rhetoric of Romans*, 93.

[155] So Paul Bowers, "Fulfilling the Gospel: The Scope of the Pauline Mission," *JETS* 30 (1987): 187. Bowers is surely correct when he says, "For Paul... conversion meant incorporation" (ibid.). Bowers understands the meaning of "fulfilling the gospel" as nurturing communities or, using a more modern missionary terminology, as "church planting." He is followed affirmatively by P. T. O'Brien, *Gospel and Mission in the Writings of Paul: An Exegetical and Theological Analysis* (Grand Rapids: Baker, 1995), 42-3.

with Paul in his future missionary projects in the western portion of the Roman Empire.[156]

It is disputed whether Paul mentions these regions simply geographically[157] or theologically[158] in his eastern missions. When Paul uses the word κύκλος, he envisions Jerusalem as the center of a circle, located in the very center of the whole world. Therefore, what Rom 15:19 portrays is the scope of Paul's mission to the nations, which are scattered around Jerusalem, the center of a circle.[159] Again, this shows his basic approach to his calling as a thoroughly Jewish apostle commissioned in the Jewish tradition. Further, Rom 15:19 should be understood in the light of Isa 66:19-20, where God comes to gather all nations to Zion in the end of time.[160] What Paul envisions here is that he is fulfilling the prophecy of Isaiah in his mission to the Gentiles.

---

[156] The soteriological significance of the role of the Gentiles in the eschatological framework of Paul's thinking will be explored in the following chapters when we discuss Rom 9-11.

[157] See, e.g., Moo, *Romans,* 894; Byrne, *Romans,* 438; Dunn, *Romans,* 2.864; Fitzmyer, *Romans,* 713-14; Stuhlmacher, *Romans,* 238.

[158] See, e.g., Bruce, *Romans,* 247, who thinks that Paul mentions Jerusalem here because Paul "regards Jerusalem as the starting-point and metropolis of the Christian movement as a whole" not because he began his ministry there (*contra* D. Zeller, *Juden und Heiden in der Mission des Paulus: Studien zum Römerbrief,* 2d ed. [Stuttgart: Katholisches Bibelwerk, 1976], 227; Moo, *ibid.*). A. S. Geyser's argument that Paul's comments in Gal 1 preclude his preaching ministry in Jerusalem seems to be right ("Un Essai d'explication de Rom. XV.19," *NTS* [1959-60]: 157) and we do not have any concrete evidence that Paul reached the Roman province of Illyria. Käsemann's comment is more theological: "The eastern part of the empire is defined by Jerusalem on the one hand as the salvation-historical center of the world and the starting point of the gospel, and by the end of the Via Aegnatia on the other hand" (*Romans,* 395).

[159] John Knox, "Romans 15:14-33 and Paul's Conception of His Apostolic Mission," *JBL* 83 (1964): 1-11. For various options to interpret the word, see James M. Scott, *Paul and the Nations: The Old Testament and Jewish Background of Paul's Mission to the Nations with Special Reference to the Destination of Galatians,* WUNT 48 (Tübingen: Mohr, 1995), 138-40 and also idem, "Paul's 'Imago Mundi' and Scripture," in *Evangelium-Schriftauslegung-Kirche: Festschrift für Peter Stuhlmacher zum 65. Geburtstag,* ed. Jostein Ådna, Scott J. Hafemann and Otfried Hofius (Göttingen: Vandenhoeck & Ruprecht, 1997), 374-78. Scott draws from Ezek 5:5 and the Table-of-Nations in Gen 10.

[160] Rainer Riesner, *Paul's Early Period: Chronology, Mission Strategy, Theology,* trans. Doug Stott (Grand Rapids: Eerdmans, 1998), 245-53; Scott, *Paul and the Nations,* 145-48; Roger D. Aus, "Paul's Travel Plans to Spain and the 'Full Number of the Gentiles' of Rom 11:25," *NovT* 21 (1979): 232-62; Dieter Zeller, "Theologie der Mission bei Paulus," in *Mission im Neuen Testament,* ed. Karl Kertelge, QD 93 (Freiburg: Herder, 1982), 184.

Now that his evangelistic missions in the eastern part of the Roman empire are completed, he plans to go to Spain (15:24, 28) for the western half of the empire.

Paul says, however, that he has to go to Jerusalem before he will be able to go to Rome (15:25-32). The reason why he is going to Jerusalem is to minister to the saints (τοῖς ἁγίοις) (15:25). Paul's planned visitation to Jerusalem is not simply to deliver the collection that he has gathered among the Gentiles but more significantly "to establish fellowship" with the poor among the saints at Jerusalem (15:26).[161] Their acceptance of the collection "would be an acknowledgment that just as they have rightfully received a share of the material blessing of the Gentiles so the Gentiles have rightfully received a share of the spiritual blessing of Israel."[162] Further, it would mean that the Gentiles and the Jews are "mutually indebted to one another and are on an equal footing within the people of God."[163] Paul's apostolic ministry as priestly service includes this important function, namely, the bringing together of the Gentiles and the Jews as a unified people of God (see 15:7-12).[164]

Paul, however, expects certain dangers in Jerusalem and also possible rejection by the saints (v. 31). Therefore, he asks the Roman Christians' support in prayer to God on his behalf (v. 30). This is crucial for Paul's plan to succeed because he cannot fulfill his obligation to preach the gospel in Spain if his visit to Jerusalem fails (v. 32). Then, he wants to be not only refreshed in their company (v. 32) but also helped on his journey (προπεμφθῆναι, 15:24) to Spain.[165] It becomes evident that Paul's visit to Rome is not to be viewed as a simple

---

[161] I follow G. W. Peterman who argues that the meaning of the phrase κοινωνίαν τινὰ ποιήσασθαι should mean "to establish fellowship" rather than the more conventional "to make a contribution" or "to share their resources" (NRSV) ("Romans 15:26: Make a Contribution or Establish Fellowship?" *NTS* 40 [1994]: 457-63). His translation is attractive mainly because it fits much better with its immediate context and also has strong support from Greco-Roman social convention (e.g., giving as a way to establish and maintain a relationship).

[162] Achtemeier, *Romans,* 320-1.

[163] Ibid., 321.

[164] Ibid., 320. Cf. Wagner, "Romans 15:8-9," 473-85.

[165] For the meaning of the word προπέμπω as "help on one's journey," see Dunn, *Romans 9-16,* 872. The word was used as a technical term for missionary support in the early church (Acts 15:3; 20:38; 21:5; 1 Cor 16:6, 11; 2 Cor 1:16; Titus 3:13; 3 John 6; Pol. *Phil.* 1.1) (Cranfield, *Romans,* II, 769, n. 4).

temporary stay but as a purposeful stopover in preparation for his missionary journey to Spain.[166]

In Rom 16:1-27, Paul finishes his letter by recommending Phoebe (vv. 1-2),[167] greeting his fellow workers in Rome (vv. 3-16), and pronouncing an eschatological warning (vv. 17-20) with a concluding doxology (vv. 25-27). According to Wuellner, these verses belong to the *pathos* section in Romans, an emotional appeal to the audience in order to stimulate their action.[168] Paul's appeal is based on the commonality Paul emphasizes in his greetings (i.e., co-workers) and the rousing doxology that Paul offers at the end of the letter.[169]

III. SUMMARY: THE SPEAKER, AUDIENCE, AND EXIGENCE

Let us now summarize our findings about the speaker, audience, and exigence in the *exordium* and *peroratio* of Romans.

The Speaker

We have shown how the speaker (in our case, obviously, Paul) has established the *ethos* with his audience in the *exordium*. In the *peroratio,* the focus is shifted from the *ethos* to the *exigence*, which can be seen as a good rhetorical strategy by the speaker who finally asks his audience for specific requests only after he establishes a proper *ethos*. Several facts about the speaker clearly emerge from our examination of these rhetorical elements: Paul was not well known to his audience; he had wanted to visit Rome many times but had not yet been successful, the reason being "the will of God," not his will; Paul wanted to come to them as an apostle sent to them, but had no intention of exercising his authority in an excessive way. The most striking feature in the *exordium* is that Paul presents himself as a Jewish apos-

---

[166] Cf. Botha, *Subject to Whose Authority?,* 155. Botha argues that Paul plays down the length of stay in Rome because of "the delicate rhetorical situation."

[167] For the possible role of Phoebe as Paul's representative in preparation for his Spanish mission, see a very imaginative theory of Robert Jewett in his "Paul, Phoebe, and the Spanish Mission," in *The Social World of Formative Christianity and Judaism,* ed. J. Neusner, *et al.* (Philadelphia: Fortress, 1988), 142-61.

[168] Wuellner, "Paul's Rhetoric of Argumentation," 137-38.

[169] Ibid., 139, 140-41.

tle in thoroughly Jewish terms. His apostleship is firmly grounded in Jewish values, rooted in the Jewish scriptures. The gospel he is commissioned to preach is also presented as one deeply rooted in the Jewish scriptures and traditions (1:2-4).[170] Also, he describes his ministry for the gospel as a cultic service in the Jewish religious traditions (ὁ θεός, ᾧ λατρεύω... ἐν τῷ εὐαγγελίτῳ τοῦ υἱοῦ αὐτοῦ). In 15:16-21, he expands and explains this theme in terms of the Spirit's powerful manifestation in securing the obedience of faith among the Gentiles. The repetition of ἐν δυνάμει in 15:19 (cf. 1:4) clearly indicates the Spirit's power as Paul explains his remarkable success in his mission work in the east.[171] Included in his ministry as God's minister is sharing χάρισμα with the audience (1:9); and that is why he wants to come to Rome and preach the gospel (εὐαγγελίσασθαι) (1:15). His sincere desire to come to Rome stems from his apostolic obligation to the Gentiles, including his audience in Rome. Paul makes clear that his audience falls within his apostolic domain, even though he did not found the church in Rome (1:6; 13b). Yet he is quite careful in asserting his authority over them. At the same time, he does not make explicit requests about his future plans. Obviously, Paul must have thought that the Romans were not yet ready to hear his requests for cooperation in his missionary projects. Especially in 1:8-13, Paul makes clear he had long desired to visit Rome but that he had been prevented by "the will of God" (1:10, 13). He is offering an explanation to a question that might have been in the mind of the Romans, namely, if he were the apostle to the Gentiles, why had he failed to visit the church where a considerable number of Gentile believers had existed for a long time?[172] But in 15:22-32, Paul resumes matters relating to the situation and makes explicit requests concerning his future plans. The tone is not so much apologetic as assertive.

The kind of *ethos* Paul establishes in the *exordium* is crucial for him to succeed in persuading his audience to accept him as their apostle and his proposal that they cooperate with him for the future mission project.[173] He comes to them as their apostle but he attributes the source of his authority to God or Jesus Christ, thus achieving an au-

---

[170] When we compare the opening of Romans with other Pauline letters, its Jewishness stands out clearly.

[171] Byrskog, "Epistolography," 44.

[172] Cf. U. Wilckens, *Der Brief an die Römer (Röm 1-5)* (EKKNT VI/1; Neukirchen/Vluyn: Zürich-Neukirchener, 1978), 79-80, who sees Paul's defensiveness when he explains his past.

[173] Sampley, "Romans in a Different Light," 119-120.

thoritative position in a non-threatening way. Paul's rhetorical strategy hinges on this very aspect in the *exordium*—he must present himself as an apostle with authority but at the same time is cautious to avoid offending his audience by unduly imposing his authority over them. Paul achieves this through his sophisticated use of rhetorical devices such as *correctio*[174] as well as through the unusually expanded sender unit of his letter prescript.

The Audience

Recently, a scholar remarked, "Pauline scholarship is in great need of conceptual discipline regarding the question of audience or reader."[175] It is impossible to disagree with him, especially in the case of Romans. Usually, the debate about the audience of Romans has been focused on the historical makeup of the Roman congregation.[176] What we are interested in here is, however, the audience inscribed and manifested in the text. Therefore, the audience here described is a construct based on the information we can extract from the text of the *exordium* and *peroratio,* which may be different from the actual historical audience of Romans. First, the audience is located in Rome. The audience that Paul targets is clearly Gentiles (1:6, 13),[177] who, however, should have been familiar with the Jewish scriptures.[178] Paul uses numerous allusions to the Jewish scriptures in his introduction, and he seems to have presupposed familiarity on the part of his audience. Richard Hays even argues that Paul's real partner in conversation in Romans is the one which is represented by these quotations and allusions and not "the addressees" who "recede curiously into the background."[179] Therefore, crucial for modern readers' understanding of Romans is the ability to hear "the intertextual echoes in the let-

---

[174] See above.

[175] Stanley K. Stowers, *A Rereading of Romans: Justice, Jews, and Gentiles* (New Haven & London: Yale University Press, 1994), 21. Borrowing from certain literary theories (e.g., *The Reader in the Text,* ed. Susan Suleiman and Inge Crosman [Princeton: Princeton University Press, 1980]), Stowers argues that "the encoded explicit" reader is clearly the Gentiles.

[176] E.g., see Werner Georg Kümmel, *Introduction to the New Testament,* rev. ed., trans. Howard Clark Kee (Nashville: Abingdon, 1975), 309-11.

[177] Nanos also sees that the "implied" audience of Paul is Christian Gentiles (*The Mystery of Romans,* 78-9).

[178] Cf. Rom 7:1.

[179] Hays, *Echoes of Scripture,* 35.

ter."[180] While I agree with Hays that we need to listen carefully to the intertextual echoes embedded in the pages of Romans, I still think that the main audience Paul is speaking to is the Romans (Gentiles) whom he wants to persuade. This has to do with his rhetorical strategy, stemming from the rhetorical situation which he has to overcome.

It is clear that Paul emphasizes that they are included in the sphere of his apostolic ministry, yet they have not seen Paul in person, nor did he found their church. Even though they are Gentiles in origin, they are already considered to have been included in the people of God, as shown by the way Paul describes them, i.e., Jewish honorific titles such as κλητοί (1:6), ἀγαπητοῖς θεοῦ (1:7) and κλητοῖς ἁγίοις (1:7). Further, they are well respected by Paul, and even in the position to benefit the author with their own spiritual gifts. Lastly, they are identified with Paul in that they share the same calling of God, thus strongly bonded by the same grace.

The Exigence

As Paul's unusual expansion of the sender unit in the letter pre-script shows, the crucial point of understanding the exigence in the *exordium* has to do much with Paul himself. His apostleship to Gentiles, the gospel that he preaches, and his future missionary plans[181] are all important factors as he begins this important letter. The first exigence is that he should be accepted as an apostle of Jesus Christ, who is sent to preach the gospel to the Gentiles in order to bring "the obedience of faith." It is not clear whether Paul had problems in claiming his apostleship to the Gentiles among the Romans, but it is evident that he desired to establish himself as a legitimate apostle, "called" and "set apart" by God to serve him. At the same time, he wanted to prove that the gospel that he preaches is based on the Jewish scriptures, whose origin actually goes all the way back to God himself (1:1c-2). As we saw in our discussion, the purpose of Paul's gospel is for "the obedience of faith," which is really directed to the Gentiles, including his audience as well. The striking Jewishness of this phrase strongly defines the nature of his apostleship: he is the Jewish apostle sent to the Gentiles.

---

[180] Ibid.

[181] The plans are not yet explicitly expressed in the *exordium*. But it is important to note that it is Paul's future projects that he has in mind when he composed his introduction, and they are to be expanded and developed further in the *peroratio*.

Paul's respect toward the Romans is shown when he says that their faith is well known around the world.[182] Still, he expresses his desire to preach to them in Rome (1:15). His subtle inclusion of the Romans within his apostolic domain in the *exordium* signals that there is something that he still wants them to understand and learn for the sake of the gospel. But it is only implied here in the *exordium* and fully explored in the *peroratio*. It is important to note, however, that already in the *exordium* Paul lays the groundwork for his persuasion later, when he describes his apostleship in terms of the Gentile mission. Paul's commission as an apostle to bring about the obedience of the Gentiles (1:5) and his desire to come to his audience (1:13) are closely related because they are also themselves Gentiles. He wants to preach the gospel (1:15) and "reap some harvest" among them (1:13). The "harvest" (καρπός) is not simply the collection that Paul gathered among the Gentile believers,[183] but refers to Paul's sense of "obligation" (ὀφειλέτης εἰμι, 1:14 with ὀφειλέται, 15:27) towards the entire Gentile world (1:5).[184] This indicates that Paul's apostolic commission was not merely gaining converts but, through their "obedience of faith," enabling the gospel to be spread throughout the world.[185] What Paul wants to reap among the Romans is their own "obedience of faith" which is manifested by their sanctified living (1:4-5; 15:18)[186] and their participation in Paul's missionary project so that their "obedience" may elicit more "obedience" among many other Gentiles.

Now this understanding of the rhetorical situation of Romans, to the degree that this is disclosed in the *exordium* and the *peroratio,* will guide and anchor our investigation of the rhetorical situation of Rom 9-11, which we will take up in the next chapter.

---

[182] See also Paul's remark in Rom 15:14 ("... αὐτοὶ μεσοί ἐστε ἀγαθ ωσύνης, πεπληρωμένοι πάσης γνώσεως, δυνάμενοι καὶ ἀλλήλους νουθετεῖν").

[183] *Contra* M. A. Kruger, *"Tina Karpon,* 'Some Fruit' in Romans 1:13," *WTJ* 49 (1987): 167-73. Cf. Keith F. Nickle, *The Collection: A Study in Paul's Strategy*, SBT 48 (Naperville, Ill.: Alec R. Allenson, Inc., 1966), 69-70.

[184] Byrne, *Romans,* 50.

[185] Cf. Müller, "Grundlinien paulinischer Theologie," 231-32.

[186] Cf. Elliott, *The Rhetoric of Romans,* 93.

CHAPTER FOUR

THE RHETORICAL UNIT AND SITUATION OF ROMANS 9-11

I. THE RHETORICAL UNIT

This study treats Romans 9-11 as a rhetorical unit. That Romans 9-11 forms an independent literary and compositional unit is universally accepted. According to Kennedy, "a rhetorical unit must have a beginning, a middle, and an end."[1] Romans 9-11 clearly has a beginning (9:1-5), a middle (9:6-11:32), and an end (11:33-36).[2] Also, Romans 9-11 forms one of the short argumentative units with which Paul proceeds in the letter (1:14-4:25; 5-8; 9-11; 12:1-15:13), each of which has a complete and autonomous *dispositio*.[3] It is striking to note that each unit ends with its own peroration (4:23-25; 8:31-39; 11:33-36; and 15:7-13) before moving on to next unit. It is evident that Paul struc-

---

[1] Kennedy, *New Testament Interpretation*, 33.

[2] We will discuss the arrangement of our unit in detail in the next chapter.

[3] J.-N. Aletti, "The Rhetoric of Romans 5-8," in *The Rhetorical Analysis of Scripture: Essays From the 1995 London Conference*, ed. Stanley E. Porter and Thomas H. Olbricht, JSNTSup 146 (Sheffield: Sheffield Academic, 1997), 295. Cf. Wuellner, "Rhetorical Criticism," 455, who points out that the rhetorical unit is different from a literary unit in that the rhetorical unit is an *argumentative* unit "affecting the reader's reasoning or the reader's imagination." Thus, "a rhetorical unit is either a convincing or a persuasive unit."

tures his letter in accordance with the rhetorical conventions of his day.[4] The implication of this observation is important in our analysis of Rom 9-11 because it is now hardly meaningful to compare Rom 1-8 and Rom 9-11 as many interpreters do when they argue for the legitimate place of Rom 9-11 in the letter as a whole.[5] It is evident that these studies are reactions to an older but prevalent view that these three chapters are an "afterglow" which Paul added after he finished his main argument. However, to compare Rom 1-8 and 9-11 to find a consistent, usually theological, theme is problematic simply because this is not what Paul intended to write. Whenever the theme of Romans has been predetermined by exegetes as "justification by faith" or the "righteousness of God," some chapters lack conformity to this theme simply because it is contrary to what Paul attempted. Such comparison is unfair to Paul. As we saw in the previous chapter, Romans has a clear rhetorical and epistolary framework that cannot be dissolved into a characterization like Rom 1-8. Further, Paul structures his letter by enclosing short argumentative units within that frame (the *exordium* and the *peroratio*) and deals with distinctive themes within each unit.[6] Therefore, the question of whether Rom 9-11 is an integral part of the letter should be asked this way: Do the *exordium* and the *peroratio* inform the audience and develop the content or theme of these three chapters? In the following section we will attempt to show that Rom 9-11 has a legitimate place in the letter because its themes are already preluded in the *exordium* and later recapitulated in the *peroratio*.

---

[4] See Aletti, "La présence," 1-24.

[5] See E. E. Johnson, *The Function of Apocalyptic and Wisdom Traditions in Romans 9-11*, SBLDS 109 (Atlanta: Scholars, 1989), 110-16, who summarized the various views of the relation between Rom 1-8 and 9-11 in four ways. Chae also provides a bird's-eye view on the question in *Paul as Apostle to the Gentiles*, 221-24. See also Richard H. Bell, *Provoked to Jealousy: The Origin and Purpose of the Jealousy Motif in Romans 9-11*, WUNT 2/63 (Tübingen: Mohr, 1994), 44-55.

[6] I do not mean, however, that Romans is not a unified letter but each rhetorical unit's distinctive themes should be respected more and they should be read in their own right. The overall theme or themes of Romans should be determined by integrating each unit's argument while maintaining its distinctive role in the whole argument.

II. THE RHETORICAL SITUATION OF ROMANS 9-11

We are now going to analyze the rhetorical situation of Rom 9-11. As we have done in the previous chapter, we will concentrate our discussion on three constituents of the rhetorical situation: the speaker, the audience and the exigence manifested in Rom 9-11.

The Speaker

In the previous chapter, we discussed how Paul establishes an authorial *ethos* that gives him a fair hearing when he begins his letter in the *exordium*. The personal tone that he uses in the *exordium* recedes into the background, however, and a kind of impersonal authorial voice emerges when he begins his main section of the letter in 1:14. The solemn declaration of his obligation to preach the gospel to the Gentiles is followed by another declaration of his confidence in the gospel for its power for salvation to the Jew and the Gentile (1:14, 16-17). This voice departs abruptly from his friendly *ethos* and takes more solemn authority.[7] As observed already, Paul's establishment of his *ethos* in the *exordium* was not simply concentrated on the friendly side but also firmly establishes him as the apostle to the audience, as one who assumes the responsibility that God has assigned him by grace. From 1:18 on, this authoritative voice, a quite impersonal one,[8] dominates the letter at least until 4:22. In 1:18-32, the authorial *ethos* is heavy and authoritative, proclaiming the revelation of God almost like an Old Testament prophet.[9] In 2:1-16, this voice directly argues against the person who is only identified by the second person singular.[10] The addressee is clearly identified as the Jew in 2:17-29, however, and this authorial voice is highly argumentative in the style of *diatribe*.[11] In 3:1-9, the

---

[7] Cf. Stowers, *Rereading Romans,* 290.

[8] Paul mentions "my gospel" in 2:16, which is exceptional considering the tone of the letter in 1:18-4:22. See Stowers, ibid.

[9] Cf. Stowers who says: "In 1:18-5(*sic!*):22 as a whole, the authorial persona is not that of a Jew or a gentile but of a prophetic admonisher of Jews and gentiles and a spokesman for God's righteousness and gentile rights" (Ibid.).

[10] The identity of this person has been widely agreed to be the Hellenistic moral teacher. See, e.g., Johnson, *Reading Romans,* 36.

[11] On Paul's use of *diatribe,* see T. Schmeller, *Paulus und die "Diatribe": eine vergleichende Stilinterpretation,* NTAbh 19 (Münster : Aschendorff, 1987)

diatribe style is continued, and in vv. 5-9, the author identifies himself with Jews for the first time,[12] but his identification with the Jews is not full-blown and he leaves the discussion hanging until he returns to the subject in full concentration in chapters 9-11. It is interesting to note that Paul as a Jew is already identified in the *exordium* but his authorial persona as a Jew does not fully blossom until chapters 9-11.[13]

Paul's use of the first person plural in 3:19 still identifies him with the Jew, which continues at least until 4:9. When Paul uses the first person plural again in 4:24, he subtly transfers the term to include believers in general, both Jew and Gentile. In 5:1-11, however, Paul makes another transition and identifies himself with his main audience, the Gentiles.[14] In 5:12-20, the author's voice becomes impersonal again but from 6:1ff, the author personally identifies himself with his Gentile audience as a believer in Christ and speaks to them directly.[15] This continues until the end of chapter 8, with an exception in 7:7-25, where the author uses a rhetorical device called *prosopopoiia* ("Speech-in-Character").[16] In these chapters, Paul uses the first person plural predominantly,[17] creating a strong rhetorical effect on his audience by creating a common bond as believers in Christ.

In Rom 9:1-5, the speaker, Paul, opens the rhetorical unit Rom 9-11 with a solemn vow. The abrupt change of tone from the previous chapter is surprising because Paul has just made a rousing affirmation

---

and S. Stowers, *The Diatribe and Paul's Letter to the Romans,* SBLDS 57 (Chico: Scholars, 1981).

[12] For a detailed analysis of this passage, see Paul J. Achtemeier, "Romans 3:1-8: Structure and Argument," in *Christ and Communities: Essays in Honor of Reginald H. Fuller*, ed. A. J. Hultgren and B. Hall (Cincinati, Ohio: Forward Movement Publication, 1990), 77-87.

[13] In a similar vein, Nils A. Dahl observes that Paul's "epistolary style is somewhat more evident in chapters 9-11 than in 1:17-8:39" ("The Future of Israel," in *Studies in Paul: Theology for the Early Christian Mission* [Minneapolis: Augsburg, 1977], 140).

[14] Stowers, *Rereading Romans,* 290.

[15] So ibid., 290-91.

[16] See ibid., 264-84. For an opposing view against Stowers' position, see Anderson, *Ancient Rhetorical Theory and Paul,* 179-83.

[17] The first person plural is used by Paul in the *exordium* also (1:5, 12) in which he identifies himself with his audience and creates a common bond in establishing the *ethos*. In 1:14-4:22, Paul uses the first person plural several times (e.g., 3:5, 9, 19, 28, 31; 4:1, 9) but these usages are quite different from his uses in the *exordium*. They lack the friendly *ethos* that he expresses in the *exordium*.

of God's love in Jesus Christ (8:31-39).[18] It is more striking, however, to see the abrupt return of the first person singular. Paul has not used the first person singular after the *exordium* except in a few isolated instances.[19] The very personal authorial persona from the *exordium* re-emerges here, but in a completely different mood. Dahl points out that Paul's "epistolary style," which he uses in Rom 1:1-15, is more evidently shown here in chapters 9-11 than in 1:17-8:39.[20] What Dahl calls "epistolary style" is Greco-Roman letter writing convention, and is typically shown in the letter opening and closing.[21] It is worth noting what Dahl observes here:[22]

1. Paul is very personal when he addresses his audience in Rom 9-11. He calls them "brethren" (10:1; 11:25) which Paul uses in the opening and closing sections of the letter (1:13, 15; 15:14, 30; 16:17) as well as in the request in 7:1, 4; 8:12; 12:1 "but not in the more essay-like parts of the letter."

2. Paul's oath-like statements (that he speaks the truth in Christ and he does not lie) as well as the reference to the Holy Spirit as his conscience's witness correspond to "epistolary sections" in his other letters (2 Cor 11:10; Gal 1:20; Rom 1:8; 2 Cor 1:12, 23; Phil 1:8).

3. Paul's expressions of his feelings, his sorrows and his intercession on behalf of the Israelites (9:1-3; 10:1) are typically seen in the opening sections of his letters (1 Cor 1:4-9; Phil 1:3-11; Phlm 4-7).

4. Dahl also observes that in the just cited examples, Paul's expressions of his feelings, thanksgiving, and the intercession are on behalf of his recipients, whereas in Rom 9-11 they concern the Israelites as a third party. Dahl points out that Paul's language is typical of recommending the third party in Rom 10:2 and 9:4-5.

---

[18] J.-N. Aletti, *Comment Dieu est-it juste? Clefs pour interpréter l'épître aux Romains* (Paris: Éditions du Seuil, 1991), 139.

[19] Both 6:19 ("Ἀνθρώπινον λέγω...") and 7:1 ("...γινώσκουσιν γὰρ νόμον λαλῶ,") are a kind of parenthetical comment inserted by Paul and we already noted the use of "I" in 7:7-25. The only exception is 8:18, where Paul solemnly declares about the glory to be revealed to both him and his audience. In what follows, however, the first person plural is used throughout.

[20] Dahl, "Future of Israel," 139-40.

[21] Stowers points out that such style is used when the writer of a letter writes "as if friends were conversing in each other's presence" (*Rereading Romans*, 291).

[22] Summarized from Dahl, "Future of Israel," 140-41. Cf. also Stowers, *Rereading Romans*, 291.

Dahl's observations may lead one to think that Paul speaks to his audience as if he is starting to write a new letter. Therefore, it is not surprising to see that many commentators have concluded that Paul is embarking on a completely new theme, detached from previous sections.[23] It is, however, a mistake to think that Paul was abruptly changing his subject and tone on a whim. In fact, what can be seen here is a highly sophisticated rhetorical strategy of Paul to persuade with maximum effect.[24] Let us now discuss how Paul presents himself in Rom 9-11.

The intense personal avowal that he is "speaking the truth in Christ" sets the tone of the whole unit: this is very personal to the speaker and he is taking this matter very seriously. Paul may be in a defensive mode here: being the apostle to the Gentiles, he may have been accused of deserting his own people.[25] When we consider the exigence of Rom 9-11, to be discussed shortly, the focus of Paul's argumentation is not himself but God. It would be a mistake to see Paul as personally defensive.[26] Since the tone is much too solemn and serious to suggest that. It is therefore not about whether Paul deserted his own people, but whether God did. At the center of Paul's heart is this matter concerning God's defense, and it results in the strongly shown *pathos* of the writer, which has often been misconstrued as arising out of a personal defensiveness.[27]

---

[23] So many commentators have taken this position that it is unnecessary to list them; see Johnson, *Romans 9-11*, 111 and her footnote 3 for examples.

[24] Cf. Stowers' remark: "The unexpectedness and pathos of the new authorial persona in 9-11 strikes as a rhetorical tour de force" (*Rereading of Romans*, 292).

[25] So O. Michel, *Der Brief an die Römer*, 14th ed. (Göttingen: Vandenhoeck & Ruprecht, 1978), 223; Wilckens, *Römer*, II, 189-90; Räisänen, "Romans 9-11," 180; F. Watson, *Paul, Judaism and the Gentiles: A Sociological Approach*, SNTSMS 56 (Cambridge: Cambridge University Press, 1986), 161: "The charge of indifference must underlie the strangely emphatic language of 9:1-5"; also, Byrne, *Romans*, 285, insists that Paul's opening here is similar to Paul's defense in 1:9-15 where he defends his failure to visit the Roman community as the apostle to the Gentiles. Dunn, *Romans 9-16*, 530, likens Paul's double protestation ("I speak the truth… I do not lie) to the beginning of chap. 6.

[26] So Cranfield, *Romans*, II, 453. *Contra* Käsemann, *Romans*, 257, who sees a forensic situation throughout 9:1-5. In short, the question is "not whether Paul is consistent, but whether God is" (Wayne A. Meeks, "On Trusting an Unpredictable God: A Hermeneutical Meditation on Romans 9-11," in *Faith and History: Essays in Honor of Paul W. Meyer*, ed. John T. Carroll, *et al.* [Atlanta: Scholars, 1990], 105).

[27] "This section [Rom 9:1-5] is marked by unmistakable pathos" (Käsemann, *ibid.*).

Paul emphatically portrays himself as a Jew[28] who is even willing to be "accursed and cut off from Christ" (9:3) for the sake of his
own people. This is consistent with the self-portrayal of Paul in the *exordium*, but now in a more emotional tone. Here it is most likely that
Paul likens himself to the person of Moses (Exod 32:31-32) in v. 3.[29]
The rhetorical effect of such an allusion is to make sure that Paul is
truly concerned about his kinsmen's salvation just as Moses was in the
Old Testament.[30] In view of his self-awareness as the apostle to the
Gentiles, Paul makes a strong statement that the salvation of the Jewish
people is not alien to his ministry but is at the core of it.[31] It is the expression of Paul's intense love for his kinspeople according to the flesh,
who are "accursed and cut off from Christ." I believe that the point that
Paul wants to make is precisely this: his own kinspeople are *anathema*,
cut off from Christ, and "ὑπὲρ τῶν ἀδελφῶν μου" he is even willing to
be anathema himself and cut off from Christ.[32] The same prayer-wish,
this time in a more positive way is expressed in 10:1 by Paul: his
heart's desire and prayer to God is for their salvation (εἰς σωτηρίαν).
Paul's willingness to do anything for their salvation is again shown in

---

[28] See the classic essay by M. Barth, "St. Paul—A Good Jew," *HBT* 1
(1979): 7-45.

[29] J. Munck (*Paul and the Salvation of Mankind*, trans. Frank Clarke
[Richmond, Va.: John Knox, 1959], 305-6; *Christ and Israel: An Interpretation of
Romans 9-11*, trans. Ingeborg Nixon [Philadelphia: Fortress, 1967], 29) has been
followed by many interpreters who see the allusion here. Among them are Cranfield, *Romans*, II, 454-55; Anthony J. Guerra, "Romans: Paul's Purpose and Audience with Special Attention to Romans 9-11," *RB* 97 (1990): 228; Fitzmyer, *Romans*, 544; John G. Lodge, *Romans 9—11: A Reader-Response Analysis*, University of South Florida International Studies in Formative Christianity and Judaism 6
(Atlanta: Scholars, 1996), 41; Moo, *Romans*, 559; Johnson, *Reading Romans*, 144-
45. Käsemann is against the idea because he believes that the force of Paul's
statement lies in the phrase, ἀπὸ τοῦ Χριστοῦ. He points out that Old Testament
parallels do not have such a point. Of course, there is no allusion in Exod 32:31-32
in reference to Christ, but the context of prayer and sacrificial suffering on behalf
of their own people make a strongly connect Moses and Paul. Further, the fact that
the story of Moses is close to Paul's mind in Rom 9-11 (e.g., 9:14-18; 10:19;
11:13-14) also points to the allusion (so Moo, *Romans*, 559).

[30] The attempt of P. Bratsiotis to connect Rom 9:3 and LXX Esth 4:17 is interesting but far-fetched and not convincing ("Eine exegetische Notiz zu Röm. IX.3
und X.1," *NovT* 5 [1962]: 299-300).

[31] Paul's repeated assertion that the order of salvation or even damnation is
for the Jews first and then the Gentiles should be noted here (1:16; 2:9-10). Cf.
Nanos, *The Mystery of Romans*, 239-288, esp. 242-47.

[32] John Piper, *The Justification of God: An Exegetical and Theological
Study of Romans 9:1-23*, 2d ed. (Grand Rapids: Baker, 1993), 45.

11:13b-14 when he says that "Inasmuch then as I am an apostle to the
Gentiles, I glorify my ministry in order to make my own people jealous, and thus save some of them." The expression of the purpose of his
apostleship to the Gentiles is striking here: his ministry for the salvation of the Gentiles is actually intended for the salvation of his kinspeople!

Finally, Paul explicitly reveals his identity in 11:1b: "I myself
am an Israelite, a descendant of Abraham, a member of the tribe of
Benjamin." Paul prefers the use of "Israel" (Ἰσραήλ, 11 times) and "Israelite" (Ἰσραηλίτης, 2 times) to more conventional "Jews" (Ἰουδαῖος,
2 times) throughout Rom 9-11. It should be noted that "Israel" and "Israelite" are not used in Romans at all outside Rom 9-11.[33] Therefore,
Paul's self-designation as an Israelite (Ἰσραηλίτης) is consistent with
his preference. Why then does Paul use the terms "Israel" and "Israelite" and call himself an "Israelite" rather than a "Jew" in Rom 9-11? D.
Fraikin is certainly correct when he says that the reason why "Paul does
not call the body of unbelieving Jews 'the Jews'" is that "there are
Christian Jews."[34]   Since "Jews are not yet defined as non-
Christians,"[35] Paul intentionally uses the term "Israel," which can be
defined as "the corporate body of the Jews as distinct from the other
nations (9:30-31), the people addressed by the prophets in the past

---

[33] Lodge, *Romans 9-11,* 34. In a stimulating essay, Calvin Roetzel argues
that since the concept of "race" is a product of the Enlightenment in Western
Europe, New Testament interpreters should not read the concept back to the New
Testament, especially Paul. His point is worth quoting at length:

> There was no concept of a Jewish race or of a race of Israel in the
> first century. The construction of race is a social phenomenon from
> the post-Enlightenment period. The category of race is one that de-
> notes inferiority, and even unintentionally when a Christian refers to
> the "race of Israel," Christianity is assumed to be normative, and the
> Jewish "race," by implication, radically defective and inferior in its
> religion. If we choose to use the term, we do well to recognize the
> mythology concealed in the language of race and its capacity to
> marginalize, to assign place, and to attempt control. Such a usage,
> whether intentional or not, makes Paul say just the opposite of what
> his letters appear to say. ("No 'Race of Israel' in Paul," in *Putting
> Body & Soul Together: Essays in Honor of Robin Scroggs,* ed. Vir-
> ginia Wiles, Alexandra Brown and Graydon F. Snyder [Valley
> Forge: Trinity Press International, 1997], 230-44; quotation from p.
> 244).

[34] "The Rhetorical Function," 100.

[35] Ibid., 100-101.

(9:27; 10:21), the people of God,"[36] to focus on their rejection of the gospel, which poses a threat to Paul's Gentile mission. The term "Israel" clearly has stronger religious connotations than the "Jews" (Ἰουδαῖος) which Paul uses to make an distinction from "Gentile" (Rom 1:16; 2:9, 10, 17, 28, 29; 3:1, 9, 29; 9:24).[37] The fact that "Israel" as the people of God has rejected the gospel[38] shakes the foundation of Paul's commission as the apostle to the Gentiles because without Israel's salvation his mission to the Gentiles is in vain.

In Rom 9-11, an unmistakable picture of the speaker clearly emerges: he is a Jew who is profoundly concerned about his kinsfolk's salvation. To his Gentile audience, this is a striking message: God sent Paul to be the apostle to them, yet even his apostleship is fundamentally Jewish in the thoroughly Jewish scheme of salvation. And in this scheme, the Jewish people are not ignored, indeed Paul's ministry is eventually for their salvation. Why does Paul use such a shocking way to discuss the subject in these chapters? I believe that this question can only be answered as we discover more about the audience and the exigence. Now let us move on to discuss the portrait of the audience in Rom 9-11.

The Audience

In chapter 3, it was argued that the audience that Paul is targeting to persuade is the Gentile Christians in the Roman church. In Rom 11:13, Paul says "Ὑμῖν δὲ λέγω τοῖς ἔθνεσιν· ἐφ᾽ ὅσον μὲν οὖν εἰμι ἐγὼ ἐθνῶν ἀπόστολος, τὴν διακονίαν μου δοξάζω." The NRSV translates this verse, "Now I am speaking to you Gentiles. Inasmuch then as I am an apostle to the Gentiles, I glorify my ministry." It sounds as if Paul's speech were directed to either the Jewish audience or the Jewish and Gentile audience, and now turns exclusively towards

---

[36] Ibid., 101. For a comprehensive treatment of uses of different names in ancient Jewish and early Christian literature, see Graham Harvey, *The True Israel: Uses of the Names Jew, Hebrew and Israel in Ancient Jewish and Early Christian Literature*, AGJU 35 (Leiden: Brill, 1996). On Paul's use of the term "Israel" in Romans, see pp. 228-32.

[37] Johnson, *Reading Romans,* 145. See also Terence L. Donaldson, *Paul and the Gentiles: Remapping the Apostle's Convictional World* (Minneapolis: Fortress, 1997), 215-48, esp. 215-26, for an interesting discussion.

[38] Of course, the notion that Israel has rejected the gospel does not mean that every individual Jew has rejected the gospel. Acknowledging this has important implications for the exegesis of 11:25-26 later.

the Gentiles.[39] The problem in this translation is whether one can render δέ with "now" which has the sense of a changed audience, as the NRSV and RSV do.[40] Lidell-Scott's Greek-English Lexicon certainly lists this possibility under the headings of the particle δέ.[41] It is to be understood in that way, however, "when the vocative stands first, then the first pronoun followed by δέ."[42] Obviously, it cannot be applied to our sentence. How should we, then, understand this sentence? In what sense does Paul use the particle δέ? Stowers points out that grammatically, 11:11, 12, and 13-14 are poorly coordinated by Paul even though they "contain three closely related thoughts" in good diatribal style.[43] He argues that the particle δέ should be understood as "merely passing from one thing to another"[44] because vv. 11, 12, and 13-14 "read almost like a list of related ideas."[45] Thus, he correctly argues that the particle δέ cannot be rendered as if in the context of turning to a new audience, or as "now at this point in the discourse."[46] Yet Stowers' translation of δέ as "yes" is problematic because it betrays his understanding of the particle as "merely passing from one thing to another." I, on the other hand, maintain that it has a corrective or contrastive force.

How should we, then, understand the sentence as a whole? The key to the correct understanding seems to lie in understanding Paul's use of combined particles, μὲν οὖν in v. 13. This combination can have the meaning of summarizing what has been said and moving to a new subject[47] or it can signal Paul's consciousness that "what he is about to say is contrary to what the Gentile Christians will be probably inclined to think."[48] It can not be seen, however, that Paul is now moving to a new subject in v. 13 only after vv. 11-12, as Dunn thinks, because vv. 11-14 contain a series of closely related thoughts as observed. Cran-

---

[39] RSV has almost same rendering except "magnify" for "glorify."

[40] They also translate δέ in 11:12 as "now."

[41] LSJ, ninth ed., 1996, s.v. II. 4.

[42] Ibid. Its example: "Μενέλαε, σοὶ δὲ τάδε λέγω..."

[43] Stowers, *Rereading Romans,* 288.

[44] Stowers cites Liddell and Scott's abridged version of 1966: "It often serves merely to pass from one thing to another, when it may be rendered *and, further.*" (ibid.).

[45] Ibid.

[46] Ibid.

[47] BDF §451.1; followed by Dunn, *Romans 9-16,* 655-6. However, BDF does not list Rom 11:13 as one of the examples.

[48] Cranfield, *Romans,* 2.559.

field's idea of contrasting force is correct but I believe that the direction is wrong. That is, this sentence occurs in the middle of a diatribal conversation and should be understood in that context. I believe that the corrective force of μὲν οὖν should be directed to *what has just been said*[49] and not to what is about to be said. That is grammatically impossible.[50] Once again, Stowers hits the mark when he says "... *men oun* must be taken adverbially with an adversative or corrective force."[51] Thus, he argues that "[t]he part of the sentence set in contrast by *menoun* corrects any mistaken impression that the discussion of Israel's future has no place in this letter so wholly addressed to gentiles and the gentile situation."[52] Further, the future of Israel and the salvation of Gentiles are more closely interrelated than his audience might have thought (11:12, 15-16, 30-32).

Therefore, the word ὑμῖν is clearly emphatic,[53] highlighting that the audience that Paul wants to communicate with is really the Gentile Christians, even though he is mainly dealing with Jewish matters and salvation. The particle δέ still has an adversative force in the sentence, resulting in the translation, "But I am speaking to you Gentiles." Thus, Rom 11:13-14 can be roughly paraphrased as follows: "But remember I am speaking to you Gentiles, even though I am dealing with the Jewish matters. Yes, I am an apostle to the Gentiles but my apostleship is also for the salvation of my own people."[54]

There is little doubt that the Roman congregation includes a substantial number of Jewish Christians.[55] Once again, however, I submit that it is the Gentile Christians whom Paul wants to persuade and move to certain actions through his letter.[56] This is what Paul says time and

---

[49] So Stowers, *Rereading Romans,* 288.

[50] See M. E. Thrall, *Greek Particles in the New Testament*, NTTS 3 (Leiden: E. J. Brill, 1962), 34-5. Cf. J. D. Denniston, *The Greek Particles*, 2d ed. (Oxford: Oxford University Press, 1954), 475-78.

[51] Stowers, *Rereading Romans,* 288.

[52] Ibid.

[53] Sanday and Headlam, *Romans,* 324.

[54] For a discussion of textual variants on 11:13 resulting from confusion on the part of ancient editors, see Stowers, *Rereading Romans,* 288-89.

[55] In fact, many scholars believe that the Roman congregation was dominated by the Jewish Christians in the beginning. See Nanos, *The Mystery of Romans,* 41-84; Dahl, "The Future of Israel," 139-42; Raymond E. Brown, "Rome," in *Antioch and Rome: New Testament Cradles of Catholic Christianity* (New York: Paulist, 1983), 94-113.

[56] *Contra* Räisänen, "Romans 9-11," 181, who asserts that it was Jewish Christians whom Paul addresses here. "Roman gentile Christians would not have

again throughout Romans. Modern readers need to listen to Paul more seriously. Anthony Guerra has recently argued that it was the Jewish Christians among the members of the Roman congregation to whom Paul was primarily speaking in order to gain favor for his mission project in the West.[57] He insists that Paul's presentation of "the Davidic Christology," (1:3) in which Paul explicitly designates Jesus as the Jewish Messiah, reflects "Paul's eagerness to affirm his orthodoxy with respect to the issue of monotheism."[58] But the most decisive evidence for Guerra that Paul is targeting the Jewish Christians in Rome is "the content and mode of argumentation of Romans 9-11."[59] Guerra argues that Paul's purpose in writing Rom 9-11 in such a way is to convince the Jewish Christians that "he is not inimical to Jewish traditions: monotheism, Scripture, the Patriarchs."[60] Guerra's reading, however, ignores Paul's direct address to the Gentiles, starting in 11:13-4.[61] Thus, his otherwise fine work is misdirected because he misconstrues the purpose and audience in the text. Simply, on the level of the text of Romans, there is no warrant that Paul was writing his letter with the purposes regarding Jewish Christians that Guerra advances.

From 11:13, Paul speaks to the Gentiles in a more direct way, using the second person in his address, while referring to the Jews in the third person plural. Paul's argument in 11:17-25a particularly reveals that among the audience there were some who had become proud in their thinking in terms of their relationship with Jews. Whether these Gentile Christians were embarrassed by Jews or the Jewish origin of

---

not cared," says Räisänen, and thus "Paul addresses those who felt the plight of Israel to be a calamity rather than a matter of course." It is, however, precisely Gentile Christians who "felt the plight of Israel" to their heart since their own salvation is at stake. See chapter 5.

[57] Guerra, "Romans 9-11," 219-37. See also the discussion in his monograph, *Romans and the Apologetic Tradition: The Purpose, Genre and Audience of Paul's Letter*, SNTSMS 81 (Cambridge: Cambridge University Press, 1995), 22-42. It was F. C. Baur who first espoused the idea of Jewish audience ("Über Zweck und Gedankengang des Römerbriefs," *Theologische Jahrbücher* 16 [1857]: 91), who is followed by F. Watson, *Paul*, 98.

[58] Guerra, "Romans 9-11," 220.

[59] Ibid., 219.

[60] Ibid., 224.

[61] He apologetically notes that "the direct address here to Gentile Christians is intended primarily to assuage Jewish Christians' fears that Paul is disdainful of Jews and their traditions" (ibid., 235, n. 63). I do not know, however, how he reached this conclusion.

the gospel is not clear.[62] What is clear is that they became proud in their salvation and they began to boast about their status as the new people of God (11:18).[63] Paul's exhortation is: "μὴ ὑψηλὰ φρόνει ἀλλὰ φοβοῦ" (11:20). Paul's use of the word φοβέομαι may be intentional if these Gentiles were former so-called "God-fearers."[64] What Paul may be saying to them is, in effect, "remember who you were and be humble." The reason they must be humble is also that their spiritual blessing was originally Israel's and they were grafted like the olive tree and have simply come to "share" it (15:27).[65]

The Exigence

There once was a time when chapters 9-11 were treated as a kind of "afterglow," something that Paul inserted or added after finishing his main argument in chapter 8.[66] The main reason for such a reading was

---

[62] *Contra* Frank Thielman, "Unexpected Mercy: Echoes of a Biblical Motif in Romans 9-11," *SJT* 47 (1994): 172-3.

[63] Nanos terms this attitude as "Christian-*gentile* exclusivism" against Jewish ethnocentric exclusivism (*The Mystery of Romans*, 9-10).

[64] Lampe, *Die stadtrömischen Christen,* 56-58, believes that the majority of the Gentiles in the Roman congregation are "God-fearers." For a review of current views on the subject, see Robert MacLennan and Thomas A. Kraabel, "The God-Fearers--A Literary and Theological Invention," *BAR* 12 (1986): 46-53 and A. Overman, "The God-Fearers: Some Neglected Features," *JSNT* 32 (1988): 17-26. It was Schmithals who proposed that the Gentile converts in Rome were former God-fearers (*Der Römerbrief als historisches Problem*, 73f., 83f.); so Beker, *Paul the Apostle*, 76. See further W.S. Campbell, *Paul's Gospel in an Intercultural Context: Jew and Gentile in the Letter to the Romans* (Frankfurt: Peter Lang, 1992), 185-87; T. Finn, "The God-Fearers Reconsidered," *CBQ* 47 (1985): 75-84; F. Siegert, "Die Gottesfürchtig und Sympathisanten," *JSJ* 4 (1973): 109-64; and Penna, "Les Juifs," 321-47.

[65] Cf. Wright, "Romans and the Theology of Paul," in *Pauline Theology III: Romans,* 58-9:

> the rhetorical force of the entire exposition of the failure of Israel is not to give Gentile Christians a sense of smugness or self-satisfaction at their contrasting success, but to highlight and emphasize the fact that they owe the Israelites a huge debt of *gratitude* (author's emphasis).

[66] This position has in recent years been largely abandoned; of the many classical positions, the representative ones are: R. Bultmann, *Theology of the New Testament*, trans. K. Grobel (New York: Charles Scribner's Sons, 1955), II, 132, who says that it is Paul's "speculative fantasy"; C. H. Dodd, *The Epistle of Paul to the Romans*, rev. ed., MNTC (London: Collins, 1959), 148; Sanday and Headlam, *Romans*, 225; F. W. Beare, *St. Paul and His Letters* (New York: Abingdon, 1962),

interpreters' ignorance of Paul's rhetorical strategy in these chapters. We have already discussed the abrupt change of authorial persona and tone in the previous section on the speaker. Some interpreters thought that such a change, combined with a new subject, was completely disjunctive with what had been said and heralded a new argument. Furthermore, when the main subject matter of these chapters was thought to be Paul's doctrine of "predestination" or the question concerning the fate of Israel, new subjects that Paul had scarcely hinted at in Rom 1-8. Increasingly, however, interpreters have joined in agreeing that these chapters are integral parts of the letter. Yet how exactly these three chapters are related or connected to the first eight chapters of the letter, not to mention the entire letter, admits of no consensus.[67] As mentioned earlier, the various proposals have not been satisfactory because they have focused on comparing and harmonizing the theological ideas of Rom 1-8 and Rom 9-11.

What we need to determine, first of all, is the exigence of Rom 9-11 and then to see if this exigence has any connection to the rest of the letter, especially to the *exordium* and the *peroratio*. If Romans is a unified letter with a rhetorically structured argumentation, a fact of which I am convinced, we can assume that the rhetorical exigence that Paul establishes in the *exordium* and recapitulates in the *peroratio*, discussed in the previous chapter, is organically connected to chapters 9-11. Rom 9-11 serve almost like one of the poles in the bridge that sustains the ongoing theme between the *exordium* and the *peroratio*—in this sense it is the pinnacle of Paul's argument in Romans.

One thing to keep in mind in the following discussion is that the question of the rhetorical exigence of Rom 9-11 is on the level of the text. Of crucial importance is the discernment that must be exercised in order to avoid falling into the trap of "filling in" the context with speculative historical information. Indeed, the subject matter of Rom 9-11 has been most elusive, plagued by modern injections of various unwarranted assumptions into the mind of Paul. One of the examples of such a phenomenon can be seen in the exegeses of continental scholars who have been preoccupied with the question of anti-Semitism in general, and the Holocaust in particular.[68]

103-4; Schmithals, *Der Römerbrief als historische Problem,* 210; and J. A. T. Robinson, *Wrestling with Romans* (London: SCM, 1979), 108.

[67] See the first section of the chapter.

[68] See various essays in Lorenzo De Lorenzi, ed., *Die Israelfrage nach Röm 9-11* (Rome: Abtei von St Paul vor den Mauern, 1977). Cf. E. Elizabeth Johnson,

More recently, interpreters have struggled to escape such a pre-occupation, attempting to find the subject matter within the pages of Romans. Among these, N. T. Wright's attempt is worth a detailed discussion.[69] Wright wants to assert that the place of Rom 9-11 within the letter is "an integral part of the argument of the letter itself."[70] In order to do that, he provides his view of the purpose of Romans, and argues that Romans was written both "to sum up Paul's theology at the end of his main activity" and "to sort out problems within the Roman church" and more.[71] He proposes that in the Roman church, which Paul wanted to use as a base of operations in his next mission project in the west, a certain problem could be foreseen, which was in fact the mirror-image of the problem he encountered in Antioch, Paul's headquarters in the east. The potential problem is

> the danger of the (largely gentile) church so relishing its status as the true people of God that it will write off ethnic Jews entirely as being not only second-class citizens *within* the church, still maintaining their dietary laws when the need for them has past, but also now beyond the reach of the gospel *outside* the church, heading for automatic damnation.[72]

Wright argues that such theological misunderstanding would lead them to adopt a different line in missionary practices so that they would "effectively stab him in the back" as the church in Antioch once did.[73] In order to prevent this, Paul wrote Romans, arguing for "total equality of Jew and Gentile within the church, and a mission to Gentiles which always includes Jews as well within its scope."[74] Wright proceeds to argue that Romans 9-11 functions as "the climax of the theological argu-

---

"Romans 9-11: The Faithfulness and Impartiality of God," in *Pauline Theology III: Romans*, ed. David M. Hay and E. Elizabeth Johnson (Minneapolis: Fortress, 1995), 211-15, who shows that the exegeses tend to focus on so-called *Israelfrage*, which is not the primary subject matter of the chapters.

[69] Wright, "Christ, the Law and the People of God: Romans 9-11," in *The Climax of the Covenant: Christ and the Law in Pauline Theology* (Minneapolis: Fortress, 1991), 231-57. Wright testifies that his essay has been well received among his students (*What St. Paul Really Said: Was Paul of Tarsus the Real Founder of Christianity* [Grand Rapids: Eerdmans, 1997], 191).

[70] Wright, "Romans 9-11," 232.

[71] Ibid., 234.

[72] Ibid. (author's emphasis).

[73] Ibid.

[74] Ibid.

ment" within this overall purpose of Romans:[75] "The whole of Romans 1-11 is... an exposition of how the one God has been *faithful*, in Jesus Christ, to the promises he made to Abraham: and this exposition must of necessity reach its climax in the historical survey of how these promises have worked out" (my emphasis).[76] I would add that the promises God made are already mentioned in 1:2 when the gospel of God is introduced by Paul and therefore they go back beyond Rom 4, where Abraham is introduced. Wright proceeds to argue that the main subject-matter of Romans 9-11 is "the covenant faithfulness of God, seen in its outworking in the history of the people of God."[77] The strength of Wright's argument is that the subject matter of Rom 9-11 is firmly put in the context of the whole letter.

Now let us examine this idea in detail. In recent years, there seems to be a consensus that the subject matter of Rom 9-11 is generally "the faithfulness of God" or "trustworthiness of God" in regard to his promises to Israel.[78] And Rom 9:6a is widely considered as the thematic statement of Rom 9-11: "It is not as though the word of God had failed." [79] It is quite puzzling that Paul's main concern of these

---

[75] Ibid.

[76] Achtemeier has already made the essentially same point concerning the structure of Romans as a whole in his commentary that the logic of Romans is that of history rather than of the doctrine:

the sweep of Paul's thought in Romans concerns not so much the spelling out of the implications of a doctrine like justification of faith as it concerns the course of the *history* of God's dealing with his creation, from its rebellion against him to its final redemption. The outline of the first eleven chapters of Romans can be seen from the course of that *history* between God and his creation (*Romans*, 13; my emphasis).

[77] Ibid., 236.

[78] See Räisänen, "Römer 9-11," 2930-36; idem, "Romans 9-11," 178 with his references there. Other recent interpreters who also agree include Johnson, "Romans 9-11," 214-5; Meeks, "On Trusting," 105-6; Wright, *The Climax of the Covenant*, 236; Chae, *Paul as Apostle to the Gentiles*, 215-6; Dunn, *Theology of Paul*, 501.

[79] Some see 9:6a representing only a transition between the introduction and the "body" of Paul's argument in Rom 9-11 (e.g., Moo, *Romans*, 572) but many commentators conclude that 9:6a is the thematic statement of Rom 9-11 (or at least 9:6-29). Among them are Käsemann, *Romans*, 261; Dahl, "The Future of Israel," 155; Cranfield, *Romans*, II, 473: "the sign and theme of the whole of chapters 9-11"; Siegert, *Argumentation bei Paulus*, 124 and 174; Byrne, *Romans*, 290; Stowers, *Rereading of Romans*, 287; Dunn, *Romans 9-16*, 539; idem, *Theology of Paul*, 501.

chapters is expressed not as an affirmative statement but in the form of denial of an implied question in 9:6a. [80] Why does Paul state his thesis in this way? Most interpreters have not asked this question, but in the present writer's view, the form of this sentence holds the key to understanding the way Paul structures his argumentation. This question can only be answered satisfactorily when we examine the arrangement and invention of Rom 9-11 in the next chapter but here we will simply entertain the idea itself.

What question is Paul answering? The question is obviously "Has the word of God failed?" The overriding issue that Paul deals with in Rom 9-11 is this crucial question concerning the character of God, or more precisely God himself. If God had once abandoned the people whom he had chosen, why wouldn't he do it again? If God gave up on the Jews whom he had elected by grace, how could the Gentiles be sure that it would not happen again? Actually, the question regarding God's character[81] was already dealt with by Paul in 3:1-8, but only briefly. In Rom 2:1-29, the Jewish people are indicted under the same judgment with which the Gentiles were indicted (1:18-32). The inevitable question arises: "What then is the advantage of the Jew?" (3:1). Ultimately it is directed to the faithfulness of God: "What if some were unfaithful? Will their faithlessness nullify the faithfulness of God? (ἡ πίστις τοῦ θεοῦ)" (3:3). This issue was not fully dealt with by Paul earlier but now in Rom 9-11 receives its full treatment.[82] Then, what Paul is most concerned with here is the defense of God's character, rather than his own gospel[83] or "the equality of Jew and Gentile in the plan of God"[84] even though these issues are all closely related to the main subject matter. Then it should be asked, is the question of God's

---

[80] In her analysis of the structure of Rom 9-11, E. Elizabeth Johnson argues that though 9:6a is not a question, the phrase οὐχ οἶον δὲ ὅτι ("it is not as though") can surely be understood as "a denial of one possible answer to a question" ("Romans 9-11," 216).

[81] Once again, I would like to submit that the focus of Rom 9-11 should be God himself, not the speaker (Paul), the audience (Gentiles), or the referent (Israelites). Too often in the history of exegesis of our passage, the wrongly focused interpretations (e.g., *Israelfrage*) have resulted in unwarranted conclusions, which do not really touch on the real concerns of the passage.

[82] Dunn, *Theology of Paul,* 502. On Rom 3:1-8 in connection with Rom 9-11, see Piper, "The Righteousness of God in Romans 3:1-8," in *The Justification of God,* 123-34.

[83] *Contra* Moo, *Romans,* 548. Moo is correct to see the chapters as a defense but is wrong on what is being defended here.

[84] Chae, *Paul as Apostle to the Gentiles,* 215-21.

trustworthiness or faithfulness in regards to his promises to the Israel-ites, manifested in their scriptures concerning their salvation, being raised for the first time in Rom 3:1-8? The answer is no, because Paul already introduced such a theme in the *exordium* of the letter, espe-cially in 1:2-4. It has already been argued that the exigence manifested in the *exordium* and the *peroratio* mainly deals with Paul's apostleship to the Gentiles, the gospel of God "which he promised beforehand through his prophets in the holy scriptures," (1:2) and his future mis-sionary plans.[85] We also saw that the way Paul presents his gospel and apostleship is strikingly Jewish, based on the Jewish scriptures. The gospel which is "promised beforehand through his prophets in the holy scriptures" finds its ultimate origin in God himself. If this gospel is the power of God to save everyone who believes (1:16), its trustworthiness is directly connected to God's character or God himself. Rom 1:17 ex-presses this idea as "the righteousness of God" and it is well docu-mented that "the righteousness of God" is pervasive in the pages of Romans.[86] "The righteousness of God" (ἡ δικαιοσύνη θεοῦ) is, of course, closely tied to the "faithfulness of God" (ἡ πίστις τοῦ θεοῦ). Paul Meyer's words hit the mark:

> ... what then becomes of God's faithfulness, that very reliability on which human trust, beginning with Abraham's, can alone depend? What about those "direct utterances" and God's calling of a people as his own, for which again Abraham is the prototype? Has God broken faith with his word, and with himself? What is at stake is not only the reality and future of Israel; it is above all a question about the God who acted in Jesus Christ... God's "faithfulness" has sev-eral levels of meaning. His trustworthiness is his power to do what he has promised (as in 4:20-21). But it involves also his constancy, the changelessness of his purpose. And another side of his reliabil-ity is the consistency with which he deals with different groups of people, i.e., the very impartiality that raised the question in the first place. In the end, these are all aspects of God's righteousness.[87]

---

[85] See chapter 3.

[86] This is not the place to review the vast amount of literature on the subject of "the righteousness of God." It will suffice to note Sam K. Williams, "The 'Righteousness of God' in Romans," *JBL* 99 (1980): 241-90 and A. Schlatter, *Romans: The Righteousness of God,* trans. S. S. Schatzmann (Peabody, Mass.: Hen-drickson, 1995), from the 1935 German original *Gottes Gerechtigkeit: Ein Kom-mentar zum Römerbrief.*

[87] Paul W. Meyer, "Romans," in *Harper's Bible Commentary*, ed. J. L. Mays, *et al* (San Francisco: Harper & Row, 1988), 1154.

How the gospel of God is promised in the Old Testament is pervasively explained in the letter as a whole by Paul (1:17; 3:21; 4:3, 6-25; 10:5-20; 15:9-12, 21).[88] There is a crucial distinction that should be made at this point. The gospel that God promised in the Old Testament is not only concerned with the salvation of the Jews, even though it is for their salvation first (1:16; 2:9, 10), but also for that of the Gentiles. The "word of God" in 9:6a should be understood in the sense that it is not confined to the promises made to the Jews concerning their salvation, but is also for the Gentiles in the salvific plan of God in the Old Testament.[89] As K. Barth put it, it is "the sum of the Gospel."[90]

It becomes quite clear then that the theme of Paul's apostleship to the Gentiles and the gospel of God manifested in the *exordium* and the *peroratio* is also manifested in Rom 9-11. Then what about his missionary plans? Paul does not elaborate his missionary plans explicitly in Rom 9-11, but rather provides the theological basis for his missionary activities, especially his ministry towards the Gentiles. As we will see in detail in the following chapter, Paul argues that his Gentile mission is carried out precisely in the context of God's grand salvific plan, to save the Jews as well as the Gentiles. Israel's temporary "stumble" but not complete "fall" allows the Gentiles, the full number of them (11:25) to come into the salvation and then "all Israel" will be saved.[91] Therefore, when Paul later asks his audience to participate with him, in prayer and in material, for his future missionary plans (travel plans to Jerusalem and eventually Spain), there is theological understanding why Paul attempts such an endeavor, even a dangerous one (15:31), with such urgency: in Paul's missions to the Gentiles the plan of God's salvation is at stake.[92] All these things hinge on the faithfulness of God in regards to his promises to Israel.

As already mentioned, deciphering the way Paul structures his argumentation in Rom 9-11 holds the key to understanding its exigence. The most crucial aspect that has been neglected in modern scholarship on Romans in general and Rom 9-11 in particular is Paul's

---

[88] Bruce, *Romans,* 68.

[89] So Chae, *Paul as Apostle to the Gentiles,* 218.

[90] *Church Dogmatics,* II/2, 13f (cited by Cranfield, *Romans,* II, 473).

[91] See Roger D. Aus, "Paul's Travel Plans to Spain and the 'Full Number of the Gentiles' of Rom. XI 25," *NovT* 21 (1979): 232-62.

[92] The reason why Paul does not mention his missionary plan in the *exordium* can be explained this way that he is careful not to burden his audience before providing them reasonable explanation throughout the letter, especially in Rom 9-11.

use of the rhetorical tool called *stasis*. In our formal rhetorical analysis of Rom 9-11, we will closely examine how Paul uses this tool in the construction of his argument.

V. SUMMARY

In this chapter, we have defined the rhetorical unit and analyzed the rhetorical situation of Rom 9-11 by focusing on Paul's presentation of the speaker, the audience, and the exigence manifested in the text of the three chapters. We have found that the speaker is portrayed as a thoroughly Jewish person who is deadly earnest for the salvation of his kinsfolk, Israel. This portrayal is consistent with the picture of the speaker we saw in the *exordium*, yet having a quite different mood.

The portrait of the audience of Rom 9-11 is again consistent with that of the *exordium* and the *peroratio*: they are the Gentile Christians in the Roman church. They are the audience that Paul attempts to persuade through his letter. Paul speaks to them, concerned that they have become proud in their salvation to the point of despising their Jewish brothers and sisters in Christ. Paul warns them not to be arrogant but to "fear" as they were formerly "God-fearers" who are indebted to the Israelites who are the original recipients of God's spiritual blessings, which they only recently came to share.

Finally, the exigence of Rom 9-11 is essentially the question of God's faithfulness or trustworthiness, succinctly expressed in Rom 9:6a. This theme is not suddenly introduced by Paul in chapter 9 but was already raised, if implicitly, in the beginning of the letter, in the *exordium*, and dealt with briefly in 3:1-8. Consistent with Paul's dealings with the issue of his apostleship to the Gentiles in the context of his missionary enterprise, the defense of God's character dominates Paul's concern in Rom 9-11.

CHAPTER FIVE

THE RHETORICAL ANALYSIS OF ROMANS 9-11

Now begins a rhetorical analysis of Romans 9-11. The arrangement of the materials will be examined first. Then, the rhetorical species of the text will be determined. In this analysis, we will examine Paul's use of invention, style, and the rhetorical devices together. The argumentative flow, however, will receive more attention than any other feature to determine whether Paul is consistent in his argumentation. Our understanding of the rhetorical situation will help us navigate one of the most difficult passages in the New Testament. At the forefront of our analysis will be Paul's use of *stasis* in his argumentation.

I. THE ARRANGEMENT OF ROMANS 9-11

There has been much scholarly debate regarding the way Paul presents his argument in Rom 9-11. It is quite plainly detected that 9:1-5 and 11:33-36 comprise the beginning and the ending of the rhetorical unit, respectively. But there are many different opinions regarding the arrangement of the middle part of the passage. Dodd's division has been standard among many commentators: 1) exordium, 9:1-5; 2) three-stage development, 9:6-29, 9:30-10:21, 11:1-32; and 3) concluding hymn, 11:33-36.[1] A perusal of various commentaries and studies yields the fact that most structural analyses do not deviate from this di-

---

[1] C. H. Dodd, *The Epistle of Paul to the Romans*, rev. ed., MNTC (London: Collins, 1959), 150.

vision except at the transition between chapters 9 and 10. A number of scholars hold that 10:1 starts a new section, 9:30-33 being a transitional section. For example, W. C. van Unnik argues that Paul's argument continues until 9:33 and that the stylistic form in 9:6-29 and 9:30-33 is identical. And with ἀδελφοί, he sees a new incision in 10:1.[2] Dahl similarly argues that 9:30-33 functions as a transition to the following section and that Paul makes a new start in 10:1-3.[3] However, at 9:30 Paul starts a new section with a *narratio,* which will be shown shortly. Further, the rhetorical invention here is quite different from the previous argument in 9:6b-29, in which he uses *stasis* extensively. Also, the metaphor of running that Paul starts to use in 9:30-33 continues until 10:4. All these elements direct us to think that Paul starts his new argument in 9:30 rather than 10:1.

We can divide Rom 9-11 in the following way:

9:1-5: *Exordium*
9:6a: *Propositio*
9:6b-11:32: *Probatio*
　　9:6b-29: Argument I (*refutatio*; defense lawyer)
　　　　I.1. 9:6b-13: Who is Israel?
　　　　　　(*stasis* of Definition)
　　　　I.2. 9:14-18: The justice of God in question
　　　　　　(*stasis* of Counterplea)
　　　　I.3. 9:19-29: The sovereignty of God
　　　　　　(*stasis* of Objection)
　　9:30-10:21: Argument II (*confirmatio*; teacher)
　　　　II.1. 9:30-10:4: Christ the end of the law
　　　　II.2. 10:5-13: No distinction between Jew and
　　　　　　　　　　Greek
　　　　II.3. 10:14-21: Israel is responsible
　　　　　　(*stasis* of Transference)
　　11:1-11:32: Argument III (*refutatio*; prosecutor)
　　　　III.1. 11:1-10: God has not rejected his people
　　　　　　(*stasis* of Conjecture)

---

[2] "Diskussion," in *Die Israelfrage nach Röm 9-11,* 121-2; so C. K. Barrett, *The Epistle to the Romans,* rev. ed. (Peabody: Hendrickson, 1991), 182.

[3] Dahl, "Future of Israel," 147; so Kuss, *Römer,* 743. Cf. also M. Theobald, *Die überströmende Gnade: Studien zu einen paulinischen Motivfeld* (Würzburg: Echter, 1982), 141, who characterizes 9:30-33 as "*transmissio*"; and Wolfgang Reinbold, "Paulus und das Gesetz: Zur Exegese von Röm 9,30-33," *BZ* 38 (1994): 253-64.

III.2. 11:11-24: The purpose of Israel's stumbling
(*stasis* of Conjecture)
III.3. 11:25-32: All Israel will be saved.
11.33-36: *Peroratio*

The first and last divisions (the *exordium* and the *peroratio*) are most easily seen since they are clearly the introduction and conclusion of the rhetorical unit.[4] 9:6a clearly puts forward the main thesis of the whole unit.[5] Then, Paul presents his argument for this thesis in three different arguments using three different methods. Paul moves from the use of *stasis* as a defense lawyer (9:6b-29) to a prosecutor (11:1-32). There is a parallelism between the first and third arguments:[6]

9:6b-29	11:1-32
Abraham, v. 7	Abraham, v. 1
(Isaac) our ancestor, v. 10	The Fathers, v. 28
Jacob, v. 13	Jacob, v. 26
To call (*passim*)	The call, v. 29
The election, v. 11	The election, vv. 5, 7, 28
To harden (σκληρύνω), v. 18	To harden (πωρόω), v. 7, 25
To have mercy, vv. 15, 16, 18	To have mercy, vv. 30, 31, 32
The mercy, v. 23	The mercy, v. 31
To love, vv. 13, 25 (2X)	To love, v. 28
A remnant, v. 27	A remnant, v. 5
"will be saved," v. 27	"will be saved," v. 26

---

[4] Of course, there are some who do not see it this way. For example, Ph. Rolland proposes a quite different structure in his analysis: 9:1-2 (introduction of the thesis); 9:3-10:21 (development of the anti-thesis in three parts, 9:3-13, 9:14-29, and 9:30-10:21); and 11:1-36 (development of the thesis in three parts, 11:1-11, 11:16-24, 11:25-32) (*Épître aux Romains: Texte grec structuré* [Rome: Biblical Institute, 1980], *ad loc*). His analysis is peculiar by either ancient or modern standards, since he understands Paul as developing the anti-thesis first before developing the thesis. Furthermore, he forces chiasm between three parts in "anti-thesis" to "thesis" (A=9:3-13 to A'=11:25-32; B=9:14-29 to B'=11:16-24; and C=9:30-10:21 to C'=11:1-11) but it is difficult to see the correspondences between these sections. Finally, his analysis neglects 11:12-15 and 11:33-36. See Aletti, *Comment Dieu est-il Juste?*, 143, for other criticisms on Rolland's structure.

[5] Aletti insists that there are three "*sub-propositio*"s in each subdivision (9:6a for 9:6-29; 10:4 for 9:30-10:21; and 11:1a for 11:1-32) (*Comment Dieu est-il Juste?*, 146-150). It is quite abnormal, however, for a Greco-Roman rhetor to pose several "*sub-propositio*"s in his argumentation. Further, as far as the present writer is aware, there is no such term as "*sub-propositio*" in the rhetorical handbooks.

The second argument (9:30-10:21) clearly has a different invention, moving from refutation to confirmation. Paul, then, comes back to 11:1-32 to conclusively argue his point less defensively but more aggressively than in 9:6b-29. Thus, the three arguments roughly form a pattern of chiasm: A-B-A'.[7] Each argument in turn has three sections. The movement of Paul's argumentation is organized to argue for the proposition that he advances from different perspectives with different rhetorical strategies. It has long been assumed that Paul's statements between Rom 9 and 11 have contradictory elements.[8] I would like to submit that it is a misunderstanding of modern scholars who do not take account of Paul's rhetorical strategy properly. All three arguments of Paul (9:6b-29; 9:30-10:21; and 11:1-32) are composed from different points of view and different strategies. Most interpreters who perceive contradictions concentrate on Paul's attitude toward the Jews.[9] Paul's attitude toward his kinsfolk is, however, also consistent in my view from the *exordium* to the *peroratio*.[10] We will support these sugges-

---

[6] The table is adapted from Alleti's diagram in Ibid., 144. His diagram includes parallels from 9:1-5 and 11:33-36, which form an *inclusio* by themselves. The omitted items are "the glory" (9:4; 11:36) and "forever. Amen" (9:5; 11:36).

[7] Aletti, *Comment Dieu est-il Juste?*, 145; Hübner, *Biblische Theologie*, 256 (although he specifies that 11:1-10 forms the latter part of the pattern).

[8] See the succinct survey in Räisänen, "Romans 9-11," 192-96.

[9] Mary Ann Getty, "Paul and the Salvation of Israel: A Perspective on Romans 9-11," *CBQ* 50 (1988): 465, rightly points out that such contradictions are mistakenly perceived when the scholars understand 9:6b ("Not all Israel is Israel") as the thesis of Rom 9-11 instead of 9:6a.

[10] The recent attempt of Charles Cosgrove, "Rhetorical Suspense in Romans 9-11: A Study in Polyvalence and Hermeneutical Election," *JBL* 115 (1996): 271-287, also tries to solve the tension from a rhetorical point of view but his assumption is still that Paul is contradictory in his attitudes toward Israel (see also his monograph, *Elusive Israel: The Puzzle of Election in Romans* [Louisville: Westminster John Knox, 1997]). Cosgrove argues that Paul uses rhetorical devices called *communicatio* and *sustentatio* in order to invite his readers to join him in the deliberation of the fate of Israel ("co-deliberation"). Above all, it is doubted whether Paul used the *communicatio* in 11:11-32 since Paul strongly denies the charge whether Israel permanently fell and disqualified herself in salvation with μὴ γένοιτο in 11:11. There is no more room to deliberate about the fate of Israel in Paul's language—they will be definitely saved. What puzzles me is Cosgrove's statement, "[s]tanding in the place of the implied readers of 11.11ff., we too must choose what we want the destiny of Paul's kinfolk to be." His reasoning is that the original audience of Romans might have had a chance to ask Paul about the subject, but we modern readers were put into perpetual "*communicatio*" which becomes a trope of hermeneutical situation. In other words, since what Paul argues is just obscure and not logical that we can conclude with any certain interpretation, we just have to wonder what it means. Furthermore, he says, "Paul himself encourages us

tions as we examine the contents of each argument after a brief discussion on the species of Rom 9-11.

II. THE RHETORICAL SPECIES OF ROM 9-11[11]

Regarding the rhetorical species[12] of Romans as a whole, there have been different suggestions over the years: epideictic,[13] deliberative,[14] protreptic,[15] or apologetic.[16] A portion of Romans such as 1:18-3:20 has been designated as forensic rhetoric[17] but it is surprising to see that there has been hardly any suggestion regarding the species of Rom 9-11 even though it has long been recognized as an independent section

---

to do just that." Since Cosgrove cannot resolve the hermeneutical tension between Rom 9 and 11, or he believes that Paul intentionally does not provide any clear answer about the fate of carnal Israel, we must decide what that fate should be. Paul's prophetic rhetoric in 11:25-26, however, simply does not allow this kind of reasoning: Paul already received "mystery" concerning the fate of Israel from God. Why should we decide what God had already decided? Furthermore, is there really an unresolved tension between Rom 9 and 11? His position is in line with those interpreters who cannot see any logical coherence between Rom 9 and 11 on the subject of Israel. However, as we have already seen, the main subject of these chapters is not really about Israel but God. Contrary to Cosgrove's strong dispute, his reasoning still resides in the circle which concerns the *Israelfrage* exclusively in Rom 9 and 11.

[11] The discussion of the rhetorical species before engaging detailed rhetorical analysis is to respond positively to Margaret Mitchell's caveat that "the designation of the rhetorical species of a text... cannot be begged in the analysis" (*Paul and the Rhetoric*, 6, 11-13).

[12] For a succinct summary of the issues involving the classification of species of ancient rhetoric, see George A. Kennedy, "The Genres of Rhetoric," in *Handbook of Classical Rhetoric*, 43-50.

[13] Kennedy, *New Testament Interpretation*, 152; Reid, "Paul's Rhetoric of Mutuality," 117-39.

[14] Wuellner, "Paul's Rhetoric of Argumentation," 330-51; Jewett, "Following the Argument of Romans," 265-77; Aletti, "La présence," 1-24.

[15] *Logos Protreptikos* (speech of exhortation) is a kind of deliberative rhetoric. Klaus Berger, *Formgeschichte des neuen Testament* (Heidelberg: Quelle & Meyer, 1984), 217; idem, "Hellenistic Gattungen im Neuen Testament," *ANRW* 2.25 (1984): 1140; Stowers, *Letter Writing*, 114; Aune, "Romans," 91-121; Guerra, *Romans and the Apologetic Tradition*, 8-22.

[16] Therefore a kind of judicial rhetoric. F. Vouga, "Römer 1,18-3,20 als *narratio*," *TGl* 77 (1987): 225-36.

[17] J.-N. Aletti, "Rm 1,18-3,20: Incohérence ou cohérence de l'argumentation paulinienne?," *Bib* 69 (1988): 47-62.

within the structure of Romans.[18] Apart from specific designation of its
species, there have been several suggestions regarding its characteristics as "defense."[19] When I consider overall rhetorical features of Rom
9-11, I am convinced that it is best described as forensic rhetoric.

Historically, the designation of rhetorical species was first made
by Aristotle,[20] and has been canonized throughout the centuries.[21] Judicial or forensic rhetoric[22] is a rhetoric used mainly in the courtroom
and it is true that the rhetorical handbooks pay most attention to it since
it was the dominant form of rhetoric in the Hellenistic period.[23] It simply concerns "the bringing and rebutting of charges,"[24] while its time
reference is the past, for it argues for defense or accusation of the actions in the past.[25] The purpose of forensic rhetoric is to establish "the
justice or injustice of some action"[26] or the person involved. Compared
to deliberative or epideictic rhetoric, forensic rhetoric is most argumentative since it should persuade the judge to make a judgment that af-
fects the business of other people.[27] In the courtroom setting, the use of
stasis is the most powerful tool since it can be used to clarify the main

---

[18] B. Fiore's designation of Rom 9-11 as forensic rhetoric is a rare exception. See "Romans 9-11 and Classical Forensic Rhetoric," *Proceedings of the
Eastern Great Lakes and Midwest Biblical Societies* 8 (1988): 117-26. Although
his analysis is very sketchy and does not use proper terminology (e.g., *stasis*), it
roughly corresponds to my own, especially on Rom 9.

[19] Piper, *Justification of God,* 15 (although he means 9:1-23 only); Guerra,
Romans and the Apologetic Tradition, 144-56; Moo, *Romans,* 547-554; Käsemann,
Romans, 257, recognizes "the forensic situation" in 9:1-5 but whether he reads the
whole Rom 9-11 as a forensic defense is doubtful.

[20] Ar. *Rhet.* 1.3.3.

[21] See *Ad. Her.* 1.2.2; Dion. Hal. *Lys.* 16; Cic. *Inv.* 1.5.7; Ar. *Top.* 23.91;
Quint. 2.21.23; 3.3-4; Aristid. *Rhetoric.* 2.502; Lausberg, *Handbook,* §§ 53-65;
Martin, *Antike Rhetorik,* 9-10, 15-210. Also see the historical survey in George A.
Kennedy, *The Art of Rhetoric in the Ancient World: 300 B.C. - A.D. 300* (Prince-
ton: Princeton University Press, 1972), 7-23.

[22] Δικανικόν (Ar. *Rhet.* 1.3.1358b.3; *Rhet. Ad Alex.* 1.1421b.7-8);
δίκαι (Ar. *Rhet.* 1.3.1359a.9); *iudicialis* (Cic. *Inv.* 1.5.7; *Top.* 24.91; *Ad. Her.* 1.2.2;
Quint. 3.3.14; 3.4.15). For further discussion, see Ar. *Rhet.* 1.10-15; *Rhet. Ad Alex.*
4, 36; Cic. *Inv.* 2.4.14-51.154; *Part. Or.* 4.14-5.15; 28-37; *Top.* 24.92-26.96; Quint.
3.9; Lausberg, *Handbook,* §§ 140-223; Martin, *Antike Rhetorik,* 15-166; Kennedy,
Roman World, 7-18.

[23] D. A. Russell and N. G. Wilson, ed. and trans., *Menander Rhetor* (Oxford: Clarendon, 1981), xxii; Mitchell, *Paul and the Rhetoric,* 9.

[24] Quint. 3.9.1.

[25] Ar. *Rhet.* 1.1358b.4; 2.18.1392a.5; Cic. *Part. Or.* 20.69.

[26] Ar. *Rhet.* 1.1358b.5; Cic. *Inv.* 2.4.12; 2.51.155-56; *Top.* 24.91.

[27] Ar. *Rhet.* 1.1354b.

issue in question (ζήτημα) to elicit the judgment (κρινόμενον) from the judge or the jury.[28]

As we will see in our analysis, Rom 9-11 exhibits the characteristics of forensic rhetoric predominantly. Paul's use of oath in 9:1-5 coupled with heavy usage of *stasis* theory throughout the rhetorical unit points us to think in that direction. As we have seen in the previous chapter, the exigence or the main point at issue (ζήτημα) is God's actions in the past:[29] whether his word had failed. The charges that are brought against God have resulted from actions by the people of God, namely Israel's failure to accept Jesus as the Messiah. The purpose of Paul's rhetoric is to defend God against these charges by refuting them and proving that God's word has not failed and therefore God is trustworthy. Now let us examine our passage from the beginning.

III. *EXORDIUM:*[30] 9:1-5

In the previous chapter, we observed that Paul's tone turns very personal as he begins this new rhetorical unit. Paul's solemn avowal not only sets the tone of the next three chapters but also introduces the subject matter which he will vehemently argue with full force. Paul's assertion that he is speaking the truth in Christ, with his conscience bearing witness (συμμαρτυρούσης[31]) in the Holy Spirit for his reliability, naturally leads his audience into the court of the law. Then Paul immediately follows this legal tone with an emotional statement, demonstrating his sophisticated use of rhetoric. That is, he skillfully establishes his *ethos* as a reliable litigator as well as appealing emotionally (*pathos*)[32] to his audience. Paul's identification of himself with his kinsfolk strikingly reminds one of Quintilian's teachings:

> ... when we desire to awaken pity, we must actually believe that the ills of which we complain have befallen our own selves... We must identify ourselves with the persons of whom we complain that they

---

[28] See chapter 1.

[29] Of course, Paul deals with future salvation of "all Israel" in Rom 11 but that is a part of the conclusion of his defense of God's past actions and therefore it does not persuade us to think it is an instance of deliberative rhetoric.

[30] For the discussion of function and use of *exordium*, see pp. 81-4.

[31] Συμμαρτυρέω is a legal term used in the court of the law (LSJ, *s.v.*).

[32] Paul's use of *pathos* is well explained by Schlier, *Römerbrief,* 284-86 and Siegert, *Argumentation bei Paulus,* 120-21.

> have suffered grievous, unmerited and bitter misfortune, and must
> plead their case and for a brief space feel their suffering as though it
> were our own...[33]

The use of emotional appeal is especially emphasized by Quintilian in forensic rhetoric because "it is this emotional power that dominates the court, it is this form of eloquence that is the queen of all."[34] Also, the sudden change of tone and mood powerfully captures the attention of the audience, as observed in chapter 4. Paul, with ultimate seriousness, introduces the problem that makes even him wish to separate himself from the love of God (cf. 8:39). This is indeed a paradoxical statement considering the passionate and rousing conclusion he just uttered in 8:31-39. Yet the serious and solemn tone of this section reveals that he is not merely playing with words. The description of his kinsfolk Israel's privileges in 9:4-5 immediately reminds his audience of the original holders of privileges the believers in Christ now have, and that he just affirmed in 8:15-33: the Israelites.[35] For example, "adoption" is mentioned by Paul in 8:15, signifying the believers' intimate privilege to call God "Abba! Father!" Later in 8:23, "adoption" is likened to the eschatological redemption of the body. Paul reminds his audience that these tremendous privileges originally belonged to the Israelites before they belonged to believers in general.[36] Similarly, the term "glory" has already been repeated twice in 8:18 and 21 (also "glorified" in 8:30). The "glory" which was lost with Adam (3:23) can only be restored through Christ (5:2), but the promise of glory still belongs to the Israel-

---

[33] Quint. 6.2.34.

[34] Ibid., 6.2.4. He also says that appealing to emotions is more powerful than arguing from proofs: "Proofs... may induce the judges to regard our case as superior to that of our opponent, but *the appeal to the emotions will do more*, for it will make them wish our case to be the better" (6.2.5; my emphasis).

[35] Scholars are divided whether these privileges still belong to the Jews (present) or belonged to them (past). The sentence is, however, clearly present ("οἵτινές εἰσιν Ἰσραηλῖται," 9:4) (so Fitzmyer, *Romans*, 545; Dunn, *Theology of Paul*, 503; Räisänen, "Romans 9-11," 181; Piper, *Justification of God*, 8; F. Mussner, *Traktat über die Juden* [Munich: Kaiser, 1979], 46-7; B. Klappert, "Traktat für Israel [Römer 9-11]," in *Jüdische Existenz und die Erneuerung der christlichen Theologie*, Abhandlungen zum christlich-jüdischen Dialog 11, ed. M. Stöhr [Munich: Kaiser, 1981], 73). *Contra* Munck, *Christ and Israel*, 31-2.

[36] Dunn points out that Paul's use and repetition of the term υἱοθεσία is surprising because the underlying thought that Israel is chosen to be God's sons is strikingly Jewish (*Theology of Paul*, 503).

ites because Israel has priority in God's purpose of salvation.[37] Therefore, it is evident that Paul uses a rhetorical device called *exuscitatio,*
which can be defined as "emotional utterance that seeks to move hearers to a like feeling."[38] Paul leads his Gentile audience to identify
themselves with the situation of the Israelites by emotionally showing
them that the Israelites are the original recipients of these privileges.[39]
In short, the problem of Israel is not completely foreign to the audience—they can be in the same situation at any moment.[40] In the following sentence, however, Paul abruptly shows that the problem of Israel's unbelief is none other than the problem of God himself, the
trustworthiness of his word (9:6a).

IV. *PROPOSITIO:*[41] 9:6A

In a forensic rhetoric, the *exordium* is usually followed by *narratio,*[42] which sets forth "the nature of the case in dispute"[43] by reporting

---

[37] Dunn, *Romans 9-16,* 533-4; Hübner, *Biblische Theologie,* 252. Ulrich
Luz finds much common vocabulary that Paul uses in Rom 1-8 and 9-11 such as
ἀδικία, δικαιοσύνη θεοῦ, δόξα, ἐκλογή, ἐπαγγελία, and ἐπίγνωσις (for a complete list, see his *Das Geschichtsverständnis des Paulus,* BevT 49 [München: Verlag, 1968], 20). Judith M. Gundry-Volf, *Paul and Perseverance: Staying and Falling Away,* WUNT 2/37 (Tübingen: Mohr, 1990), 161-62, also points out that there
are common motifs and the terminology in 8:14-39 and 9:4-13 (sonship, glory, calling, election, divine predestination, and divine love).

[38] Lanham, *Handlist,* 77.

[39] Elliott, *Rhetoric of Romans,* 262-3:
[t]he echoes of 8.17-39 in 9.1-5 suggest that Paul is less concerned
to bolster a Gentile-Christian audience's estimate of *their own* salvation-historical status, than to invite them to share his profound and
anxious compassion *for the Jews* who have not yet embraced the ful-
fillment of what is properly *their* destiny (author's emphasis).

[40] Cf. Wright, "Romans and the Theology of Paul," 59. Wright sees that
"the whole apparently negative emphasis of Romans 9 and 10 is to be read as an
appeal for a *sympathetic understanding,* on the part of the Gentile church in Rome,
of the plight of the Jews" (my emphasis). I think, however, what Paul wants to
achieve in this section is more than simply to espouse "a sympathetic understanding" but to let his audience know that the plight of the Jews can be their own at any
time, which is precisely the underlying question that the argument of Paul refutes in
Rom 9-11.

[41] For discussions on *propositio* (πρόθεσις in Aristotle's term, see Ar. *Rhet.*
3.13, 1414b, 9), see *Ad. Her.* 1.10.17; Cic. *Inv.* 1.22.31-23.33; Quint. 3.9.2-5, 4.2.7,
4.2.30, 4.4.1-5.28; and Lausberg, *Handbook,* §§ 262, 289.

the events that have occurred or might have occurred.[44] In Rom 9-11, the *narratio* is missing. Paul's blunt statement in 9:6a shows his assumption that the audience understands "the nature of the case in dispute." It also reveals his rhetorical strategy with the sudden stating of the proposition and movement into the main argument. Paul could omit the *narratio* since the juxtaposition of 8:31-39 with 9:1-5 amply indicates the nature of the problem:[45] if the Israelites are not saved because of their rejection of Christ, then what kind of God does the audience trust?[46]

In his discussion of the form of *propositio,* Cicero states that it should have three qualities: brevity, completeness, and conciseness.[47] Since its function is to make clear the point in dispute, what Cicero teaches makes sense. What Paul states in 9:6a certainly has these qualities: it states the point in dispute briefly, completely, and concisely. Further, the sentence, Οὐχ οἷον δὲ ὅτι ἐκπέπτωκεν ὁ λόγος τοῦ θεοῦ, introduces God as a defendant in a court of law with Paul as defense lawyer and the Gentiles as prosecutors who also need to make κρινόμενον.[48] Certainly, Paul poses this sentence as a denial of the charge that the word of God had failed. Now Paul's defense begins by dealing with the definition of the term "Israel."

---

[42] Quntilian divides the forensic speech into five parts: the *exordium,* the *statement of facts* (*narratio*), the *proof* (*probatio*), the *refutation* (*refutatio*), and the *peroration* (Quint. 3.9.1). See also ibid., 4.2.31-3.1. For a comprehensive view of divisions by various rhetorical theoreticians, see a convenient chart in Lausberg, *Handbook,* 122-3.

[43] Quint. 4.2.31.

[44] *Ad. Her.* 1.3.4.

[45] Cf. Fiore, "Romans 9-11," 119-20. It is probable that Paul did not want to put the problem in words since the possibility of failure of God's word is already on the border of blasphemy. John Calvin's description of Paul's dilemma is pertinent: "Entweder ist die Wahrheit der göttlichen Verheißung fraglich, oder Jesus, den Paulus predigte, ist nicht der Messias der Herrn" (*Iohannis Calvini commentarius in epistolam Pauli ad Romanos,* ed. T.H.L. Parker [Leiden : E. J. Brill, 1981], 115; cited by Siegert, *Argumentation bei Paulus,* 121).

[46] Hübner, *Gottes Ich,* 15.

[47] Cic. *Inv.* 1.22.32. Cicero's term is *partitio,* which is equivalent to *propositio.*

[48] Fiore, "Romans 9-11," 124, concurs that it is the Gentiles who are prosecuting the case because they "are concerned about the reliability of the promises made to them on the basis of their faith commitment." I am also tempted to say that the Jews are in the position of the jury or the judge but that may be too far-fetched.

V. *PROBATIO*:[49] 9:6B-11:32

Argument I: 9:6b-9:29

In this first argument, Paul uses the *stasis* theory extensively to prove his point.[50] He uses three different *stases* in his argument, namely, *stasis* of Definition, *stasis* of Counterplea, and *stasis* of Objection.

I.1: Who is Israel? (9:6b-13). The first argument that Paul advances in support of his thesis concerns the definition of Israel. The *stasis* of Definition (*constitutio definitiva or propritas,* ὅρος) arises when the definition of a fact is called into question. We can reconstruct Paul's argument with his opponent in the following way:

P(rosecution): God is not trustworthy since his word to Israel has failed.

D(efense): God's word has not failed.

P: But Israel has been deserted.

D: Israel has not been deserted "because not all from Israel are Israel (οὐ γὰρ πάντες οἱ ἐξ Ἰσραήλ οὗτοι Ἰσραήλ)" (9:6b).

---

[49] For discussions on *probatio=argumentatio* (πίστις in Ar. *Rhet.* 3.13.4), see *Ad. Her.* 1.10.18-2.29.46; Cic. *Inv.* 1.24.34-51.97; Quint. 5; and Lausberg, *Handbook,* §§ 348-9.

[50] This is not to say that we should look at the argument of Paul only in terms of Greco-Roman rhetorical theories. That Paul uses midrashic method in his argumentation cannot be denied. Indeed, I believe that understanding this holds an important key to understanding Paul's argumentation (see, esp., William R. Stegner, "Romans 9.6-29—A Midrash," *JSNT* 22 [1984]: 37-52 and James W. Aageson, "Scripture and Structure in the Development of the Argument in Romans 9-11," *CBQ* 48 [1986]: 265-89). Paul's use of scripture in Rom 9-11 has been the subject of numerous studies, most notably Hübner, *Gottes Ich und Israel,* Koch, *Schrift als Zeuge,* and Hays, *Echoes of Scripture,* 63-83. One lamentably ignored aspect of Paul's use of scripture in terms of its rhetorical function in his argument has now been taken up by Christopher D. Stanley, "Biblical Quotations as Rhetorical Devices in Paul's Letter to the Galatians," in *SBL 1998 Seminar Papers* (Atlanta: Scholars, 1998), 700-30. See also his discussion on methodology in idem, "The Rhetoric of Quotations: An Essay on Method," *Early Christian Interpretation of the Scriptures of Israel: Investigation and Proposals,* eds. Craig A. Evans and James A. Sanders (Sheffield: Sheffield Academic, 1997), 44-58. He reports that he is working on a book-length study on the subject in which we hope he will deal with the rhetorical function of Paul's quotations in Rom 9-11.

Paul's denial points out that the name Israel has been misunderstood and thus a charge based on such a misunderstanding is not valid. Who, then, is Israel according to Paul's definition? I believe the key word to understanding Paul's argument not only in 9:6b-13 but also 9:14-29 is the word καλεῖν (9:7, 12, 24, 25, 26).[51] The calling of God is the determining factor in who Israel is. Paul refutes the definition of Israel by physical descent first in 9:7-9: not all of Abraham's children are his "seed" (σπέρμα); this status is determined by God's calling in Isaac (Gen 21:12). Not the children of the flesh (τὰ τέκνα τῆς σαρκὸς) but the children of promise (τῆς ἐπαγγελίας) are the children of God. Paul goes on to refute another definition of Israel by election in 9:10-13: election is determined by God's calling and not by works (οὐκ ἐξ ἔργων ἀλλ᾽ ἐκ τοῦ καλοῦντος) (9:12).[52] Therefore, the definition of Israel should be determined by none other than God's calling; any other definition of Israel is wrong. The trustworthiness of God's word cannot be questioned by an allegation based on a faulty definition of Israel.

   I.2: The justice of God in question (9:14-18). Paul now moves on to refute another charge alleged of God. He uses the *stasis* of Counterplea (Justification; ἀντίληψις), a sub-*stasis* of *stasis* of Quality (*constitutio qualitas* or *generalis*, ποιότης). Through this *stasis* the lawyer claims that what the defendant committed was actually necessary and honorable, and thus justified. Again, we reconstruct the courtroom proceeding in the following manner:

> P: What God has done is not just because God made God's choice without any consideration on the part of human beings.
> D: There is no injustice on God's part because God has freedom to choose whomever he wishes; and moreover, the result of his actions is mercy upon all.

---

[51] Hübner, *Biblische Theologie*, 253: "*Berufen, καλεῖν,* ist das dominante theologische Wort aus *Röm 9,6-29*" (author's emphasis); Dunn, *Theology of Paul*, 510.
[52] I understand the term ἐξ ἔργων as the abbreviated form of ἐξ ἔργων νόμου (*contra* Hübner, *Gottes Ich und Israel*, 25) to mean the badges of Israel's ethnic privileges. See further, Michael Cranford, "Election and Ethnicity: Paul's View of Israel in Romans 9.1-13," *JSNT* 50 (1993): 39-40; Dunn, *Romans 9-16*, 549.

The accusation that God is not just is caused by Paul's assertion that God's call determines who is to be loved and to be hated without any consideration of their actions. Paul argues that the quality of God's act is not something that can be debated because God has freedom to do whatever God wills. We should, however, pay close attention to the context of Paul's two quotations from Exodus: "I will have mercy on whom I will have mercy and will have compassion on whom I have compassion" (33:19) and "For this purpose have I raised you up, for the very purpose of showing my power in you, so that my name may be proclaimed in all the earth" (9:16). These two texts are closely related to God's name (ὄνομα) since the context of Exod 33 is where God's name is proclaimed or God's glory is manifested by showing "his propensity to show mercy and his sovereign freedom in its distribution."[53] These texts demonstrate God's sovereign freedom, whether in mercy or hardening, by preserving and displaying the glory of God's name.[54] The overwhelming focus, however, is on God's mercy in God's freedom—when God calls, God's calling is designed to have mercy and compassion. Even the "hardening" has his divine purpose to save more, as the audience will find out later (11:25). Thus, God's actions cannot be accused of being unjust because they are actually honorable. Paul's assertion that God has sovereign freedom leads the prosecutor to another accusation in the following verses.

I.3: The Sovereignty of God (9:19-29). In this argument, Paul allows the prosecution to speak for itself: "Why then does he still find fault? For who can resist his will?" Against this accusation, Paul employs the last class of *stasis*, the *stasis* of Objection (*constitutio translatio*, μετάληψις). Through this *stasis*, Paul refutes the claim by pointing out an illegitimacy in the legal proceeding. The argument can be reconstructed as follows:

P: How can God still find fault in human actions when nobody can resist God's will?
D: You cannot accuse God this way because you are God's creatures.

---

[53] Piper, *The Justification of God,* 88, 100 (quotation).
[54] Christian Müller, *Gottes Gerechtigkeit und Gottes Volk: Eine Untersuchung zu Römer 9-11*, FRLANT 86 (Göttingen: Vandenhoeck & Ruprecht, 1964), 31; cf. Dahl, "The Future of Israel," 144.

Paul shows that human beings do not possess the legal right to argue with God simply because God is their creator. Paul's use of vocative, ὦ ἄνθρωπε, highlights the unworthiness of the accuser and the potter-clay analogy underscores this (9:21-22).[55] Thus the charge is dismissed on the basis of legal incompetence. Paul's argument sounds very dogmatic and does not offer any elaboration.[56] Indeed, the *stasis* of Objection was the last resort that a lawyer could use and it was not popular among the rhetorical educators.[57] Paul's bluntness is balanced in the following verses when he emphasizes the ultimate purpose of God's sovereign act as "mercy." Dunn hits the mark when he says: "Paul did not hesitate to state forthrightly the sovereign right of God over his creation, for he was confident that the ultimate purpose of God was that of mercy."[58] Paul also makes an important point by identifying the "vessels of mercy" as not only including Jews but also Gentiles (9:24). Paul proves this by quoting several Old Testament verses: "Those who were not my people I will call 'my people,' and her who was not beloved I will call 'beloved.' And in the very place where it was said to them, 'You are not my people,' there they shall be called children of the living God" (Hos 2:23; 1:10). Again, Paul quotes from Isaiah: "Though the number of children of Israel were like the sand of the sea, only a remnant of them will be saved." Thus, the "vessels of mercy" includes both historic Israel and Gentiles: "the redefinition of Israel in terms of divine call does not mean a disowning of historic Israel, but simply a reminder of the character of historic Israel's call to be Israel."[59] Paul argues that all of this has been done according to God's word—therefore, God's word has not failed.

It is interesting to note that Paul's first argument proceeds by using three different *stases*, in the order of defensibility specified by Quintilian and others.[60] He begins with *stasis* of Definition, then Quality (Counterplea), and then Objection to complete his argument. Surely it is no accident that Paul's use of *stasis* is organized this way. Certainly, there is Paul's intention to show that he can defend the infallibility of God's word from different accusations.

---

[55] Fiore, "Romans 9-11," 121.

[56] Dahl, "Future of Israel," 144: "Paul's reply does not even attempt a rational explanation. It simply recalls that God is God and man is a sinner who has no right to make complaints against his Creator."

[57] See chapter 1.

[58] Dunn, *Theology of Paul*, 513.

[59] Ibid., 514.

[60] See the table in chapter 4.

Argument II: 9:30-10:21

The second argument of Paul takes a different tack and shifts from legal refutation to a more expository argument (*confirmatio*[61]). This has led some commentators to think that Paul's argument in 9:30-10:21 is a sort of digression: "9:30-10:21 ought to be studied as an independent section, which... must nevertheless be interpreted on its own merits."[62] Munck notes that 11:1 clearly resumes "the thread of 9:29" but that 9:30-10:21 is "not some incidental parenthesis, but a necessary and basic explanation."[63] Dahl agrees with Munck on this point although he does not agree with his exegesis:

> it is important to recognize that Romans 10 is not a part of Paul's answer to the question of whether or not God had repudiated his promises to Israel. The chapter is a delayed explanation of the factors which caused him to raise that question. From 10:4 onward Paul digresses from his main line of argumentation, though at the conclusion of the section he returns to it. At the end of chapter 10 Paul repeats the same point he made at the end of chapter 9: the Gentiles have found the God they did not seek, while Israel has proven to be a disobedient and recalcitrant people.[64]

It is incorrect, however, to say that Paul digresses from his main point of argument in this passage; rather, he is dealing with the same problem from a different angle. Paul had been arguing from God's perspective in 9:6b-29 but here he shifts to a human perspective.[65] He is still answering the charge that God's word has failed in this section, only now in a different way.[66] Furthermore, by employing *confirmatio* Paul is trying to buttress his refutation in the previous sections before proceeding to his next refutation. Especially in 9:30-10:13, Paul employs *dia-*

---

[61] *Confirmatio* is a sub-division of *probatio*, which is used to demonstrate the correctness of one's own view. Cic. *Inv.* 1.24: "Confirmation [*confirmatio*]... is the part of the oration which by marshalling arguments lends credit, authority, and support to our case." See also Lausberg, *Handbook,* §§ 348, 430.

[62] Munck, *Christ and Israel,* 90.

[63] Ibid.

[64] Dahl, "The Future of Israel," 148.

[65] Cf. Hübner, *Biblische Theologie,* 254:
Paulus argumentiert in der Israelfrage weiter, *Röm 9,30-10,21*- nur freilich jetzt auf einer anderen Ebene, nämlich auf der *Ebene des menschlichen Sich-Verhaltens.* Auf den ersten Blick wirkt *Röm 9,30-10,21* als eklatanter Widerspruch zu 9,6-29 (author's emphasis).

[66] Cf. Wright, *The Climax of the Covenant,* 239-40.

tribe extensively, using questions in a different way from the previous sections.[67] The tone is strikingly that of teaching, confirming the observations made by Stanley Stowers in his book, *The Diatribe and Paul's Letter to the Romans*[68] that the *diatribe* was a teaching tool that was used to instruct the believers.[69]

II.1: Christ the end of the law (9:30-10:4). Paul starts this section with a *narratio,* which states the current situation of Israel and the Gentiles (9:30-33). This *narratio,* whose earlier absence was discussed in the previous section, succinctly summarizes the problem that causes the "great sorrow and unceasing anguish" in the apostle's heart (9:2):[70] Gentiles attained righteousness but Israel did not. The reason is that Israel pursues righteousness "not by faithfulness but as if by works" (οὐκ ἐκ πίστεως ἀλλ᾽ ὡς ἐξ ἔργων). In other words, they pursue it based not on Christ's faithfulness but on their ethnic privileges.[71] Indeed, Christ became a stumbling stone for them.[72] In this section, Paul

---

[67] The way Paul uses questions in 9:14 and 9:19 (in the form of the opponent's response) is certainly different from his uses in 9:30, 32, and 10:8. The former usage is followed by refutations whereas the latter ones are followed by explanations. Paul's use of questions is important to detect his argumentative strategy but it should be recognized that he uses them in a variety of ways. Elizabeth Johnson's argument ("Romans 9-11," 216-7) that the rhetorical questions in Rom 9-11 hold the key to the structure of the passage is basically correct but she fails to detect different usage of these questions by Paul. Furthermore, without considering Paul's rhetorical strategy in using different forms of argument, she is simply blinded from seeing how Paul proceeds with his argument and therefore her analysis of Paul's structure is unsatisfactory. Cf. also Moo's criticism of her structure from a different angle in his "The Theology of Romans 9-11: A Response to E. Elizabeth Johnson," in *Pauline Theology III: Romans,* 242-3. Moo is equally blinded from seeing Paul's *inventio* correctly.

[68] SBLDS 57 (Chico: Scholars, 1981).

[69] Ibid., 175-83.

[70] Cf. Meyer, *Romans,* 1157: "Now for the first time Paul's readers get a clear glimpse of the reason for his pain in 9:2."

[71] For interpretation of ἐκ πίστεως as Christ's faithfulness, see Stowers, *Rereading of Romans,* 303. See also idem, "ΕΚ ΠΙΣΤΕΩΣ and ΔΙΑ ΠΙΣΤΕΩΣ in Romans 3:30," *JBL* 108 (1989): 665-74.

[72] The identification of the "stone" has been debated extensively over the years. Paul Meyer's identification of it as "Torah" ("Romans 10:4 and the End of the Law," in *The Divine Helmsman: Studies on God's Control of Human Events, Presented to Lou H. Silberman,* ed. James L. Crenshaw and Samuel Sandmel [New York: KTAV, 1980], 59-64; he later changed his position and asserts instead that it should denote God himself [*Romans,* 1157]) challenged the traditional reading of it as "Christ." Still the traditional reading has its strong support from the usual early Christian tradition of interpreting the "stone" of Isa 28:16 and 8:14 in conjuction

uses the imagery of a footrace with words like διώκω ("run"),
φθάνω ("reach"), καταλαμβάνω ("attain"), and τέλος ("goal").[73] Israel
as a runner in a footrace has stumbled over the stumbling stone.[74] The
use of such imagery or metaphor, what the rhetoricians call *trope*
(μεταφοά), is recommended by Quintilian when the rhetor needs "to
make [his] meaning clearer."[75] A *trope* is

> the transference of expressions from their natural meaning and prin-
> cipal signification to another, with a view to the embellishment of
> style or... the transference of words and phrases from the place
> which is strictly theirs to another to which they do not properly be-
> long.[76]

What Paul argues in this section should be understood in the light of his
use of *trope,* that is, the imagery of footrace; otherwise, as the history
of exegesis amply shows, we will arrive at a conclusion that was never
intended by the apostle.[77] Simply put, Israel did not reach the goal line
(τέλος) because they did not follow the rule of the race (οὐκ ἐκ
πίστεως ἀλλ' ὡς ἐξ ἔργων) and stumbled on the rock, even though they
had zeal for the race. The prize of the race, ἡ δικαιοσύνη has been

---

with Ps 117:22 LXX as "Christ" (so Steven Richard Bechtler, "Christ, the *Telos* of
the Law: The Goal of Romans 10:4," *CBQ* 56 [1994]: 295; E. P. Sanders, *Paul, the
Law, and the Jewish People* [Minneapolis: Fortress, 1983], 37 and 60-1, n. 98).
Yet I follow Meeks's position that we do not have to force a choice because Paul
does not seem to make a simple allegory or typology:

> ... Hays's comparison with the poetic trope "echo" or "metalepsis"
> is most helpful, for it suggests a range of connections and meanings
> within which a text may resound. Thus we need not choose whether
> it is Torah, Christ, or God himself that is signified in the verse about
> a rock that is both obstacle and reliable foundation, as if one ex-
> cluded the other ("On Trusting," 115).

[73] Paul uses the same vocabulary in Phil 3:12-16 (except τέλος) in the same
imagery of race (also, 1 Cor 9:24 has καταλαμβάνω) (Bechtler, "Romans 10:4,"
292, n. 15). Bechtler is wrong to think that τέλος in 10:4 does not carry on the rac-
ing imagery.

[74] Meyer, "Romans 10:4," 62; G. Stählin, "προσκόπτω, πρόσκομμα," *TDNT*
6.755, n. 57.

[75] Quint. 8.6.6.

[76] Examples of *trope* include: metaphor, metonymy, antonomasia, metalep-
sis, synecdoche, catachresis, allegory, and hyperbole. Quint. 9.1.4-5 (quotation
from 9.1.4). See further Cic. *De Or.,* 27, 92-93; Lausberg, *Handbook,* §§ 552-98;
Martin, *Antike Rhetorik,* 261-70.

[77] See Robert Badenas, *Christ the End of the Law: Romans 10.4 in Pauline
Perspective,* JSNTSup 10 (Sheffield: JSOT, 1985), 7-37 for a survey of various
conclusions.

won by Gentiles because they ran the race according to the rule (ἐκ πίστεως), even though they were not even trying to win it!

II.2: No distinction between Jew and Greek (10:5-13). Paul introduces this section with γάρ, which sets it as a scriptural warrant for what he argued in the previous section. Paul cites Lev 18:5 and Deut 9:4, 30:12-14 to contrast ἡ δικαιοσύνη ἐκ τοῦ νόμου (v. 5) with ἡ δικαιοσύνη ἐκ πίστεως (vv. 6-8). The first citation, "the person who does these things will live by them" does not indicate the necessity of complete obedience to the law, but "rather, primarily intended to indicate the way life should be lived by the covenant people."[78] The second citation is put in the mouth of ἡ δικαιοσύνη ἐκ πίστεως itself, a form of προσωποποιΐα.[79] Προσωποποιΐα is a rhetorical device, one of *fictio personae*, which is "the introduction of non-personal things as persons capable of speech and other forms of personified behavior."[80] It is a bolder form of *figure*, which can be used by a rhetor "to put words of advice, reproach, complaint, praise or pity into the mouths of appropriate persons" without sacrificing the rhetor's credibility.[81] In order to use this device, the rhetor should possess great powers of eloquence.[82] The effect of this device is powerful but the rhetor should be careful to use it because "either they will move our hearers with exceptional force ... or they will be regarded as empty nothings."[83] Here, "the righteousness from faithfulness" pronounces words of "reproach" from Deuteronomy (with Paul's explanatory glosses)[84] against the Jewish pursuit of righteousness, which is apart from Christ, and this is "symptomatic of Israel's exclusivistic understanding of its privilege as

---

[78] Dunn, *Theology of Paul*, 516.

[79] Anderson, Jr., *Ancient Rhetorical Theory*, 211; Stowers, *Rereading Romans*, 309.

[80] Lausberg, *Handbook*, § 826.

[81] Quint. 9.2.29-30.

[82] Ibid., 9.2.33.

[83] Ibid.

[84] The original version of Deut 30:11-14 LXX reads:

For this commandment which I command you today is not too excessive, nor far from you. It is not up in heaven saying, "Who will go up for us into heaven and get it for us; and having heard it we shall do it?" Neither is it across the sea saying, "Who will go across to the other side of the sea for us and get it for us; and he will make it audible to us and shall do it?" But the word is near you, in your mouth and in your heart and in your hands, so that you can do it (Dunn's translation, *Theology of Paul*, 516).

the people of God's covenant."[85] Paul's use of προσωποποιΐα here effectually put these words of reproach from Deuteronomy to the mouth of the personified "righteousness from faithfulness," thus dramatically stressing that what he is arguing is not from his own ideas but from the one who speaks through the Mosaic law. Again, from the larger argumentation of Paul in Rom 9-11, this passage also proves that God's word has not failed.

Now Paul moves on to expound his theology of salvation in 10:9-13. "The word about faithfulness" (τὸ ῥῆμα τῆς πίστεως) that Paul and his colleagues are preaching concerns the faithfulness of God shown in the Christ-event. The only thing that believers have to do to be saved is to confess that Jesus is Lord with their lips (because the word is near on their lips) and to trust[86] that God raised Christ from the dead with their hearts (because the word is near in their hearts).[87] Therefore, there is no distinction between Jew and Greek in salvation "for 'everyone who calls on the name of the Lord shall be saved'" (10:13). The idea of "calling on" (ἐπικαλέω) God should be contrasted to the idea of God's calling of Israel in chapter 9. It clearly shows that Paul is arguing from the perspective of human beings in 9:30-10:21. The call of God constitutes the true Israel; conversely, the people who call on the name of the Lord meet the Lord's requirement to become identified as Israel, without regard for ethnicity.[88]

II.3: Israel is responsible (10:14-21). In the third and last section of the second argument, Paul returns to use *stasis* once more, this time the *stasis* of Transference (μετάστασις), a sub-*stasis* of Quality. Let us examine how the argument proceeds. The argument begins with a series of four questions (vv. 14-15a), which forms the charge of the prosecutor. The third charge ("how are they to hear without someone to proclaim him?") and the fourth charge ("how are they to proclaim him unless they are sent?") are answered by Paul with a quotation from

---

[85] Bechtler, "Romans 10:4," 305.

[86] Gk. πιστεύειν. I understand this word to mean "trust" rather than conventional "believe" because of the context of this verse ("trust with heart" makes much better sense than "believe with heart") and the following quotation from Isa 28:16 ("No one who trusts in him will be put to shame") in v.11.

[87] I affirm Dunn's idea of relating "with the heart" to "trust" and "with the mouth" to "commitment" (*Theology of Paul*, 517).

[88] Cf. Dunn, *Theology of Paul*, 518: "God's openness in Christ to the "all who trust" corresponds to the definition of Israel in terms of God's call (9.7-13, 24-26). In the definition of Israel, the correlate to God's call is not ethnic distinctiveness or works, but faith in God's Christ."

Isa 52:7: "How beautiful are the feet of those who bring good news!"[89]
The second charge ("how are they to believe in one of whom they
never heard?") is answered by Paul in v.18 ("But I ask, have they
heard? Indeed they have; for 'Their voice has gone out to all the earth,
and their words to the ends of the world'"). Therefore, only one charge
remains: "how are they to call on one in whom they have not believed?" It is this first charge that is the source of the following three
charges. Paul's rhetorical strategy is to answer the charges moving
from the lesser to the greater ones. And his countercharge is found in
vv. 16-17, 19-21. In his rebuttal, Paul shows that God did everything
he could to reach out to the Israelites but it is they who did not hear and
trust him. We can reconstruct the argument in the following way:

> P: God is responsible for the Israelites' failure to call on him be-
> cause they have never heard him; nobody was sent to proclaim the
> good news to them; how can they trust the one whom they never
> heard?
> D: But they did hear the good news because God sent someone to
> proclaim him and their voice was heard even at the ends of the
> world. But not all obeyed the good news. And God even tried to
> make them jealous to make them call on him and even stretched
> out his hands to them. But they never listened. Therefore, God is
> not responsible but Israel is.

Therefore, the guilty one is not God but Israel. The charge is transferred to Israel. Paul raises a serious question concerning the character
of Israel in the course of this argument. When they heard (ἤκουσαν)
the message (ἡ ἀκοή), they did not trust (ἐπίστευσαν). They even understood the message (10:19) but they did not obey (ὑπήκουσαν).[90] On
the contrary, the portrait of God, the accused, in this passage is "a long-
suffering and persistent seeker of the well-being of the alleged victims."[91] Therefore, the charge that God is responsible for Israel's unbelief is thrown out and the alleged victims are instead found responsible
for their own situation.

    Paul's argumentation in 9:30-10:21 is not some kind of *digressio*
or excursus to the whole argument of Rom 9-11 but a powerful confir-

---

[89] Dodd, *Romans,* 169-70; so Fiore, "Romans 9-11," 122.

[90] Paul's play on words, ἀκούω, ἀκοή, ὑπακούω and πιστεύω is evident.
We already observed such wordplay in chapter 3 in the discussion of ὑπακοὴ
πίστεως.

[91] Fiore, "Romans 9-11," 123.

mation for the main thesis.[92] Paul continues to argue that God is trust-worthy because his word has not failed even in the case of Israel's stumbling and not reaching the goal line (yet); for the word of God has already established that there is no distinction between Jew and Greek for salvation; and Israel's stumbling is not God's fault but her own.

Argument III: 11:1-32

Paul's third argument differs in mood from the preceding argument in that it resumes a highly legal tone, but this time a much more aggressive tone than in the first argument. In a way, Paul sounds like a prosecutor himself, asking questions rather than answering questions. Thus, the use of *stasis* in this argument is different from the previous arguments. In this argument, Paul speaks to his audience more directly, challenging its members' positions.

III.1: God has not rejected his people (11:1-10). Paul begins this argument with a question expecting a negative answer. The charge is exactly the same charge that has been refuted, namely, whether God's word has failed (9:6a). The question is responded to by a strong μὴ γένοιτο.[93] Paul employs *stasis* of Conjecture (*constitutio coniecturalis*, στοχασμός) to deny the charge. The argument can be reconstructed in the following way:

P: God has rejected people.
D: By no means! God has not rejected his people.

Paul then gives examples,[94] the example of himself first and then the example of Elijah's seven thousand people who had not bowed the knee to Baal. Paul's point is simple: the proof that God has not rejected

---

[92] Cf. Meeks, "On Trusting," 113, who argues that 9:30-10:21 is "the centerpiece of [Paul's] argument in chaps. 9-11."

[93] For the use of this phrase in Paul and Epictetus, see Abraham Malherbe, "*Mê Genoito* in the Diatribe and Paul," *HTR* 73 (1980): 231-40.

[94] In Greco-Roman rhetorical theories, "example" is a part of *logos*, which is, in turn, part of proofs and is expressed in various names: i.e., παράδειγμα (Ar. *Rhet.* 1.2.1357a.13; 2.20.1393a.1; Quint. 5.11.1-2); *exemplum* (Cic. *Inv.* 1.30.49; Quint. 5.11.6). The author of *Rhet. Ad Alex.* defines examples (παραδείγματα) as "actions that have occurred previously and are similar to, or the opposite of, those which we are now discussing" (8.1429a.21). For full discussion, see Ar. *Rhet.* 2.20; *Rhet. Ad Alex.* 8; Cic. *Inv.* 1.30.49; Quint. 5.11; Lausberg, *Handbooks,* §§ 410-26; Martin, *Antike Rhetorik,* 119-24.

his people can be easily seen because he himself is an Israelite. The point of Elijah's example is that God has not rejected his people; even when it seemed that way, a remnant (λεῖμμα; 11:5)[95] is allowed to remain.[96]   This remnant is chosen by grace (χάρις) and not ἐξ ἔργων (11:6). Once again, Paul highlights the fact that God's election is by God's own initiative (cf. καλεῖν [9:7] and πίστις [9:32]) and not based on ethnic privileges.

    III.2: The purpose of Israel's stumbling (11:11-24). In this section, Paul again begins with a question expecting a negative answer and another μὴ γένοιτο follows. It is plain that he again employs the *stasis* of Conjecture and denies the charge. A reconstructed argument is as follows:

    P: Israel has stumbled so as to fall (permanently).
    D: By no means! She stumbled in order for the Gentiles to be saved, so as to make Israel jealous.

From 11:11, Paul unpacks his reasons why he believes that God's word has never failed with regard to his promises to Israel. The stumbling of Israel has its purposes and in the end all Israel will be saved. N. T. Wright writes that "11.1-10 raises, and answers, the question: can *any* Jews then be saved?... 11.11-24 then asks the consequent question: can any *more* Jews be saved?"[97] The answer is a resounding yes but the present unbelief of Israel has to be explained in terms of God's salvation plan. Paul explains by employing another *trope* of footrace. Paul's question in 11:11 reiterates his discussion of Israel's stumbling in 9:32-33 and asks a serious question: whether that stumbling (not pursuing righteousness according to the rule and thus falling behind the goal line) caused Israel to fall and lose in the race completely.[98] Paul's answer is no—Israel just stumbled but did not completely fall so they are still alive in the race. Through her stumbling, the Gentiles now have a chance to advance in the race but since their advance is seen by Israel, she will become jealous and zealous to run harder in the race. The meaning of παράπτωμα (v.12) should be understood not only in terms of footrace ("misstep") but also the theological meaning of

---

[95] Cf. ὑπόλειμμα in Rom 9:27.

[96] Aageson, "Scripture and Structure," 280.

[97] Wright, *Climax of the Covenant,* 247 (author's emphasis).

[98] Stowers, *Rereading Romans,* 312-3. Stowers points out that Isa 28:16 clearly says that it is God who laid the "stone of stumbling in Zion."

"transgression."[99] Israel's παράπτωμα serves as a springboard for the Gentiles to be saved but eventually God's purpose is to save Israel also. Paul's use of the *trope* of footrace with a comparison[100] between ἥτημμα ("defeat") and πλήρωμα ("completion") powerfully illustrates the purpose of Israel's stumble.[101] The implication of this imagery is that Israel's παράπτωμα is only temporary but she will soon catch up in the race toward the goal line. Thus, when Paul's direct address to his Gentile audience makes clear that his priority in his mission is for his own people,[102] it should not be surprising. In 11:15, Paul compares Israel's acceptance (πρόσλημψις) into the family of God to the resurrection of Christ.[103] Paul, then, employs other *tropes,* the imagery of "dough," "root," "branches," and "olive trees." The point of the "parabolic admonition"[104] is directed toward Gentile Christians that they should not look down on Jewish non-Christians ("branches broken off") but "be in awe" (φοβοῦ).[105]

III.3: All Israel will be saved (11:25-32). Paul's direct admonition toward his audience continues in v. 25: he will tell them a mystery so that they may not mistakenly think they are wise (φρόνιμοι).[106] Paul makes his final case toward the prosecutors concerning the reliability of God's word in dramatic terms.[107] The mystery of God's plan is that God reverses the *Heilsgeschichte* (cf. Rom 1:16) and lets the Gentiles believe in the gospel first until their full number comes in by partially hardening Israel (πώρωσις ἀπὸ μέρους τῷ Ἰσραὴλ). And in this manner (οὕτως) all Israel will be saved. Therefore, the content of "this mystery" is not so much that "all Israel" will be saved nor the harden-

---

[99] Ibid., 313: "The imagery of the footrace would have been unmistakable to the ancient reader. At the same time the 'misstep' of the race serves as a trope for 'transgression' against God's plan."

[100] For rhetorical use of comparison, see Ar. *Rhet.* 2.20.1393a.2; 1393b.4.

[101] Stowers argues that ἥτημμα does not denote the complete loss of a race or contest but "any sort of failure or mistake in a competition" in Greco-Roman literature (*Rereading Romans,* 314).

[102] For a detailed exegesis of 11:13-14, see chapter 4.

[103] Wright argues that Israel's behavior resembles Adam's sin and the pattern of Messiah (compare 5:12-21 with 11:11-12 and 5:10 with 11:15) (*Climax of the Covenant,* 247-8).

[104] Elliott's phrase, *Rhetoric of Romans,* 270.

[105] Wright, *Climax of the Covenant,* 248.

[106] There certainly is a clear echo of Paul's warning in 11:20— "μὴ ὑψηλὰ φρόνει" (so Dunn, *Romans 9-16,* 679).

[107] Aletti is correct to see that vv. 25-32 form the climax of Rom 9-11 (*Comment Dieu est-il juste?* 183).

ing motif[108] but the reason for the reversal of the salvation order and *how* all Israel will be saved.[109]   The identity of "all Israel" (πᾶς Ἰσραήλ) has been hotly debated[110] but it should be clearly understood to denote "historic, ethnic Israel,"[111] Israel as a whole, but "not as necessarily including every individual Israelite."[112] Paul envisions the whole generations of the Jews, including "the remnant" (11:5) and "the elect" (11:7) and "the rest" (11:7).[113] The salvation of all Israel will be reality with the coming of "the Deliverer out of Zion," which points to

---

[108] Beker, *Paul,* 334; Nanos, *The Mystery of Romans,* 259.

[109] The time of revelation of this mystery has been debated vigorously in recent times. Bent Noack's assertion that Paul received the revelation at the very moment of his dictating 11:13-36 has been popular among some circles ("Current and Backwater in the Epistle to the Romans," *ST* [1965]: 165-6; so N. Walter, "Zur Interpretation von Römer 9-11," *ZTK* 81 [1984]: 176; David E. Aune, *Prophecy in Early Christianity and the Mediterranean World* [Grand Rapids: Eerdmans, 1983], 252). Considering Paul's rhetorical strategy and plan that we have observed, this cannot be supported. Seyoon Kim recently reasserted his thesis that Paul received the revelation on the Damascus road with his call to apostleship, but it only represents the other extreme position of Noack's ("The 'Mystery' of Rom 11.25-6 Once More," *NTS* 43 [1997]: 412-29). I wonder why we have to know the exact time of the revelation; what can it prove?

[110] For a succinct summary of various positions, see Moo, *Romans,* 720-3.

[111] Fitzmyer, *Romans,* 623: "The phrase *pas Israel,* a Hebraism for *kol-Yisrae'el,* occurs 148 times in the OT and always designates historic, ethnic Israel,... For Paul, *pas Israel* means Israel in the ethnic sense and diachronically." So Dunn, *Theology of Paul,* 527; Cf. Wright, *Climax of the Covenant,* 249-50, who argues that "all Israel" is a typical "Pauline redefinition" of Israel, whose "the privileges and attributes" have been transferred to "the Messiah and his people." That is, now "all Israel" is composed of Jews and Gentiles who are brought into the new covenant community.

[112] Sanday and Headlam, *Romans,* 335. "When all Israel is saved, there may yet be indifferent, unbelieving Jews, but there will then be no longer a synagogue nor any Jews who reject Jesus on the basis of their Law" (Leonard Goppelt, *Jesus, Paul and Judaism: an Introduction to New Testament Theology,* tr. Edward Schroeder [New York: Thomas Nelson, 1964], 161; cited by Reidar Hvalvik, "A 'Sonderweg' for Israel: A Critical Examination of a Current Interpretation of Romans 11.25-27," *JSNT* [1990]: 101, n. 91).

[113] James M. Scott is correct to see that "all Israel" is "the people of Israel taken as a whole from their initial election to their ultimate salvation." Scott's conclusion is based on the usage of Israel in the Deuteronomic tradition, which he argues frames Romans 9-11: "Israel is a unity in a historical continuum" ("Restoration of Israel," in *Dictionary of Paul and His Letters,* ed., Gerald F. Hawthorn, *et al.* [Downers Grove, Ill.: InterVarsity, 1993]: 804). See also his article, "Paul's Use of Deuteronomic Tradition," *JBL* 112 [1993]: 645-65, esp., 664-65). *Contra* Moo, *Romans,* 723, who argues that "all Israel" is limited to "denote the corporate entity of the nation of Israel as it exists at a particular point in time."

the second coming of Jesus.[114] Through the completion of the salvation of "all Israel," the distinction between ethnic Israel and the Gentiles will truly be abolished. Of course, Paul already declared that there is no such distinction (10:12) but its true realization will come only through the final salvation of the Jews in God's plan.[115] That "the gifts and the calling of God are irrevocable" strongly echoes his proposition of Rom 9-11 that God's word has not failed. Rom 11:30-32 contrasts the Gentiles' or Jews' "disobedience" (ἀπειθεία and ἀπειθέω) and God's "mercy" (ἔλεος and ἐλεέω); even human beings' disobedience is within God's sovereign plan of salvation for all. Paul assures his Gentile audience that they "can have utter confidence in that God, however his plan may seem to be going awry," because "God can use even rebellion and disobedience in his plan of mercy on all."[116]

VI. *PERORATIO*:[117] 11:33-36

Paul finishes the whole rhetorical unit with a rousing praise to God. It is a fitting finish for a long and tortuous argument for the faith-

---

[114] Christopher D. Stanley's argument that it is not Christ but Yawheh himself who will come to save his people is not convincing ("The Redeemer Will Come ἐκ Σιων: Romans 11.26-27 Revisited," in *Paul and the Scriptures of Israel,* ed. C. A. Evans and J. A. Sanders [Sheffield: Sheffield Academic, 1993], 118-42, esp., 140-42). It is true that Paul does not mention Jesus Christ explicitly but that does not mean that Jesus is not involved with the final salvation of Israel; it simply shows the emphasis that Paul put forward in Romans 9-11, that is, the faithfulness of God in God's promises to Israel. Stanley's conclusion inevitably resembles the now well-known position of the "Sonderweg" theory, which has been increasingly refuted by various scholars (so Dieter Sänger, "Rettung der Heiden und Erwählung Israels: Einige vorläufige Erwägunge zu Römer 11,25-27," *KD* 32 [1986]: 99-119; idem, *Die Verkündigung des Gekreuzigten und Israel: Studien zum Verhältnis von Kirche und Israel bei Paulus und im frühen Christentum,* WUNT 75 [Tübingen: Mohr, 1994], 151-83; so Dan G. Johnson, "The Structure and Meaning of Romans 11," *CBQ* 46 [1984]: 102). For reviews of various positions, see F. Refoulé, *"... et ainsi tout Israël sera sauvé" Romains 11.25-32,* LD 117 (Paris: Cerf, 1984) and Hvalvik, "Sonderweg," 87-101.

[115] It is evident that the concept "already and not yet" flows as an undercurrent of Paul's thinking. Dunn convincingly shows this concept at work in Paul's thinking throughout his book, *Theology of Paul,* especially in his section on "Israel" (pp. 499-532).

[116] Achtemeier, *Romans,* 189.

[117] For the function and use of *peroratio* in Greco-Roman rhetoric, see pp. 84-6.

fulness of God. The *peroratio* here certainly takes the form of *amplificatio* (*adfectus*/αὔξησις), which is used to arouse the emotions of the audience to strengthen the case.[118] Paul does not use *repetitio*, which would be to recapitulate the argument here, because he has already done that in the previous section.[119] In his exposition of the use of *peroratio,* Cicero teaches that careful consideration must be given to the choice of the language because "[a]mplification ... is a sort of weightier affirmation, designed to win credence in the course of speaking by arousing emotion. This is accomplished... by the nature of the language used..."[120] One of the examples that Cicero gives in application of this principle is to "introduce matters that are supposed to be of high importance"[121] in the course of peroration. "The matters of high importance" can be adduced from "our experience of them" whose examples include "love of the gods, love of country, love of parents."[122] Paul's use of language in this section is in accordance with what the rhetorical handbooks teach. His rhetorical skill is powerfully shown in the use of language in *peroratio.*[123] Yet Paul's creative invention is that he puts these words in a hymnic form.[124]

The hymnic nature of Rom 11:33-36 has been widely recognized by various exegetes over the years.[125] E. Norden points out that there are nine strophes with parallels in the following structure:[126]

---

[118] See p. 85 and references there.

[119] Cf. Johnson, *Romans 9-11,* 173: "Just as 11:28-32 provide the 'logical' conclusion to the argument, so 11:33-36 offer the 'liturgical' counterpart." Johnson is following her teacher, Paul Meyer, who also says that 11:25-27 is the "prophetic conclusion" ("Romans," 1159-60).

[120] Cic. *Part. Or.,* 15.52.

[121] Ibid., 16.55.

[122] Ibid., 16.56.

[123] Käsemann, *Romans,* 318: "... along with the unity and logic of the chapters they display the rhetorical skill of the apostle even to points of detail."

[124] As far as the Greco-Roman rhetoric is concerned, the use of hymn in peroration is not specifically discussed. However, the language of the hymnic materials is in line with what the rhetorical teachers taught.

[125] See E. Norden, *Agnostos Theos: Untersuchungen zur Formgeschichtlichte religiöser Rede* (Leipzig/Berlin: Teubner, 1913), 240-50; R. Deichgräber, *Gotteshymnus und Christus-hymnus in der frühen Christenheit,* SUNT 5 (Göttingen: Vandenhoeck & Ruprecht, 1967), 60-4; G. Bornkamm, "The Praise of God: Romans 11:33-36," in *Early Christian Experience* (London: SCM, 1967), 105-11; W. H. Gloer, "Homologies and Hymns in the New Testament: Form, Content, and Criteria for Identification," *Perspectives in Religious Studies* 11 (1984): 115-32; Johnson, *Romans 9-11,* 164-74.

[126] *Agnostos Theos,* 241.

11.33 Ὦ βάθος πλούτου καὶ σοφίας καὶ γνώσεως θεοῦ
ὡς ἀνεξεραύνητα τὰ κρίματα αὐτοῦ
καὶ ἀνεξιχνίαστοι αἱ ὁδοὶ αὐτοῦ.
11.34 Τίς γὰρ ἔγνω νοῦν κυρίου;
ἢ τίς σύμβουλος αὐτοῦ ἐγένετο;
11.35 ἢ τίς προέδωκεν αὐτῷ,
καὶ ἀνταποδοθήσεται αὐτῷ;
11.36 ὅτι ἐξ αὐτοῦ καὶ δι᾽ αὐτοῦ καὶ εἰς αὐτὸν τὰ
πάντα:
αὐτῷ ἡ δόξα εἰς τοὺς αἰῶνας, ἀμήν.

Basically, the hymn has three parts: 1) two exclamations (v. 33);
2) three rhetorical questions from Isa 40:13 LXX (vv. 34-5); and 3) the
concluding doxology (v. 36). The two exclamations highlight three attributes of God with the "depth" (βάθος) with three dependent genitival
constructions: πλούτου, σοφίας, and γνώσεως θεοῦ. The next three
rhetorical questions in turn address each attribute in reverse order; thus
there is a chiastic structure between them.[127] The concluding doxology
also has three prepositional phrases ascribing "all things" to God: He is
the source (ἐξ αὐτοῦ), the sustainer (δι᾽ αὐτοῦ), and the goal
(εἰς αὐτον).[128] Finally, "To him be the glory, Amen" reminds the audience of the doxology in 9:5. Further, it is evident that 11:33-36 forms
an *inclusio* with 9:1-5. It is clear, therefore, that Paul intends this *peroratio* to be the conclusion of the rhetorical unit of Rom 9-11, rather
than his argument from 1:16 up to this point as some exegetes hold.[129]
The thesis that "God's word has not failed" cannot be measured with
human wisdom and knowledge; his ways are inscrutable and his judgments are unsearchable![130] Therefore, Paul invites his audience to join

---

[127] Bornkamm, "The Praise of God," 107:

πλούτου	(v. 33a)
σοφίας	(v. 33a)
γνώσεως	(v. 33a)
ἔγνω	(v. 34a)
σύμβουλος	(v. 34b)
προέδωκεν	(v. 35a)

[128] Achtemeier, *Romans*, 189.

[129] So Moo, *Romans*, 740; Cranfield, *Romans*, 2.589; John Murray, *The
Epistle to the Romans*, NICNT (Grand Rapids: Eerdmans, 1959-65), 2.105; Schlier,
Römerbrief, 348. *Contra* Bruce, *Romans*, 211; and Fitzmyer, *Romans*, 632. Also
cf. Johnson, *Romans 9-11*, 174, who holds that 11:28-32 with 11:33-36 conclude
the whole of Romans 1:16-11:27.

him in worshipping God and giving glory to him at the end of his argumentation. What an appropriate ending!

---

[130] Cf. Isa 55:8-11:

> For my plans are not your plans, nor are my ways your ways, says
> Yahweh. For as the heavens are higher than the earth, so are my
> ways higher than your ways, and my plans than your plans. For as
> the rain and the snow come down from the heavens and do not re-
> turn there until they drench the earth, making it bring forth and
> sprout, giving seed to the one who sows and grain to the one who
> eats, so shall my word[c] that goes out from my mouth; it shall not re-
> turn to me empty-handed, for it shall accomplish that which I desire,
> and succeed in the thing for which I sent (my translation).

I am convinced that Second Isaiah (Isa 40-55) with its theology of the word of God
should be the most relevant Old Testament background for Paul's logic and argument in Rom 9-11. Probing this aspect, however, is beyond the scope of our project. Cf. Hays, *Echoes of Scripture,* 63 and more recently, idem, "'Who Has Believed Our Message?': Paul's Reading of Isaiah," *SBL 1998 Seminar Papers: Part
One* (Atlanta: Scholars, 1998), 205-24.

SUMMARY AND CONCLUSION

This study was prompted by the need for a fresh approach to Rom 9-11. There has been an impasse among scholars regarding the theological content of these chapters. Stemming often from modern interpreters' lack of understanding of Paul's rhetorical arguments, Paul has been accused of being an inconsistent thinker and it has been maintained that the presentation of his ideas in Rom 9-11 is virtually impossible to follow. This study demonstrates that Paul is indeed consistent and that he follows through on his thesis clearly and methodically. We have employed the method of rhetorical criticism to support our thesis. In chapter one, we saw that concentration on Paul's theological ideas without due consideration of his rhetorical usage and strategy could not advance our understanding of Rom 9-11 and it was argued that the rhetorical critical method is the best alternative to historical and theological approaches. The strength of Betz's rhetorical criticism was noted for its emphasis on invention and arrangement, in contrast to the previous attempts which almost exclusively emphasize style. Betz's rhetorical criticism eventually led New Testament scholars to pay more attention to "argumentation" in Paul's letters. It was in Kennedy's methodology, however, that we found the "vigorous methodology" for understanding Paul's argumentation in his letters. Reviewing and evaluating Kennedy's methodology, we realized that his explanation of the theory of rhetorical situation and the theory of *stasis* is not adequate. An examination of the theory of *stasis* yielded the conclusion that this important ancient rhetorical theory has been neglected by rhetorical critics although it could help greatly in understanding Paul's argumentation. The *stasis* theory has been claimed as "a key tool in invention,"[1] which can then help interpreters of the New Testament to discover "resources

---

[1] Malcom Heath, "Invention," in *Handbook of Classical Rhetoric,* 90.

for discursive persuasion latent in any given rhetorical problem."[2] Also, "identifying the issue [*stasis*] and working through its division provides a firm underlying structure of argument, without which all subsequent elaborations would be ineffective."[3] And this has exactly been the case in our investigation of Rom 9-11—identifying the various *stases* that Paul employed has led to the discovery of Paul's underlying structure of argument. This useful tool has been grossly neglected by New Testament rhetorical critics, in part because of confusion about terminology, and in part because of general neglect of the argumentative side of rhetoric in the New Testament. In the end, the theory developed and summarized by Quintilian appeared to be most applicable to our analysis of Rom 9-11.

Chapter two examined theories of the historical situation and the rhetorical situation. Historical criticism and rhetorical criticism do not have to be in an antithetical relationship for New Testament exegetes. Since rhetorical criticism belongs to the realm of historical criticism, they can complement each other by providing checks and balances. In order to enhance their complementary, interpretive roles, effort was concentrated on delineating the similarities and differences between the historical situation and the rhetorical situation. The rhetorical situation cannot be equated with the historical situation and the crucial differentiating factor is the focus of the exegete's investigation, which is on the text level in the case of the rhetorical situation. In establishing the rhetorical situation, the rhetorical critic focuses on the intended audience whom the speaker wants to persuade through his/her rhetoric. Historical makeup, on the other hand, is the criterion of the historical situation. The speaker's situation is likewise extracted on the level of text in the rhetorical situation rather than the actual, historical situation of the speaker, which may be obtained from external sources in the historical situation. In the case of the exigence, or the "imperfection" that the speaker perceives and wishes to change, it is investigated exclusively from the text itself in the rhetorical situation, rather than depending on extraneous sources as in the historical situation. Yet rhetorical criticism cannot ignore historical aspects of the text, simply because the New Testament is an historical document. The possibility that the rhetorical situation can help establish the actual, historical situation is raised and should be investigated further for its theoretical development and application.

---

[2] Ibid., 89.
[3] Idem, *Hermogenes,* 23.

Chapter three examined the rhetorical situation of Romans to the degree that it can be exposed in the *exordium* and the *peroratio*. Paul establishes his *ethos*, from the beginning of the letter, as the apostle with authority invested by God. Paul presents himself as a Jewish apostle in thoroughly Jewish terms. The gospel he preaches is firmly rooted in the Jewish scriptures and his ministry as the apostle is described as a cultic service in the Jewish religious tradition. This is striking because the members of the rhetorical audience on whom Paul intends to make an impact are the Gentile Christians in the Roman congregation. It becomes clear, however, that the nature of the subject in Rom 9-11 is closely related to the Jewish scriptures and Jewish values. It also becomes clear why Paul establishes himself as the expert in this area, apart from the fact that he himself is personally involved with the subject matter that he argues in Rom 9-11. Paul also makes clear that the audience is included in the sphere of his ministry, namely, that they are within his apostolic responsibility. Paul establishes his authority over his audience very carefully, using a highly sophisticated rhetorical device such as *correctio*, because not having seen him in person, he was a virtual stranger to them. His establishment of a proper *ethos* in the beginning of the letter is crucial for him to succeed in persuading his audience to accept him as their apostle and his proposal that they cooperate with him for the future mission project. As already noted, the audience that Paul wants to persuade is the Gentile Christians in the Roman congregation. They are called by Paul as the people of God, and given typically Jewish honorific titles such as "called," "beloved by God," and "called to be saints." Paul forms a strong bond with his audience by pointing out that they share the same calling of God and the same grace of God. The exigence that is manifested in the *exordium* and the *peroratio* of Romans is first of all that Paul himself is to be accepted as the apostle to the audience. Paul makes careful assertions in order to establish himself as a legitimate apostle, "called" and "set apart" by God for bringing "the obedience of faith" to the Gentiles. In the beginning of the letter, Paul makes clear that the subject matter of his argument is the gospel of God (1:1), its promise (1:2), its content (1:3), its power (1:4), and its result (1:5). What Paul argues in Romans has to do with the gospel of God, in one way or another, and all these aspects should be kept in mind in our interpretation. "The obedience of faith" especially needs to be understood in the context of Romans, not exclusively as a theological concept, but in a missionary context, especially in the situation of his audience. Paul asks his audience to participate with him in bringing about "the obedience of faith" among the Gentiles in his future missionary endeavor.

Chapter four argued that Rom 9-11 forms a rhetorical unit. Rom 9-11 is complete with an autonomous *dispositio.* The rhetorical situation of Rom 9-11 was analyzed in terms of the portrait of the speaker, the audience, and the exigence. In Rom 9-11, the very personal authorial persona emerges and dominates throughout the rhetorical unit. His intense personal avowal sets the tone of the whole unit from the beginning. He emphatically portrays himself as a Jew who is even willing to sacrifice himself for the sake of his kinsfolk. This is seen to be consistent with Paul's portrayal of himself in the *exordium.* Paul presents himself as the apostle to the Gentiles but he makes clear that at the core of his apostolic ministry is the salvation of the Jewish people. Throughout the rhetorical unit of Rom 9-11, he consistently portrays himself as the one who is gravely concerned for the salvation of the Jewish people—even his ministry for the salvation of the Gentiles is actually intended for the salvation of his kinsfolk according to the flesh. Therefore, the argument that Paul's attitude towards Jews is not consistent and contradictory is groundless. The rhetorical audience in Rom 9-11, the intended audience that Paul wishes to impact, is the Gentile Christians, which is again consistent with the audience in the *exordium.* Paul emphasizes that it is the Gentiles to whom he wants to communicate and persuade, even though he is dealing mainly with Jewish matters and salvation. Also, the argument in 11:17-25a reveals that there were some Gentiles who became proud in their salvation and despised the Jewish people. Paul exhorts them not to be proud but "be in awe." The exigence in Rom 9-11 is straightforwardly the defense of "the faithfulness of God." The gospel of God which is set forth in the *exordium* includes God's promise through "his prophets in the holy scriptures" (1:2). Also, this gospel is concerned with (περὶ) his Son who was born of the seed of David according to the flesh. In other words, the origin of the gospel of God is thoroughly Jewish and God's promise was given first to the Jewish people through his prophets. If Israel is not saved because of her rejection of this gospel, then, some maintained that this proved that God is not faithful in his promise to his own people. Thus, Paul had to defend the counterproposition that God's word had not failed, especially with regard to his promise towards Israel.

Chapter five presented a rhetorical analysis of Rom 9-11. It was argued that Rom 9-11 is forensic rhetoric in which Paul defends God's faithfulness. We saw that Paul consistently argues, by means of a carefully composed argument, for his main thesis that the word of God has not failed. Paul's use of *stasis* was explored in the context of a forensic setting. Paul uses different *stases* to defend the reliability of God's word, and eventually, the faithfulness of God, throughout these chapters. The accusations that have been raised against God center on the fate of Israel, caused by her unbelief within the current situation. Paul maintains that God's word has not failed precisely because the term "Israel" has been misunderstood to mean genetic descent. Rather, Paul maintains, it refers to that Israel which God called and which has always been saved. Then Paul refutes the charge against God that God's action is not just by pointing out that his actions are actually necessary and honorable. The following charge against God (9:19-29) is dismissed by Paul on the basis that the charge represents a faulty legal proceeding. In 9:30-10:4, Paul expounds the current situation of Israel by comparing it to a footrace: Israel fell behind in the race because she stumbled on the stone that was laid by God, but the Gentiles, who were not even in the race, reached the goal line and won the prize first because they had inadvertently followed the rule, which was to accept the faithfulness of Christ. Paul then supports what he just argued in 9:30-10:4 with scriptural proofs. He asserts that there is no distinction between Jew and Greek in salvation. In these two sections (9:30-10:4 and 10:5-13), Paul does not refute any charge but tries to support his refutations of 9:6b-29. The tone of his argument is surprisingly that of teaching in the form of *diatribe*, employing the metaphor of footrace and proofs from scripture to illustrate his point. In 10:14-21, Paul returns to his use of the *stasis* theory to refute the charge that God is responsible for Israel's unbelief. Here he refutes the charge by proving that it is not God but Israel who is responsible for her own unbelief. In Rom 11:1-10, Paul directly refutes the charge that God has rejected his people by giving the examples of himself and Elijah that God's remnant still remains. Paul follows with yet another refutation of the charge that Israel fell and is permanently damned from salvation. By no means! Paul shows that Israel's stumbling is only temporary so that the full number of Gentiles can come into salvation, and then "all Israel" will be saved. Paul ends his argument with a rousing hymn, praising God and giving glory to him.

As we follow Paul's argumentation closely, we observe that the focus of that argument is concentrated on the refutation of the charges that God's word has failed, and therefore God is not faithful. Paul's argumentation is well designed and follows logically step by step. Was Paul successful in his persuasion of his audience in Rom 9-11? We cannot know the answer but one thing is clear: Paul presented a power-

ful case that God is faithful and reliable as demonstrated in the faithfulness toward Israel regarding her salvation. Now the Gentiles can be
assured that their salvation is secure as long as they trust in that God
through Jesus Christ.

Paul's use of rhetoric in Rom 9-11 is indeed crucial for understanding his argumentation. His rhetorical argument is shaped by the
need to meet the rhetorical exigence, the need to defend God's faithfulness. In his defense, he organizes his material so as to use the theory of
stasis effectively and, at the same time, teach his Gentile audience
about the order of salvation in God's plan. In the course of his argument, he vigorously argues for the trustworthiness and faithfulness of
God, revealing his theological convictions. Since Paul was not writing
a systematic theology in the sense that a modern theologian such as
Karl Barth did, we cannot satisfactorily demand of Paul his argument
for certain theological points such as predestination, the relationship
between Jews and Gentiles, or salvation. This does not mean, however,
that we cannot delineate any theological conviction of Paul. This study
simply argues that without proper understanding of Paul's rhetorical
arguments, we cannot possibly follow his reasoning, with the result that
his theology cannot be fairly (to him) and profitably (to us) understood.[4] Understanding Paul's rhetorical arguments is only a beginning
step for understanding his theology; studying Paul's theology in Rom
9-11 is a topic for another day.

In our examination of rhetoric and situation in Rom 9-11, we
found that Paul's main concerns in these chapters are God and God's
character; his kinsfolk Israel's salvation; and for his Gentile audience,
that their trust in God would be assured. Hence, the title of this
study—God, Israel and the Gentiles.

---

[4] The recent remark by Ben Witherington, *The Paul Quest,* 280, echoes my
thought well:

> Paul's theology is embedded within rhetorical arguments, which in
> turn are found in an epistolary framework. Theology cannot just be
> read off the surface of the letters; often the meaning of a text will be
> missed if one does not recognize the rhetorical function of a given
> piece of material. In each letter Paul has an overall argumentative
> focus, purpose and strategy, and the parts and individual arguments
> need to be seen in relationship to the whole. Careful attention to the
> *propositio...* or the *peroratio...* of these letters will provide definite
> clues as to Paul's rhetorical aims and main concerns and how he
> may use theological material to address those aims.

SELECTED BIBLIOGRAPHY

I. REFERENCE WORKS

Bauer, Walter A. *A Greek-English Lexicon of the New Testament and Other Early Christian Literature.* Trans., adapted, and augmented by William F. Arndt, F. Wilbur Gingrich, and Frederick W. Danker. 2d ed. Chicago: University of Chicago Press, 1979.

Blass, F., and A. Debrunner. *A Greek Grammar of the New Testament and Other Early Christian Literature.* Trans. and rev. by Robert W. Funk. Chicago: University of Chicago Press, 1961.

Brown, F., S. R. Driver and C. A. Briggs. *A Hebrew and English Lexicon of the Old Testament.* Oxford: Clarendon, 1972.

Buttrick, George Arthur, and Keith Crimm, eds. *The Interpreter's Dictionary of the Bible.* 5 vols. Nashville: Abingdon, 1962, 1976.
　　S.v. "Letter," by Nils A. Dahl. Sup.: 538-40.
　　S.v. "Obedience," by F. W. Young. 3: 580-81.

Enos, Theresa, ed. *Encyclopedia of Rhetoric and Composition.* New York: Garland, 1996.
　　S.v. "Hermagoras," by Omar Swartz. 315-16.

Hawthorn, Gerald F., and Ralph P. Martin, eds. *Dictionary of Paul and His Letters.* Downers Grove, Ill.: InterVarsity, 1993.
　　S.v. "Restoration of Israel," by James M. Scott. 796-805.
　　S.v. "Rhetorical Criticism," by G. W. Hansen. 822-26.

Kittel, Gerhard, ed. *Theological Dictionary of the New Testament.* 10 vols. Trans. G. W. Bromiley. Grand Rapids: Eerdmans, 1964-76.
　　S.v. "ἀπόστολος," by K. H. Rengstorf. 1: 407-47.
　　S.v. "προσκόπτω, πρόσκομμα," by G. Stählin. 6: 745-58.

Lanham, Richard. *A Handlist of Rhetorical Terms.* Berkeley: University of California Press, 1968.

Liddell, Henry George, and Robert Scott. *A Greek-English Lexicon.* 9th ed. Rev. by Henry Stuart Jones and Roderick McKenzie. Oxford: Clarendon, 1996.

Louw, Johannes P., and Eugene A. Nida, ed. *Greek-English Lexicon of the New Testament: Based on Semantic Domains*, 2d ed. New York: United Bible Societies, 1989.

Smyth, Herbert Weir. *Greek Grammar.* Rev. by Gordon M. Massing. Cambridge: Harvard University Press, 1956.

The New Encyclopaedia Britannica. 11th ed. 1975.
S.v. "Rhetoric: Rhetoric in Literature," by T. O. Sloan. 758-62.

II. ANCIENT TEXTS AND TRANSLATIONS

Aristotle. *The Art of Rhetoric.* Trans. John Henry Freese. LCL. Cambridge: Harvard University Press, 1926.

_____. *Aristotle on Rhetoric: A Theory of Civic Discourse.* Trans. George A. Kennedy. Oxford: Oxford University Press, 1991.

_____. *The Politics.* Trans. H. Rackham. LCL. Cambridge: Harvard University Press, 1932.

_____. *Topica.* Trans. E. S. Forster. LCL. Cambridge: Harvard University Press, 1960.

Biblia Hebraica Stuttgartensia. Ed. K. Elliger, W. Rudolph, *et al.* Stuttgart: Deutsche Bibelgesellschaft, 1983.

Cicero. *Brutus, Orator.* Trans. G. L. Hendrickson and H. M. Hubbell. LCL. Cambridge: Harvard University Press, 1939.

_____. *De Inventione, De Optimo, Genere Oratorum, Topica.* Trans. H. M. Hubbell. LCL. Cambridge: Harvard University Press, 1949.

_____. *The Letters to Atticus.* Trans. E. O. Winstedt. 3 vols. LCL. Cambridge: Harvard University Press, 1912-18.

_____. *The Letters to His Friends.* Trans. W. Glynn Williams, M. Cary, and Mary Henderson. 4 vols. LCL. Cambridge: Harvard University Press, 1927-72.

_____. *De Oratore, De Fato, Paradoa Stoicorum, De Partitione Oratoria.* Trans. E. W. Sutton and H. Rackam. 2 vols. LCL. Cambridge: Harvard University Press, 1942.

[_____]. *Rhetorica ad Herennium.* Trans. Harry Caplan. LCL. Cambridge: Harvard University Press, 1954.

The Cynic Epistles. A Study Edition. Ed. Abraham J. Malherbe. Missoula, Mont.: Scholars, 1977.

Demetrius. *On Style.* Trans. W. Hamilton Fyfe and W. Rhys Roberts. LCL. In Aristotle vol. 23, *The Poetics.* Cambridge: Harvard University Press, 1932.

Demosthenes. Trans. C. A. Vince and J. H. Vince. 7 vols. LCL. Cambridge: Harvard University Press, 1926-49.

Dio Chrysostom. *Orations.* Trans. J. W. Cohoon and H. L. Crosby. 5 vols. LCL. Cambridge: Harvard University Press, 1932-51.

Epictetus. *The Discourses as Reported by Arrian, The Manual, and Fragments.* Trans. A. W. Oldfather. 2 vols. LCL. Cambridge: Harvard University Press, 1926-28.

Hermogenes. *Hermogenes* On Issues: *Strategies of Argument in Later Greek Rhetoric.* Trans. Malcom Heath. Oxford: Clarendon, 1995.

_____. *Hermogenis Opera.* Ed. H. Rabe. Rhetores Graeci VI. Lipsiae: Teubner, 1913.

Isocrates. Trans. George Norlin and Larue Van Hook. 3 vols. LCL. Cambridge: Harvard University Press, 1928-45.

Josephus. Trans. H. St. J. Thackeray, R. Marcus, and L. H. Feldman. 9 vols. LCL. Cambridge: Harvard University Press, 1956-65.

Longinus. *On the Sublime.* Trans. W. H. Fyfe. LCL. In Aristotle vol. 23, *The Poetics.* Cambridge: Harvard University Press, 1927.

Lucian of Samosata. Trans. A. M. Harmon and M. D. Macleod. 8 vols. LCL. Cambridge: Harvard University Press, 1913-67.

Menandor Rhetor. Edited with translation and commentary by D. A. Russell and N. G. Wilson. Oxford: Clarendon, 1981.

New Testament Apocrypha. Ed. E. Hennecke, W. Schneemelcher, R. McL. Wilson. 2 vols. Philadelphia: Westminster, 1963, 1965.

Novum Testamentum Graece. 27th ed. Rev. and ed. K. Aland *et al.* Stuttgart: Deutsche Bibelgesellschaft, 1993.

The Old Testament Pseudepigrapha. Ed. J. H. Charlesworth. 2 vols. Garden City, N.Y.: Doubleday, 1983-85.

Orosius, Paulus. *The Seven Books of History against the Pagans.* Trans. Roy J. Deferrari. Washington, D.C.: Catholic University of America Press, 1964.

Philo. Trans. F. H. Colson, G. H. Whitaker, *et al.* 12 vols. LCL. Cambridge: Harvard University Press, 1912.

Plato. 12 vols. Trans. H. N. Fowler, W.R.M. Lamb, *et al.* LCL. Cambridge: Harvard University Press, 1914-35.

_____. *The Collected Dialogues.* Ed. Edith Hamilton and Huntington Cairns. Princeton: Princeton University Press, 1961.

Pliny. *Letters, Panegyricus.* Trans. B. Radice. 2 vols. LCL. Cambridge: Harvard University Press, 1969.

Plutarch. *Lives.* Trans. B. Perrin. 11 vols. LCL. Cambridge: Harvard University Press, 1914-26.

Quintilian. *Institutio Oratoria.* Trans. H. E. Butler. 4 vols. LCL. Cambridge: Harvard University Press, 1920-22.

Rhetorica ad Alexandrum. Trans. H. Rackam. LCL. Cambridge: Harvard University Press, 1983.

Septuaginta. Ed. A. Rahlfs. Stuttgart: Deutsche Bibelgesellschaft, 1935.

Sextus Empiricus. Trans. R. G. Bury. Vol. 4: *Against the Professors.* LCL. Cambridge: Harvard University Press, 1949.

Suetonius. *The Lives of the Caesars.* Trans. J. C. Rolfe. 2 vols. LCL. Cambridge: Harvard University Press, 1914.

Tacitus. *The Histories and the Annals.* Trans. C. H. Moore and J. Jackson. 4 vols. LCL. Cambridge: Harvard University Press, 1925-37.

III. COMMENTARIES ON ROMANS

Achtemeier, Paul J. *Romans.* IBC. Atlanta: John Knox, 1985.

Barrett, C. K. *A Commentary on the Epistle to the Romans.* 2d ed. Peabody, Mass.: Hendrickson, 1991.

Barth, K. *The Epistle to the Romans.* Oxford: Oxford University Press, 1933.

Bruce, F. F. *The Letter of Paul to the Romans.* 2d ed. Tyndale New Testament Commentaries. Grand Rapids: Eerdmans, 1985.

Byrne, Brendan, S.J. *Romans.* SacPag 6. Collegeville, Minn.: The Liturgical Press, 1996.

Cranfield, C. E. B. *A Critical and Exegetical Commentary on the Epistle to the Romans.* 2vols. ICC. Edinburgh: T. & T. Clark, 1975, 1979.

Dodd, C. H. *The Epistle of Paul to the Romans.* rev. ed. MNTC. London: Collins, 1959.

Dunn, James D. G. *Romans 1-8.* WBC 38a. Dallas: Word, 1988.

_____. *Romans 9-16.* WBC 38b. Dallas: Word, 1988.

Fitzmyer, Joseph A. *Romans: A New Translation with Introduction and Commentary.* AB 33. New York: Doubleday, 1993.

Johnson, Luke Timothy. *Reading Romans: A Literary and Theological Commentary.* New York: Crossroad, 1997.

Kuss, Otto, *Der Römerbrief übersetzt und erklärt.* 3 vols. Regensburg: Puster, 1957-1978.

Meyer, Paul W. "Romans." In *Harper's Bible Commentary*, ed. J. L. Mays, 1130-67. San Francisco: Harper & Row, 1988.

Michel, O. *Der Brief an die Römer*, 14th ed. Göttingen: Vandenhoeck & Ruprecht, 1978.

Calvin, John. *Iohannis Calvini commentarius in epistolam Pauli ad Romanos*, ed. T.H.L. Parker. Leiden : E. J. Brill, 1981.

Murray, John. *The Epistle to the Romans,* NICNT. 2 vols. Grand Rapids: Eerdmans, 1959-65.

Moo, Douglas. *The Epistle to the Romans.* NICNT. Grand Rapids: Eerdmans, 1996.

Nygren, Anders. *Commentary on Romans.* Trans. C. C. Rasmussen. Philadelphia: Fortress, 1949.

Sanday, W. and A. C. Headlam. *A Critical and Exegetical Commentary on the Epistle to the Romans.* ICC. New York: Charles Scribner's Sons, 1926.

Schlatter, A. *Romans: The Righteousness of God.* Trans. S. S. Schatzmann. Peabody, Mass.: Hendrickson, 1995.

Schlier, Heinrich. *Der Römerbrief.* HTKNT. Freiburg: Herder, 1988.

Stuhlmacher, Peter. *Paul's Letter to the Romans.* Trans. S. J. Hafemann. Louisville: Westminster/John Knox, 1994.

Wilckens, U. *Der Brief an die Römer.* EKKNT. 3 vols. Neukirchen/Vluyn: Zürich-Neukirchener: Banziger, 1978-81.

IV. OTHER MONOGRAPHS AND ARTICLES

Aageson, James W. "Scripture and Structure in the Development of the Argument in Romans 9-11." *CBQ* 48 (1986): 265-89.

Achtemeier, Paul J. *"Omne Verbum Sonat*: The New Testament and the Oral Environment of Late Western Antiquity." *JBL* 109 (1990): 3-27.

_____. "Romans 3:1-8: Structure and Argument." In *Christ and Communities: Essays in Honor of Reginald H. Fuller*, 77-87, ed. A. J. Hultgren and B. Hall. Cincinati, Ohio: Forward Movement Publication, 1990.

_____. "Unsearchable Judgments and Inscrutable Ways: Reflections on the Discussion of Romans." In *Pauline Theology, IV: Looking Back, Pressing on*, ed. E. Elizabeth Johnson and David M. Hay, 3-21. Atlanta: Scholars, 1997.

Ådna, Jostein, S. J. Hafemann and Otfried Hofius, eds. *Evangelium, Schriftauslegung, Kirche: Festschrift für Peter Stuhlmacher zum 65. Geburtstag.* Göttingen: Vandenhoeck & Ruprecht, 1997.

Aletti, J.-N. "L'argumentation paulinienne en Rm 9." *Bib* 68 (1987): 41-56.

_____. "Rm 1,18-3,20: Incohérence ou cohérence de l'argumentation paulinienne?," *Bib* 69 (1988): 47-62.

_____. *Comment Dieu est-it juste? Clefs pour interpréter l'épître aux Romains.* Paris: Éditions du Seuil, 1991.

_____. "La *dispositio* rhétorique dans les épîtres pauliniennes." *NTS* 38 (1992): 385-401.

_____. "La présence d'um modèle rhétorique en Romains: Son rôle et son importance." *Bib* 71 (1990): 1-24.

_____. "The Rhetoric of Romans 5--8." In *The Rhetorical Analysis of Scripture: Essays From the 1995 London Conference*, ed. Stanley E. Porter and Thomas H. Olbricht, 294-308. JSNTSup 146. Sheffield: Sheffield Academic, 1997.

Allen, L. C. "The Old Testament Background of (ΠΡΟ)΄ΟΡΙΖΕΙΝ in the New Testament." *NTS* 17 (1970-71): 104-8.

Anderson, R. Dean, Jr. *Ancient Rhetorical Theory and Paul.* Contribution to

Biblical Exegesis and Theology 18. Kampen: Kok Pharos, 1996.

Aune, David E. "Romans As a *Logos Protreptikos* in the Context of Ancient Religious and Philosophical Propaganda." In *Paulus und das antike Judentum*, ed. Martin Hengel and Ulrich Heckel, 91-124. WUNT 58. Tübingen: Mohr, 1991.

_____. *Prophecy in Early Christianity and the Mediterranean World.* Grand Rapids: Eerdmans, 1983.

Aus, Roger D. "Paul's Travel Plans to Spain and the 'Full Number of the Gentiles' of Rom 11:25." *NovT* 21 (1979): 232-62.

Badenas, R. *Christ the End of the Law: Romans 10.4 in Pauline Perspective.* JSNTSup 10. Sheffield: JSOT Press, 1985.

Barclay, John M. G. "Mirror-Reading a Polemical Letter: Galatians As a Test Case." *JSNT* 31 (1987): 73-93.

Barth, M. "St. Paul--A Good Jew." *HBT* 1 (1979): 7-45.

Barwick, Karl. "Zur Rekonstruktion der Rhetorik des Hermagoras von Temnos." *Philogus* 109 (1965): 186-218.

Baur, F. C. *Paul the Apostle of Jesus Christ.* Ed. E. Zeller. London: William & Norgate, 1876.

_____. "Über Zweck und Veranlassung des Römerbriefs und der damit zusammenhängenden Verältnisse der römischen Gemeinde." *Tübinger Zeitschrift für Theologie* 3 (1836): 59-178.

_____. "Über Zweck und Gedankengang des Römerbriefs." *Theologische Jahrbücher* 16 (1857): 60-108, 184-209.

Beare, F. W. *St. Paul and His Letters.* New York: Abingdon, 1962.

Bechtler, Steven Richard. "Christ, the *Telos* of the Law: The Goal of Romans 10:4." *CBQ* 56 (1994): 288-308.

Beker, J. C. *Paul the Apostle: The Triumph of God in Life and Thought.* Philadelphia: Fortress, 1980.

_____. "Romans 9-11 in the Context of the Early Church." *Princeton Seminary Bulletin* Supp.1 (1990): 40-55.

Bell, Richard H. *Provoked to Jealousy: The Origin and Purpose of the Jealousy Motif in Romans 9-11.* WUNT 2/63. Tübingen: Mohr, 1994.

Benko, S. "The Edict of Claudius of A.D. 49 and the Instigator Chrestus," *TZ* 25 (1969): 406-18.

Berger, Klaus. "Hellenistische Gattungen im Neuen Testament." In *ANRW II. Principat 25,2. Religion*, ed. H. Temporini and W. Haase, 1031-432, 1831-85. Berlin and New York: Walter de Gruyter, 1984.

_____. *Formgeschichte des neuen Testament.* Heidelberg: Quelle & Meyer, 1984.

Berliner, A. *Geschichte der Juden in Rom von der ältesten Zeit bis zur Gegenwart (2050 Jahre).* 2 vols. Frankfurt: Kauffmann, 1893.

Betz, Hans-Dieter. *Galatians: A Commentary on Paul's Letter to the Churches in Galatia.* Hermeneia. Philadelphia: Fortress, 1979.

_____. "The Literary Composition and Function of Paul's Letter to the Galatians." *NTS* 21 (1975): 353-79.

_____. "The Problem of Rhetoric and Theology According to the Apostle Paul." In *L'Apôtre Paul. Personalitè, Style et concêption du ministère*, ed. A. Vanhoye, 16-48. BETL 73. Leuven: Leuven University Press, 1986.

The Bible and Culture Collective. "Rhetorical Criticism." In *The Postmodern Bible*, ed. Elizabeth A. Castelli, *et al.*, 149-86. New Haven: Yale University Press, 1995.

Bitzer, Lloyd F. "Functional Communication: A Situational Perspective." In *Rhetoric in Transition: Studies in the Nature and Uses of Rhetoric*, ed. Eugene E. White, 21-38. University Park: The Pennsylvania State University Press, 1980.

_____. "The Rhetorical Situation." *Philosophy and Rhetoric* 1 (1968): 1-14.

Black, C. C. "Rhetorical Criticism." In *Hearing the New Testament: Strategies for Interpretation*, ed. Joel B. Green, 256-77. Grand Rapids: Eerdmans, 1995.

_____. "Rhetorical Criticism and Biblical Interpretation." *ExpTim* 100 (1989): 252-8.

_____. "Rhetorical Questions: The New Testament, Classical Rhetoric, and Current Interpretation." *Dialog* 29 (1990): 62-70.

Boer, Martinus C. de. "Narrative Criticism, Historical Criticism, and the Gospel of John." *JSNT* 47 (1992): 35-48.

Bonner, S. F. *Education in Ancient Rome: From the Elder Cato to the Younger Pliny.* Berkeley: University of California Press, 1977.

Borg, M. "A New Context for Romans XIII," *NTS* 19 (1972-73): 205-18.

Bornkamm, G. "The Praise of God: Romans 11:33-36." In *Early Christian Experience,* 105-11. London: SCM, 1967.

Botha, Jan. *Subject to Whose Authority? Multiple Readings of Romans 13.* Emory Studies in Early Christianity 5. Atlanta: Scholars, 1994.

Bowers, Paul. "Fulfilling the Gospel: The Scope of the Pauline Mission." *JETS* 30 (1987): 185-98.

Bowers, W. P. "Jewish Communities in Spain in the Time of Paul the Apostle." *JTS* 26 (1975): 395-402.

Braet, Antoine. "The Classical Doctrine of *status* and the Rhetorical Theory of Argumentation." *Philosophy and Rhetoric* 20 (1987): 79-93.

Brändle, Rudolf and Ekkehard W. Stegemann. "Die Entstehung der ersten 'christlichen Gemeinde' Roms im Kontext der jüdischen Gemeinden." *NTS* 42 (1996): 1-11.

Brandt, William J. *The Rhetoric of Argumentation.* Indianapolis: Bobbs-Merrill, 1970.

Bratsiotis, P. "Eine exegetische Notiz zu Röm. IX.3 und X.1." *NovT* 5 (1962): 299-300.

Bring, R. "Paul and the Old Testament: A Study of the Ideas of Election, Faith and Law in Paul with Special Reference to Rom ix:30-x:21." *ST* 25 (1971): 21-60.

Brinton, Alan. "Situation in the Theory of Rhetoric." *Philosophy and Rhetoric* 14 (1981): 234-48.

Brown, R. E. "Rome." In *Antioch and Rome: New Testament Cradles of Catholic Christianity,* 94-113. New York: Paulist, 1983.

Bruce, F. F. *Commentary on the Book of Acts.* Grand Rapids: Eerdmans, 1966.

Bullmore, Michael A. *St. Paul's Theology of Rhetorical Style: An Examination of 1 Corinthians 2:1-5 in the Light of First Century Graeco-Roman Culture.* San Francisco: International Scholars Publications, 1995.

Bultmann, Rudolf. *Theology of the New Testament.* 2 vols. Trans. Kendrick Grobel. New York: Charles Scribner's Sons, 1951 and 1955.

Bünker, Michael. *Briefformular und rhetorische disposition im 1. Korintherbrief.* GTA 28. Göttingen: Vandenhoeck und Ruprecht, 1983.

Buren, Paul M. van. "The Church and Israel: Romans 9-11." *Princeton Seminary Bulletin* Supp. 1 (1990): 5-18.

Burke, Kenneth. *A Rhetoric of Motives.* Berkeley: University of California Press, 1969.

Byrne, Brendan, S.J. "Rather Boldly (Rom 15:15): Paul's Prophetic Bid to Win the Allegiance of the Christians in Rome." *Bib* 74 (1993): 83-96.

Byrskog, Samuel. "Co-Senders, Co-Authors and Paul's Use of the First Person Plural." *ZNW* 87 (1996): 230-50.

_____. "Epistolography, Rhetoric, and Letter Prescript: Romans 1.1-7 As a Test Case." *JSNT* 65 (1997): 27-46.

Caird, G. B. "Predestination--Romans ix.-xi." *ExpTim* 68 (1956-57): 324-27.

Campbell, W. S. *Paul's Gospel in an Intercultural Context: Jew and Gentile in the Letter to the Romans.* Frankfurt: Peter Lang, 1992.

Chae, Daniel Jong-Sang. *Paul As Apostle to the Gentiles: His Apostolic Self-Awareness and Its Influence on the Soteriological Argument in Romans.* Paternoster Biblical and Theological Monographs. Carlisle: Paternoster, 1997.

Clark, D. L. *Rhetoric in Greco-Roman Education.* New York: Columbia University Press, 1957.

Clarke, M. L. *Higher Education in the Ancient World.* Albuquerque: University of New Mexico Press, 1971.

Classen, Carl Joachim. "Paulus und die antike Rhetorik." *ZNW* 82 (1991): 1-33.

_____. "St. Paul's Epistles and Ancient Greek and Roman Rhetoric." In *Rhetoric and the New Testament: Essays From the 1992 Heidelberg Conference*, ed. Stanley E. Porter and Thomas H. Olbricht, 265-91. JSNTSup 90. Sheffield: Sheffield Academic, 1993.

Consigny, Scott. "Rhetoric and Its Situations." *Philosophy & Rhetoric* 7 (1974): 175-86.

Corbett, Edward P. J. *Classical Rhetoric for the Modern Student.* 3d ed. Oxford: Oxford University Press, 1990.

Cosgrove, Charles H. *Elusive Israel: The Puzzle of Election in Romans.* Louisville, Ky.: Westminster John Knox Press, 1997.

_____. "Rhetorical Suspense in Romans 9-11: A Study in Polyvalence and Hermeneutical Election." *JBL* 115 (1996): 271-287.

Craffert, Pieter F. "Relationships Between Social-Scientific, Literary, and Rhetorical Interpretation of Texts." *BTB* 26 (1996): 45-55.

Crafton, Jeffery A. *The Agency of the Apostle: A Dramatistic Analysis of Paul's Responses to Conflict in 2 Corinthians*. Sheffield: JSOT Press, 1991.

_____. "Paul's Rhetorical Vision and the Purpose of Romans: Toward a New Understanding." *NovT* 32 (1990): 317-39.

Cranford, Michael. "Election and Ethnicity: Paul's View of Israel in Romans 9.1-13." *JSNT* 50 (1993): 27-41.

Dahl, Nils A. *Studies in Paul: Theology for the Early Christian Mission*. Minneapolis: Augsburg, 1977.

Davies, W. D. "Paul and the People of Israel." *NTS* 24 (1977-1978): 4-39.

Deichgräber, R. *Gotteshymnus und Christus-hymnus in der frühen Christenheit*. SUNT 5. Göttingen: Vandenhoeck & Ruprecht, 1967.

Denniston, J. D. *The Greek Particles*. 2d ed. Oxford: Oxford University Press, 1954.

Dieter, O. A. L. "Stasis." *Speech Monographs* 17 (1950): 345-69.

Dinkler, E. "The Historical and the Eschatological Israel in Romans, Chapters 9-11: A Contribution to the Problem of Predestination and Individual Responsibility." *JR* 36 (1956): 109-27.

Dinter, Paul E. "The Remnant of Israel and the Stone of Stumbling According to Paul (Romans 9-11)." Dissertation, Union Theological Seminary in New York, 1979.

Donaldson, Terence L. *Paul and the Gentiles: Remapping the Apostle's Convictional World*. Minneapolis: Fortress, 1997.

_____. "'Riches for the Gentiles' (Rom 11:12): Israel's Rejection and Paul's Gentile Mission." *JBL* 112 (1993): 81-98.

Donfried, K. P., ed. *The Romans Debate: Revised and Expanded Edition*. Peabody, Mass.: Hendrickson, 1991.

Dreyfus, François. "Le Passé et le présent d'Israël (Rom 9,1-5; 11,1-24)." In *Die Israelfrage Nach Römer 9-11*, ed. L. De Lorenzi, 131-92. Rome: Abtei von St. Paul.

du Toit, A. B. "Romans 1,3-4 and the Gospel Tradition: A Reassessment of the Phrase *Kata Pneuma Hagiosune.*" In *The Four Gospels 1992: Festschrift Frans Neirynck, V. 1*, ed. F. van Segbroeck, *et al.*, 249-56. Leuven: Leuven University Press, 1992.

Dunn, James D. G. *The Theology of Paul the Apostle.* Grand Rapids: Eerdmans, 1998.

Dworkin, Gerald, ed., *Determinism, Free Will, and Moral Responsibility.* Englewood Cliffs, N.J.: Prentice-Hall, 1970.

Elliott, N. *The Rhetoric of Romans: Argumentative Constraint and Strategy and Paul's Dialogue with Judaism.* JSNTSup 45. Sheffield: Sheffield Academic, 1990.

Ellis, E. E. *Paul's Use of Old Testament.* Grand Rapids: Baker, 1957.

Eriksson, Anders. "'Women Tongue Speakers, Be Silent': A Reconstruction Through Paul's Rhetoric." *Biblical Interpretation* 6 (1998): 80-104.

Fee, Gordon D. *God's Empowering Presence: The Holy Spirit in the Letters of Paul.* Peabody, Mass.: Hendrickson, 1994.

Finn, T. "The God-Fearers Reconsidered." *CBQ* 47 (1985): 75-84.

Fiore, B. "Romans 9-11 and Classical Forensic Rhetoric." *Proceedings of the Eastern Great Lakes and Midwest Biblical Societies* 8 (1988): 117-26.

Fiorenza, E. S. "Rhetorical Situation and Historical Reconstruction in 1 Corinthians." *NTS* 33 (1987): 386-403.

_____. "The Rhetoricity of Historical Knowledge: Pauline Discourse and Its Contextuality." In *Religious Propaganda and Missionary Competition in the New Testament World: Essays Honoring Dieter Georgi*, ed. Lukas Bormann, *et al.*, 443-70. Leiden: E. J. Brill, 1994.

Fraikin, D. "The Rhetorical Function of the Jews in Romans." In *Anti-Judaism in Early Christianity: Volume I: Paul and the Gospels*, ed. P. Richardson, 91-105. Studies in Christianity and Judaism 2. Waterloo, Ontario: Wilfrid Laurier University, 1986.

Funk, R. W. "The Apostolic 'Parousia': Form and Significance." In *Christian History and Interpretation: Studies Presented to John Knox*, ed. W.R. Farmer, C.F.D. Moule and R. R. Niebuhr, 249-68. Cambridge: Cambridge University Press, 1967.

Furnish, Victor P. *Theology & Ethics in Paul.* Nashville: Abingdon, 1968.

Gamble, Jr., Harry. *The Textual History of the Letter to the Romans: A Study in*

Textual and Literary Criticism. Studies and Documents 42, ed. I. A. Sparks. Grand Rapids: Eerdmans, 1977.

Garlington, D. B. *Faith, Obedience, and Perseverance: Aspects of Paul's Letter to the Romans*. WUNT 79, ed. Martin Hengel and Otfried Hofius. Tübingen: Mohr, 1994.

_____. *'The Obedience of Faith': A Pauline Phrase in Historical Context*. WUNT 2/38, ed. Martin Hengel and Otfried Hofius. Tübingen: Mohr, 1991.

Getty, Mary Ann. "Paul and the Salvation of Israel: A Perspective on Romans 9-11." *CBQ* 50 (1988): 456-69.

Geyser, A. S. "Un Essai d'explication de Rom. XV.19." *NTS* (1959-60): 156-59.

Giblin, Charles H. "'As It Is Written…' A Basic Problem in Noematics." *CBQ* 20 (1958): 477-98.

Glad, Clarence E. *Paul and Philodemus : Adaptability in Epicurean and Early Christian Psychagogy*. NovTSup 81. Leiden: E. J. Brill, 1995.

Gloer, W. H. "Homologies and Hymns in the New Testament: Form, Content, and Criteria for Identification," *Perspectives in Religious Studies* 11 (1984): 115-32.

Goppelt, Leonard. *Jesus, Paul and Judaism: an Introduction to New Testament Theology*. Trans. Edward Schroeder. New York: Thomas Nelson, 1964.

Gorday, P. *Principles of Patristic Exegesis: Romans 9-11 in Origen, John Chrysostom, and Augustine*. Studies in the Bible and Early Christianity 4. New York: E. Mellen, 1983.

Guerra, Anthony J. "Romans: Paul's Purpose and Audience with Special Attention to Romans 9-11." *RB* 97 (1990): 219-37.

_____. *Romans and the Apologetic Tradition: The Purpose, Genre and Audience of Paul's Letter*. SNTSMS 81. Cambridge: Cambridge University Press, 1995.

Gundry-Volf, Judith M. *Paul and Perseverance: Staying and Falling Away*. WUNT 2/37. Tübingen: Mohr, 1990.

Guterman, S. *Religious Toleration and Persecution in Ancient Rome*. London: Aiglon Press, 1951.

Haacker, K. "Das Evangelium Gottes und die Erwählung Israels." *TBei* 13 (1982): 59-72.

Haenchen, E. *Die Apostelgeschichte.* MeyerK 3. 5th ed. Göttingen: Vandenhoeck & Ruprecht, 1965.

Hafemann, S. J. "The Salvation of Israel in Romans 11:25-32: A Response to Krister Stendahl." *Ex Auditu* 4 (1989): 38-58.

Hall, Sidney G. III. *Christian Anti-Semitism and Paul's Theology.* Minneapolis: Fortress, 1993.

Harnack, A. *The Mission and Expansion of Christianity in the First Three Centuries.* 2d ed. New York: Putnam, 1908.

Harvey, A. E. *Jesus and the Constraints of History.* Philadelphia: Westminster, 1982.

Harvey, Graham. *The True Israel: Uses of the Names Jew, Hebrew and Israel in Ancient Jewish and Early Christian Literature.* AGJU 35. Leiden: E. J. Brill, 1996.

Hay, David M. and E. E. Johnson, eds. *Pauline Theology, Volume III: Romans.* Minneapolis: Fortress, 1995.

Hays, Richard B. *Echoes of Scripture in the Letters of Paul.* New Haven: Yale University Press, 1989.

_____. "Adam, Israel, Christ: The Question of Covenant in the Theology of Romans: A Response to Leander E. Keck and N. T. Wright." In *Pauline Theology III: Romans,* 68-86.

_____. "'Who Has Believed Our Message?': Paul's Reading of Isaiah." *SBL 1998 Seminar Papers: Part One,* 205-24. Atlanta: Scholars, 1998.

Heath, Malcom. *Hermogenes On Issues: Strategies of Argument in Later Greek Rhetoric.* Oxford: Clarendon, 1995.

_____. "The Substructure of *Stasis*-Theory From Hermagoras to Hermogenes." *Classical Quarterly* 44 (1994): 114-29.

_____. "Invention." In *Handbook of Classical Rhetoric,* 89-119.

Hengel, Martin. *Judaism and Hellenism: Studies in their Encounter in Palestine during the Early Hellenistic Period.* Trans. John Bowden. Minneapolis: Fortress, 1974.

_____. *Acts and the History of Earliest Christianity.* Philadelphia: Fortress, 1979.

_____. *The Hellenization of Judea in the First Century After Christ.* Philadelphia: Trinity Press International, 1989.

Hengel, Martin and R. Deines. *The Pre-Christian Paul.* Valley Forge, Pa.: Trinity Press International, 1991.

Hester, Jack. *Doing History.* Bloomington: Indiana University Press, 1971.

Hoeber, R. O. "The Decree of Claudius in Acts 18:2." *CTM* 31 (1960): 691-92.

Holtz, Traugott. "Die historischen und theologischen Bedingungen des Römerbriefes." In *Evangelium-Schriftauslegung-Kirche: Festschrift für Peter Stuhlmacher zum 65. Geburtstag,* ed. Jostein Ådna, Scott J. Hafemann and Otfried Hofius, 238-54. Göttingen: Vandenhoeck & Ruprecht, 1997.

Horak, Franz. "Die rhetorische Statuslehre und der moderne Aufbau des Verbrechensbegriffs." In *Festgabe für Arnold Herdlitczka,* ed. Franz Horak and W. Waldstein, 121-42. München/Salzburg, 1972.

Hübner, Hans. *Biblische Theologie des Neuen Testaments, Band 2: Die Theologie des Paulus und ihre neutestamentaliche Wirkungsgeschichte.* Göttingen: Vandenhoeck & Ruprecht, 1993.

_____. *Gottes Ich und Israel: Zum Schriftgebrauch des Paulus in Römer 9-11.* FRLANT 136. Göttingen: Vandenhoeck & Ruprecht, 1984.

_____. "Die Rhetorik und die Theologie: Der Römerbrief und die rhetorische Kompetenz des Paulus." In *Die Macht des Wortes: Aspekte gegenwärtiger Rhetorikforschung,* ed. Carl Joachim and Heinz-Joachim Müllenbrock, 165-79. Ars Rhetorica 4. Marburg: Hitzeroth, 1992.

Hunsaker, David M. and Craig R. Smith. "The Nature of Issues: A Constructive Approach to Situational Rhetoric." *Western Speech Communication* 40 (1976): 144-56.

Hvalvik, R. "A 'Sonderweg' for Israel: A Critical Examination of a Current Interpretation of Romans 11.25-27." *JSNT* 38 (1990): 87-107.

Janne, H. "Impulsore Chresto." *Annuaire de l'Institut de philologie et d'histoire orientales* 2 (1934): 533-35.

Jervis, L. Ann. *The Purpose of Romans: A Comparative Letter Structure Investigation.* JSNTSup 55. Sheffield: Sheffield Academic, 1991.

Jewett, Robert. "Following the Argument of Romans." In *The Romans Debate: Revised and Expanded Edition,* ed. Karl P. Donfried, 265-77. Peabody, Mass.: Hendrickson, 1991.

_____. "Paul, Phoebe, and the Spanish Mission." In *The Social World of Formative Christianity and Judaism,* ed. J. Neusner, *et al.,* 142-61. Philadelphia: Fortress, 1988.

_____. "The Redaction and Use of an Early Christian Confession in Romans 1:3-4." In *The Living Text: Essays in Honor of Ernest W. Saunders*, ed. Dennis E. Groh and Robert Jewett, 99-122. Lanham, Md.: University Press of America, 1985.

_____. "Romans As an Ambassadorial Letter." *Int* 36 (1982): 5-20.

Johnson, D. G. "The Structure and Meaning of Romans 11." *CBQ* 46 (1984): 91-103.

Johnson, E. Elizabeth. "Romans 9-11: The Faithfulness and Impartiality of God." In *Pauline Theology III: Romans*, ed. David M. Hay and E. Elizabeth Johnson, 211-39. Minneapolis: Fortress, 1995.

_____. *The Function of Apocalyptic and Wisdom Traditions in Romans 9-11*. SBLDS 109. Atlanta: Scholars, 1989.

Juster, J. *Les Juifs dans l'Empire Romain*. Pairs: Paul Geuthner, 1914.

Käsemann, E. *Commentary on Romans*. Trans. G. W. Bromiley. Grand Rapids: Eerdmans, 1980.

Keck, Leander E. "The Premodern Bible in the Postmodern World." *Int* 50 (1996): 130-41.

_____. "Searchable Judgments and Scrutable Ways: A Response to Paul J. Achtemeier." In *Pauline Theology, Volume IV: Looking Back, Pressing on*, ed. E. Elizabeth Johnson and David M. Hay, 22-32. Atlanta: Scholars, 1997.

_____. "What Makes Romans Tick?" In *Pauline Theology, Volume III*, ed. David M. Hay and E. Elizabeth Johnson, 3-29. Minneapolis: Fortress, 1995.

_____. "Will the Historical-Critical Method Survive? Some Observations." In *Orientation by Disorientation: Studies in Literary Criticism and Biblical Literary Criticism: Presented in Honor of William A. Beardslee*, ed. Richard A. Spencer, 115-28. Pisttsburgh: Pickwick, 1980.

Kennedy, George A. "The Genres of Rhetoric." In *Handbook of Classical Rhetoric*, 43-50.

_____. *The Art of Rhetoric in the Ancient World: 300 B.C. - A.D. 300*. Princeton: Princeton University Press, 1972.

_____. *A New History of Classical Rhetoric*. Princeton: Princeton University Press, 1994.

_____. *New Testament Interpretation Through Rhetorical Criticism*. Chapel Hill: University of North Carolina Press, 1984.

Kim, Seyoon. "The 'Mystery' of Rom 11.25-6 Once More." *NTS* 43 (1997): 412-29.

Kingsbury, Jack D. "Reflections on 'the Reader' of Matthew's Gospel." *NTS* 34 (1988): 442-60.

Kinneavy, J. L. *Greek Rhetorical Origins of Christian Faith: An Inquiry.* New York: Oxford University Press, 1987.

Klappert, B. "Traktat für Israel (Römer 9-11)," in *Jüdische Existenz und die Erneuerung der christlichen Theologie*, ed. M. Stöhr, 58-137. Abhandlungen zum christlich-jüdischen Dialog 11. Munich: Kaiser, 1981.

Knox, John. "Romans 15:14-33 and Paul's Conception of His Apostolic Mission." *JBL* 83 (1964): 1-11.

Koch, Dietrich-Alex. *Die Schrift als Zeuge des Evangliums: Untersuchungen zur Verwendung und zum Verständnis der Schrift bei Paulus.* BHT 69. Tübingen: Mohr, 1986.

Koskenniemi, H. *Studien zur Idee und Phraseologie des griechischen Briefes bis 400 n. Chr.* Helsinki: Akateeminen Kirjakauppa, 1956.

Krentz, E. *The Historical-Critical Method.* Philadelphia: Fortress, 1975.

Kruger, M. A. "*Tina Karpon,* 'Some Fruit' in Romans 1:13." *WTJ* 49 (1987): 167-73.

Kümmel, Werner Georg. *Introduction to the New Testament.* rev. ed. Trans. Howard Clark Kee. Nashville: Abingdon, 1975.

_____. "Die Probleme von Römer 9-11 in der gegenwärtigen Forschungslage." In *Die Israelfrage Nach Römer 9-11*, ed. L. De Lorenzi, 13-33. Rome: Abtei van St. Paul vor den Mauern, 1977.

Lampe, Peter. *Die stadtrömischen Christen in den ersten beiden Jahrhunderten.* 2d ed. WUNT 2/18. Tübingen: Mohr, 1989.

Lausberg, H. *Handbook of Literary Rhetoric: A Foundation for Literary Study.* Ed. David E. Orton and R. Dean Anderson. Trans. Matthew T. Bliss, Annemiek Jansen and David E. Orton. Leiden: Brill, 1998.

_____. *Handbuch Der Literarischen Rhetorik: Eine Grundlegung Der Literaturwissenschaft.* 3d ed. 2 vols. Stuttgart: Franz Steiner, 1960.

_____. *Elemente der literarischen Rhetorik.* Munich: Hueber, 1967.

Leon, H. *The Jews of Ancient Rome.* Philadelphia: The Jewish Publication Society of America, 1960.

Lieberman, Saul. *Hellenism in Jewish Palestine.* New York: Jewish Theological Seminary of America, 1954.

Lincoln, Andrew T. "Abraham Goes to Rome: Paul's Treatment of Abraham in Romans 4." In *Worship, Theology and Ministry in the Early Church: Essays in Honor of Ralph P. Martin,* ed. M. Wilkins and T. Paige, 163-79. JSNTSup 87. Sheffield: JSOT Press, 1992.

_____. "From Wrath to Justification: Tradition, Gospel, and Audience in the Theology of Romans 1:18-4:25." In *Pauline Theology, Volume III: Romans,* ed. David M. Hay and E. Elizabeth Johnson, 130-59. Minneapolis: Fortress, 1995.

Lindberg, Gertrud. "Hermogenes of Tarsus." *ANRW* II 34.3 (1997): 1978-2063.

Linnemann, Eta. *Historical Criticism of the Bible: Methodology or Ideology?* Grand Rapids: Baker, 1990.

Litfin, Duane. *St. Paul's Theology of Proclamation: 1 Corinthians 1-4 and Greco-Roman Rhetoric.* STNSMS 79. Cambridge: Cambridge University Press, 1994.

Lodge, John G. *Romans 9--11: A Reader-Response Analysis.* University of South Florida International Studies in Formative Christianity and Judaism 6. Atlanta: Scholars, 1996.

Longenecker, Bruce W. "Different Answers to Different Issues: Israel, the Gentiles and Salvation History in Romans 9-11." *JSNT* 36 (1989): 95-123.

De Lorenzi, Lorenzo, ed. *Die Israelfrage nach Röm 9-11.* Rome: Abtei von St Paul vor den Mauern, 1977.

Louw, Johannes P. *Semantics of New Testament Greek.* SBLSS. Philadelphia; Chico: Fortress; Scholars, 1982.

Lübking, Hans-Martin. *Paulus und Israel im Römerbrief: Eine Untersuchung zu Römer 9-11.* Europäische Hochschulschriften. Frankfurt am Main: Peter Lang, 1986.

Luedemann, G. *Paul, Apostle to the Gentiles: Studies in Chronology.* Trans. F. S. Jones. Philadelphia: Fortress, 1984.

Luz, U. *Das Geschichtsverständnis des Paulus,* BevT 49. München: Verlag, 1968.

Mack, Burton L. *Rhetoric and the New Testament.* GBS. Minneapolis: Fortress, 1990.

MacLennan, Robert and Thomas A. Kraabel. "The God-Fearers--A Literary and Theological Invention." *BAR* 12 (1986): 46-53.

Maier, Gerhard. *The End of the Historical-Critical Method*. Trans. Edwin W. Leverenz and Rudolph F. Norden. St. Louis: Concordia Publishing House, 1974.

Malherbe, Abraham J. "*Mê Genoito* in the Diatribe and Paul," *HTR* 73 (1980): 231-40.

_____. "Determinism and Free Will in Paul: The Argument of 1 Corinthians 8 and 9." In *Paul in Hellenistic Context,* ed. Troels Engberg-Pedersen, 231-55. Minneapolis: Fortress, 1995.

Malina, Bruce J. and Jerome H. Neyrey, *Portraits of Paul: An Archaeology of Ancient Personality*. Louisville: Westminster John Knox, 1996.

Marrou, Henri I. *A History of Education in Antiquity.* Trans. George Lamb. New York: Sheed & Ward, 1956.

Marcel, Simon. *Verus Israel: A Study of the Relations between Christians and Jews in the Roman Empire, 135-425.* Trans. H. McKeating. Oxford: Oxford University Press, 1986.

Marshall, I. H. "Historical Criticism." In *New Testament Interpretation: Essays on Principles and Methods*, ed. I. H. Marshall, 126-38. Grand Rapids: Eerdmans, 1977.

Martin, Dale B. *The Corinthian Body*. New Haven: Yale University Press, 1995.

_____. *Slavery As Salvation: The Metaphor of Slavery in Pauline Christianity*. New Haven: Yale University Press, 1990.

Martin, Josef. *Antike Rhetorik: Technik und Methode*. Handbuch Der Altertumswissenschaft II/3. München: Beck, 1974.

Martin, Troy. "Apostasy to Paganism: The Rhetorical Stasis of the Galatian Controversy." *JBL* 114 (1995): 437-61.

Matthes, Dieter. "Hermagoras von Temnos, 1904-1955." *Lustrum* 3 (1958): 58-214.

Meeks, Wayne A. "On Trusting an Unpredictable God: A Hermeneutical Meditation on Romans 9-11." In *Faith and History: Essays in Honor of Paul W. Meyer*, ed. John T. Carroll, *et al.*, 105-24. Atlanta: Scholars, 1990.

Melanchton, Philip. *Loci communes, 1521*. Werke in Auswahl 2.1, ed. R. Stupperich. Gütersloh: Bertelsmann, 1952.

Meyer, Paul W. "Romans 10:4 and the End of the Law." In *The Divine Helmsman: Studies on God's Control of Human Events, Presented to Lou H. Silberman*, ed. James L. Crenshaw and Samuel Sandmel, 59-78. New York: KTAV, 1980.

Meynet, R. "Histoire de 'l'analyse rhétorique' en exégèse biblique." *Rhetorica* 8 (1990): 291-312.

Migliore, Daniel L., ed. *The Princeton Seminary Bulletin Supplemenatry Issue No. 1 (on Romans 9-11)*. Princeton: Princeton Theological Seminary, 1990.

Miller, Arthur B. "Rhetorical Exigence." *Philosophy and Rhetoric* 5 (1972): 111-18.

Mitchell, Margaret M. *Paul and the Rhetoric of Reconciliation: An Exegetical Investigation of the Language and Composition of 1 Corinthians*. HUT 28. Tübingen: Mohr, 1991.

Moo, Douglas. "The Theology of Romans 9-11: A Response to E. Elizabeth Johnson." In *Pauline Theology III: Romans,* 240-58.

Muilenburg, James. "Form Criticism and Beyond." *JBL* 88 (1969): 1-18.

Müller, Christian. *Gottes Gerechtigkeit und Gottes Volk: Eine Untersuchung zu Römer 9-11*. FRLANT 86. Göttingen: Vandenhoeck & Ruprecht, 1964.

Müller, Peter. "Grundlinien paulinischer Theologie (Röm 15,14-33)." *KD* 35 (1989): 212-35.

Munck, Johannes. *Christ and Israel: An Interpretation of Romans 9-11*. Trans. Ingeborg Nixon. Philadelphia: Fortress, 1967.

_____. *Paul and the Salvation of Mankind*. Trans. Frank Clarke. Richmond: John Knox, 1959.

Mussner, Franz. *Traktat über die Juden*. Munich: Kaiser, 1979.

Nadeau, R. "Classical Systems of Stases in Greek: Hermogoras to Hermogenes." *GRBS* 2 (1959): 51-71.

_____. "Hermogenes' *On Stases*: A Translation with an Introduction and Notes." *Speech Monographs* 31 (1964): 361-421.

Nanos, Mark D. *The Mystery of Romans: The Jewish Context of Paul's Letter*. Minneapolis: Fortress, 1996.

Nations, Archie L. "Historical Criticism and the Current Methodological Crisis." *SJT* 36 (1983): 59-71.

Nickle, Keith F. *The Collection: A Study in Paul's Strategy*. SBT 48. Naperville, Ill.: Alec R. Allenson, Inc., 1966.

Noack, Bent. "Current and Backwater in the Epistle to the Romans." *ST* 19 (1965): 155-66.

Norden, E. *Agnostos Theos: Untersuchungen zur Formgeschichtlichte religiöser Rede.* Leipzig/Berlin: Teubner, 1913.

O'Brien, P. T. *Gospel and Mission in the Writings of Paul: An Exegetical and Theological Analysis.* Grand Rapids: Baker, 1995.

Ong, W. J. *Orality and Literacy: The Technologizing of the Word.* New York: Methuen, 1982.

Overman, A. "The God-Fearers: Some Neglected Features." *JSNT* 32 (1988): 17-26.

Patton, J. H. "Causation and Creativity in Rhetorical Situations: Distinctions and Implications." *Quarterly Journal of Speech* 65 (1979): 36-55.

Perelman, C. and L. Olbrechts-Tyteca. *The New Rhetoric: A Treatise on Argumentation.* Trans. J. Wilkinson and P. Weaver. Notre Dame: Notre Dame University Press, 1969.

Penna, R. "Les Juifs à Rome au temps de l'Apôtre Paul." *NTS* 28 (1982): 321-47.

_____. *Paul the Apostle: Jew and Greek Alike: A Theological and Exegetical Study.* 2 vols. Trans. T. P. Wahl. Collegeville, Minn.: The Liturgical Press, 1996.

Perry, E. "The Meaning of *'emuna* in the Old Testament." *JBR* 21 (1953): 255-56.

Peterman, G. W. "Romans 15:26: Make a Contribution or Establish Fellowship?" *NTS* 40 (1994): 457-63.

Peterson, Brian K. *Eloquence and the Proclamation of the Gospel in Corinth.* SBLDS 163. Atlanta: Scholars, 1998.

Peterson, Erik. "Das Amulett von Acre." In *Frühkirche, Judentum und Gnosis: Studien und Untersuchungen,* 346-54. Rome: Herder, 1959.

Philipps, Gerald M. "The Place of Rhetoric in the Babylonian Talmud." *Quarterly Journal of Speech* 43 (1957): 390-93.

_____. "The Practice of Rhetoric at the Talmudic Academies." *Speech Monographs* 26 (1959): 37-46.

Piper, John. *The Justification of God: An Exegetical and Theological Study of Romans 9:1-23.* 2d ed. Grand Rapids: Baker, 1993.

Plag, Christoph. *Israel's Wege zum Heil: Eine Untersuchung zu Römer 9 bis 11.* Arbeiten zur Theologie 40. Stuttgart: Calwer, 1969.

Plank, Karl A. *Paul and the Irony of Affliction.* SBLSS. Atlanta: Scholars, 1987.

Pogoloff, S. M. *Logos and Sophia: The Rhetorical Situation of 1 Corinthians.* SBLDS 134. Atlanta: Scholars, 1992.

Porter, Stanley E. "Paul of Tarsus and His Letters." In *Handbook of Classical Rhetoric in the Hellenistic Period 330 B. C.-A.D. 400*, ed. Stanley E. Porter, 533-86. Leiden: Brill, 1997.

_____. "The Theoretical Justification for Application of Rhetorical Categories to Pauline Epistolary Literature." In *Rhetoric and the New Testament: Essays From the 1992 Heidelberg Conference*, ed. Stanley E. Porter and Thomas H. Olbricht, 100-22. JSNTSup 90. Sheffield: JSOT Press, 1993.

_____., ed. *Handbook of Classical Rhetoric in the Hellenistic Period 330 B.C.-A.D. 400.* Leiden: Brill, 1997.

Porter, Stanley E. and Thomas H. Olbricht, eds. *Rhetoric and the New Testament: Essays From the 1992 Heidelberg Conference.* JSNTSup 90. Sheffield: Sheffield Academic, 1993.

_____, eds. *The Rhetorical Analysis of Scripture: Essays From the 1995 London Conference.* JSNTSup 146. Sheffield: Sheffield Academic, 1997.

Powell, Mark A. *What Is Narrative Criticism?* GBS, ed. Dan O. Via. Minneapolis: Fortress, 1990.

Probst, Hermann. *Paulus und der Brief: Die Rhetorik des antiken Briefes als Form der paulinischen Korintherkorrespondenz (1 Kor 8--10).* WUNT 2/45. Tübingen: Mohr, 1991.

Räisänen, H. "Paul, God, and Israel: Romans 9-11 in Recent Research." In *The Social World of Formative Christianity and Judaism: Essays in Tribute to Howard Clark Kee*, ed. J. Neusner, *et al.*, 178-206. Philadelphia: Fortress, 1988.

_____. "Römer 9-11: Analyse eines geistigen Ringens." *ANRW* 2.25.4 (1987): 2891-939.

Reed, Jeffrey T. "Using Ancient Rhetorical Categories to Interpret Paul's Letters: A Question of Genre." In *Rhetoric and the New Testament: Essays From 1992 Heidelberg Conference*, ed. Stanley E. Porter and Thomas H. Olbricht, 292-324. JSNTSup 90. Sheffield: JSOT Press, 1993.

Refoulé, François. *"...et ainsi tout Israël sera sauvé": Romains 11,25-32.* LD 117. Paris: Cerf, 1984.

_____. "Cohérence ou incohérence de Paul en Romains 9-11?" *RB* 98 (1991): 51-79.

Reid, M. L. "A Consideration of the Function of Rom 1:8-15 in Light of Greco-Roman Rhetoric." *JETS* 38 (1995): 181-91.

_____. "Paul's Rhetoric of Mutuality: A Rhetorical Reading of Romans." In *SBL 1995 Seminar Papers*, ed. Eugene H. Lovering, Jr., 117-39. Atlanta: Scholars, 1995.

_____. "A Rhetorical Analysis of Romans 1:1-5:21 with Attention Given to the Rhetorical Function of 5:1-21." *Perspectives in Religious Studies* 19 (1992): 255-72.

Reinbold, Wolfgang. "Israel und das Evangelium: Zur Exegese von Römer 10,19-21." *ZNW* 86 (1995): 122-29.

_____. "Paulus und das Gesetz: Zur Exegese von Röm 9,30-33." *BZ* 38 (1994): 253-64.

Rese, M. "Israel und Kirche in Römer 9." *NTS* 34 (1988): 208-17.

_____. "Die Rettung der Juden nach Römer 11." In *L'Apôtre Paul: Personnalité, style et conception du ministè*, ed. A. Vanhoye, 422-30. BETL 73. Louvain: Leuven University/Peeters, 1986.

Reumann, John. "Methods in Studying the Biblical Text Today." *CTM* 40 (1969): 663-70.

Riesner, Rainer. *Paul's Early Period: Chronology, Mission Strategy, Theology*. Trans. Doug Stott. Grand Rapids: Eerdmans, 1998.

Roetzel, Calvin J. "No 'Race of Israel' in Paul," in *Putting Body & Soul Together: Essays in Honor of Robin Scroggs*, ed. Virginia Wiles, Alexandra Brown and Graydon F. Snyder, 230-44. Valley Forge, Pa.: Trinity Press International, 1997.

Rolland, Ph. *Épître aux Romains: Texte grec structuré*. Rome: Biblical Institute, 1980.

Rowe, Galen O. "Style." In *Handbook of Classical Rhetoric in the Hellenistic Period 330 B.C.-A.D. 400*, ed. Stanley E. Porter, 121-57. Leiden: Brill, 1997.

Ruether, R. *Faith and Fratricide: The Theological Roots of Anti-Semitism*. New York: Crossroad, 1974.

Russell, D. A. *Greek Declamation*. Cambridge: Cambridge University Press, 1983.

Russell, D. A. and N. G. Wilson, ed. and trans., *Menander Rhetor*. Oxford: Clarendon, 1981.

Sampley, J. Paul. "Romans in a Different Light: A Response to Robert Jewett," in *Pauline Theology III: Romans*, ed. David M. Hay and E. Elizabeth Johnson, 109-29. Minneapolis: Fortress, 1995.

Sanders, E. P. *Paul, the Law, and the Jewish People*. Minneapolis: Fortress, 1983.

_____. *Paul and Palestinian Judaism: A Comparison of Patterns of Religion*. Minneapolis: Fortress, 1977.

Sänger, Dieter. "Rettung der Heiden und Erwählung Israels: Einige vorläufige Erwägungen zu Römer 11,25-27." *KD* 32 (1986): 99-119.

_____. *Die Verkündigung des Gekreuzigten und Israel: Studien zum Verhältnis von Kirche und Israel bei Paulus und im frühen Christentum*. WUNT 75. Tübingen: Mohr, 1994.

Satake, A. "Apostolat und Gnade bei Paulus." *NTS* 15 (1968-69): 96-107.

Saw, Insawn. *Paul's Rhetoric in 1 Corinthians 15: An Analysis Utilizing the Theories of Classical Rhetoric*. Lewiston: Mellen Biblical Press, 1995.

Schmeller, T. *Paulus und die "Diatribe": eine vergleichende Stilinterpretation*, NTAbh 19. Münster: Aschendorff, 1987.

Schmithals, Walter. *Der Römerbrief als historisches Problem*. SNT 9. Gütersloh: Gütersloher Verlagshaus Gerd Mohn, 1975.

Schneider, B. "Κατὰ Πνεῦμα Ἁγιωσύνης (Romans 1,4)." *Bib* 48 (1967): 359-87.

Schnider, Franz and Werner Stenger. *Studien zum neutestamentlichen Briefformular*. NTTS 11. Leiden: E. J. Brill, 1987.

Schürer, Emil. *The History of the Jewish People in the Age of Jesus Christ (175 B.C.—A.D. 135,* a new English version rev. and ed. Geza Vermes, Fergus Millar, and Matthew Black; original trans. John Macpherson. 3 vols. Edinburgh: T. & T. Clark, 1979.

Scott, James M. *Adoption As Sons of God: An Exegetical Investigation Into the Background of* ΥΙΟΘΕΣΙΑ *in the Pauline Corpus*. WUNT 2/48. Tübingen: Mohr, 1992.

_____. *Paul and the Nations: The Old Testament and Jewish Background of Paul's Mission to the Nations with Special Reference to the Destination of Galatians*. WUNT 48. Tübingen: Mohr, 1995.

_____. "Paul's Use of Deuteronomic Tradition." *JBL* 112 (1993): 645-65.

_____. "Paul's *"Imago Mundi"* and Scripture." In *Evangelium-Schriftauslegung-Kirche: Festschrift für Peter Stuhlmacher zum 65.*

Geburtstag, ed. Jostein Ådna, Scott J. Hafemann and Otfried Hofius, 366-81. Göttingen: Vandenhoeck & Ruprecht, 1997.

Scramuzza, V. M. *The Emperor Claudius.* Cambridge: Harvard University Press, 1940.

_____. "The Policy of the Early Roman Emperors towards Judaism," in *The Beginnings of Christianity,* ed. F. J. Foakes Jackson and Kirsopp Lake, 5: 277-97. London: MacMillan, 1920-33.

Siegert, F. *Argumentation bei Paulus: gezeigt an Röm 9-11.* WUNT 34. Tübingen: Mohr, 1985.

_____. "Die Gottesfürchtig und Sympathisanten." *JSJ* 4 (1973): 109-64.

Slingerland, Dixon. "Chrestus: Chritus?" In *New Perspectives on Ancient Judaism,* 4:133-44, ed. Alan J. Avery-Peck, The Literature of Early Rabbinic Judaism: Issues in Talmudic Redaction and Interpretation. Lanham: University Press of America, 1989.

_____. "Suetonius *Claudius* 25.4, Acts 18, and Paulus Orosius' *Historiarum Adversum Paganos Libri VII*: Dating the Claudian Expulsion(s) of Roman Jews." *JQR* 83 (1992): 127-44.

_____. "Suetonius *Claudius* 25.4 and the Account in Cassius Dio." *JQR* 79 (1989): 305-22.

Snyman, A. H. "Style and the Rhetorical Situation of Romans 8:31-39." *NTS* 34 (1988): 218-31.

Stamps, D. L. "Rethinking the Rhetorical Situation: The Entextualization of the Situation in New Testament Epistles." In *Rhetoric and the New Testament: Essays From the 1992 Heidelberg Conference*, ed. Stanley E. Porter and Thomas H. Olbricht, 193-210. JSNTSup 90. Sheffield: JSOT Press, 1993.

_____. "Rhetorical Criticism and the Rhetoric of New Testament." *LT* 6 (1992): 268-79.

_____. "Rhetorical Criticism of the New Testament: Ancient and Modern Evaluations of Argumentation." In *Approaches to New Testament Study*, ed. Stanley E. Porter and David Tombs, 129-69. JSNTSup 120. Sheffield: Sheffield Academic, 1995.

Stanley, Christopher D. "Biblical Quotations as Rhetorical Devices in Paul's Letter to the Galatians." In *SBL 1998 Seminar Papers,* 700-30. Atlanta: Scholars, 1998.

_____. "The Rhetoric of Quotations: An Essay on Method." In *Early Christian Interpretation of the Scriptures of Israel: Investigation and*

Proposals, ed. Craig A. Evans and James A. Sanders, 44-58. Sheffield: Sheffield Academic, 1997.

_____. "The Redeemer Will Come ἐκ Σιων: Romans 11.26-27 Revisited." In *Paul and the Scriptures of Israel,* ed. C. A. Evans and J. A. Sanders, 118-42. Sheffield: Sheffield Academic, 1993.

Stegner, W. R. "Romans 9.6-29--a Midrash." *JSNT* 22 (1984): 37-52.

Stern, M. "The Jewish Diaspora." In *The Jewish People in the First Century: Historical Geography, Political History, Social, Cultural and Religious Life and Institutions.* ed. by S. Safrai and M. Stern in co-operation with D. Flusser and W. C. van Unnik, 1: 117-83. Philadelphia: Fortress, 1974.

_____. *Greek and Latin Authors on Jews and Judaism.* 2 vols. Jerusalem: Israel Academy of Sciences and Humanities, 1974-1984.

Stowers, Stanley K. *The Diatribe and Paul's Letter to the Romans.* Chico: Scholars, 1981.

_____. "ΕΚ ΠΙΣΤΕΩΣ and ΔΙΑ ΠΙΣΤΕΩΣ in Romans 3:30." *JBL* 108 (1989): 665-74.

_____. *A Rereading of Romans: Justice, Jews and Gentiles.* New Haven: Yale University Press, 1994.

Stuhlmacher, Peter. *Historical Criticism and Theological Interpretation of Scripture: Toward a Hermeneutics of Consent.* Trans. Roy A. Harrisville. Philadelphia: Fortress, 1977.

_____. "Zur Interpretation von Röm 11,25-32." In *Probleme biblischer Theologie: Festschrift für Gerhard von Rad zum 70,* ed. H. W. Wolff, 555-70. Munich: Kaiser, 1971.

Suhl, A. *Paulus und seine Briefe.* SNT 11. Gütersloh: Mohn, 1975.

Suleiman, Susan and Inge Crosman, eds. *The Reader in the Text.* Princeton: Princeton University Press, 1980.

Theobald, Michael. "'Dem Juden zuerst und auch dem Heiden': Die paulinische Auslegung der Glaubensformel Röm 1,3f." In *Kontinuität und Einheit für Franz Mussner,* ed. Paul-Gerhard Müller and Werner Stenger, 376-92. Freiburg: Herder, 1981.

_____. *Die überströmende Gnade: Studien zu einen paulinischen Motivfeld.* Würzburg: Echter, 1982.

_____. "Glaube und Vernunft: Zur Argumentation des Paulus im Römerbrief." *Theologische Quartalschrift* 169 (1989): 287-301.

_____. "Kirche und Israel nach Röm 9-11." *Kairos* 29 (1987): 1-22.

Thielman, Frank. *Paul & the Law: A Contextual Approach*. Downers Grove, Ill.: InterVarsity, 1994.

_____. "Unexpected Mercy: Echoes of a Biblical Motif in Romans 9-11." *SJT* 47 (1994): 169-81.

Thiselton, Anthony C. "New Testament Interpretation in Historical Perspective." In *Hearing the New Testament: Strategies for Interpretation*, ed. Joel B. Green, 10-36. Grand Rapids: Eerdmans, 1995.

Thrall, M. E. *Greek Particles in the New Testament*. NTTS 3. Leiden: E. J. Brill, 1962.

Thurén, Lauri. *The Rhetorical Strategy of 1 Peter: With Special Regard to Ambiguous Expressions*. Åbo: Åbo Academy Press, 1990.

Toews, John E. "The Law in Paul's Letter to the Romans: A Study of Romans 9:30-10:13." Dissertation, Northwestern University, 1977.

Tompkins, P. K., J. H. Patton and Lloyd F. Bitzer. "The Forum: Tompkins on Patton and Bitzer, Patton on Tompkins, and Bitzer on Tompkins (and Patton)." *Quarterly Journal of Speech* 66 (1980): 85-95.

van Unnik, W. C. "Tarsus or Jerusalem: The City of Paul's Youth." In *Sparsa Collecta: The Collected Essays of W. C. van Unnik*, part I: *Evangelia Paulina Acta,* 259-320. NovTSup 29. Leiden: E. J. Brill, 1973.

Vatz, Richard E. "The Myth of the Rhetorical Situation." *Philosophy & Rhetoric* 6 (1973): 154-61.

Vogelstein, H. and P. Rieger. *Geschichte der Juden in Rom*. 2 vols. Berlin: Mayer & Müller, 1895-96.

Vorster, J. N. "The Context of the Letter to the Romans: A Critique on the Present State of Research." *Neot* 28 (1994): 127-45.

_____. "Toward an Interactional Model for the Analysis of Letters." *Neot* 24 (1990): 107-30.

_____. "The Rhetorical Situation of the Letter to the Romans--an Interactional Approach." Unpublished DD dissertation. University of Pretoria, 1991.

Vorster, W. S. "The Historical Paradigm--Its Possibilities and Limitations." *Neot* 18 (1984): 104-23.

Vouga, F. "Römer 1,18-3,20 als *narratio*." *TGl* 77 (1987): 225-36.

Wacholder, Ben Z. *Nicolaus of Damascus.* Berkeley: University of California Press, 1962.

Wagner, Ross. "The Christ, Servant of Jew and Gentile: A Fresh Approach to Romans 15:8-9." *JBL* 116 (1997): 473-86.

Walter, N. "Zur Interpretation von Römer 9-11." *ZTK* 81 (1984): 172-95.

Walters, James C. *Ethnic Issues in Paul's Letter to the Romans: Changing Self-Definitions in Earliest Romans Christianity.* Valley Forge, Pa.: Trinity Press International, 1994.

Wasserberg, Guenter. "Romans 9-11 and Jewish Christian Dialogue: Prospects and Provisos." In *1998 SBL Seminar Papers: Part One*, 1-11. Atlanta: Scholars, 1998.

Watson, Duane F. "The Contributions and Limitations of Greco-Roman Rhetorical Theory for Constructing the Rhetorical and Historical Situations of a Pauline Letter." Paper presented at the Malibu Conference of Rhetoric and Religion, Pepperdine University, Malibu, Calif., 1996.

_____. "The Integration of Epistolary and Rhetorical Analysis of Philippians." In *The Rhetorical Analysis of Scripture: Essays From the 1995 London Conference*, ed. Stanley E. Porter and Thomas H. Olbricht, 398-426. JSNTSup 146. Sheffield: Sheffield Academic, 1997.

_____. *Invention, Arrangement, and Style: Rhetorical Criticism of Jude and 2 Peter.* SBLDS 104. Atlanta: Scholars, 1988.

_____. "Rhetorical Criticism of the Pauline Epistles Since 1975." *Currents in Research: Biblical Studies* 3 (1995): 219-48.

Watson, Duane F. and Alan J. Hauser, eds. *Rhetorical Criticism of the Bible: A Comprehensive Bibliography with Notes on History and Method.* Biblical Interpretation Series 4. Leiden: E. J. Brill, 1994.

Watson, Francis. *Paul, Judaism and the Gentiles: A Sociological Approach.* SNTSMS 56. Cambridge: Cambridge University Press, 1986.

Wedderburn, A.J.M. *The Reasons for Romans.* 1988; reprint, Minneapolis: Fortress, 1991.

_____. "The Purpose and Occasion of Romans Again." In *The Romans Debate*, 195-202.

Weima, Jeffrey A. "What Does Aristotle Have to Do with Paul? An Evaluation of Rhetorical Criticism." *Calvin Theological Journal* 32 (1997): 458-68.

Wengert, Timothy J. "Philip Melanchthon's 1522 Annotations on Romans and the

Lutheran Origins of Rhetorical Criticism." In *Biblical Interpretation in the Era of the Reformation: Essays Presented to David C. Steinmetz in Honor of His Sixtieth Birthday*, ed. Richard A. Muller and John L. Thompson, 118-40. Grand Rapids: Eerdmans, 1996.

White, John L. "Apostolic Mission and Apostolic Message: Congruence in Paul's Epistolary Rhetoric, Structure and Imagery." In *Origins and Method: Towards a New Understanding of Judaism and Christianity: Essays in Honour of John C. Hurd*, ed. Bradley H. McLean, 145-61. Sheffield: Sheffield Academic, 1993.

Williams, Sam K. "The 'Righteousness of God' in Romans." *JBL* 99 (1980): 241-90.

Wink, Walter. *The Bible in Human Transformation: Toward a New Paradigm for Biblical Study*. Philadelphia: Fortress, 1973.

Winter, Bruce W. *Philo and Paul Among the Sophists*. SNTSMS 96. Cambridge: Cambridge University Press, 1997.

_____. "Is Paul among the Sophists?" *Reformed Theological Review* 53 (1994): 28-38.

_____. "The Entries and Ethics of Orators and Paul (1 Thessalonians 2:1-12)." *TynBul* 44 (1993): 55-74.

Wire, A. C. "'Since God Is One': Rhetorical as Theology and History in Paul's Romans." In *The New Literary Criticism and the New Testament*, ed. E. S. Malbon and E. V. McKnight, 210-27. JSNTSup 109. Sheffield: Sheffield Academic, 1994.

_____. *The Corinthians Women Prophets: A Reconstruction Through Paul's Rhetoric*. Minneapolis: Fortress, 1990.

_____. "Review of M. M. Mitchell, *Paul and the Rhetoric of Reconciliation: An Exegetical Investigation of the Language and Composition of 1 Corinthians.*" *JBL* 112 (1993): 539-40.

Wischmeyer, O. "Das Adjective ΑΓΑΠΗΤΟΣ in den paulinischen Breifen. Eine traditionsgeschichtliche Miszelle." *NTS* 32 (1986): 476-80.

Wisse, J. *Ethos and Pathos: From Aristotle to Cicero*. Amsterdam: Adolf M. Hakkert, 1989.

Witherington, Ben, III. *The Paul Quest: The Renewed Search for the Jew of Tarsus*. Downers Grove, Ill.: InterVarsity, 1998.

Wright, N. T. *The Climax of the Covenant: Christ and the Law in Pauline Theology*. Minneapolis: Fortress, 1992.

_____. "Romans and the Theology of Paul." In *Pauline Theology III: Romans,* 30-67.

_____. *What St. Paul Really Said: Was Paul of Tarsus the Real Founder of Christianity?* Grand Rapids: Eerdmans, 1997.

Wuellner, Wilhelm. "Paul's Rhetoric of Argumentation in Romans: An Alternative to the Donfried-Karris Debate Over Romans." In *The Romans Debate: Revised and Expanded Edition,* ed. Karl P. Donfried, 128-46. Peabody, Mass.: Hendrickson, 1991.

Yeo, Khiok-Khng. *Rhetorical Interaction in 1 Corinthians 8 and 10: A Formal Analysis with Preliminary Suggestions for a Chinese, Cross-Cultural Hermeneutic.* Biblical Interpretation Series 9. Leiden: E. J. Brill, 1995.

Zeller, Dieter. *Juden und Heiden in der Mission des Paulus.* 2d ed. FB 8. Stuttgart: Katholisches Bibelwerk, 1976.

_____. "Theologie der Mission bei Paulus." In *Mission im Neuen Testament,* ed. Karl Kertelge, QD 93. Freiburg: Herder, 1982.

Zielinski, T. "L'empereur Claude et l'idée de la domination mondiale des Juifs." *Revue de l'Universite de Bruxelles* 32 (1926-27): 143-44.